D1593947

WITHDRAWN

TX 338.278 Goo $ 29.95   SM
Goodwyn, Lawrence.
Texas oil, American
   dreams : a study of the
Texas Inde............6521

TX 338.278 Goo $ 29.95   SM
Goodwyn, Lawrence.
Texas oil, American
   dreams : a study of the
Texas Independen 92406521

3 4028 02760 8109

AUG 2 7 1997
SM

There's A Branch
Near You

HARRIS COUNTY PUBLIC LIBRARY

HOUSTON, TEXAS

Texas Oil, American Dreams

TEXAS OIL, AMERICAN DREAMS

A *Study of the Texas Independent Producers and*

Royalty Owners Association

LAWRENCE GOODWYN

Published for the Center for American History
by the Texas State Historical Association

Copyright © 1996 by the Texas State Historical Association, Austin, Texas.
All rights reserved.
Printed in the United States of America.

Frontispiece: Boomtown by Thomas Hart Benton, 1927–1928. Oil on canvas 46⅛ × 54¼ inches. *Courtesy Memorial Art Gallery of the University of Rochester.*

ISBN 0-87611-158-4

Published for the Center for American History by the Texas State Historical Association in cooperation with the Center for Studies in Texas History at the University of Texas at Austin.

Number five in the Barker Texas History Center Series
Senior editor, Don E. Carleton

The paper used in this book meets the minimum requirements of the American National Standard for Information Science—Permanence of Paper for Printed Library Materials, ANSI Z39.84-1984.

For Patillo Higgins
Anthony Lucas
John Galey
Dad Joiner
and their descendants

CONTENTS

FOREWORD

Texas Oil, American Dreams: A Study of the Texas Independent Producers and Royalty Owners Association is the fifth volume in the Barker Texas History Center series, a cooperative publication program of the University of Texas at Austin Center for American History (CAH) and the Texas State Historical Association. CAH is a special collections library, archive, and museum that facilitates research and sponsors programs on the historical development of the United States. Its components include the Barker Texas History Collections, the Sam Rayburn Library and Museum (in Bonham, Texas), the Winedale Historical Center (near Round Top, Texas), the Littlefield Southern History Collections, and the Congressional History Collections.

The Barker series was established to encourage and support the publication of historical studies based mainly on CAH's Barker Texas History Collections, which includes the nation's largest Texana library as well as extensive holdings of archival, cartographic, newspaper, sound, and photographic material. Texas Oil, American Dreams was selected for the series because a significant portion of the book is based on the Barker Collections' especially rich holdings documenting the history of the Texas oil industry. These include an extensive archive produced by a pioneering oral history project funded in 1952 by Mrs. Walter B. Sharp to preserve the memories and records of individuals who participated in the discovery and development of early Texas oil fields, including Spindletop and East Texas; an oral history collection documenting the legal and political battle waged between Texaco and Pennzoil over control of the Getty Oil Company; the papers of Texas railroad commissioner E. O. Thompson; and the papers of several prominent Texans who played key roles in the history of Texas oil.

CAH's collections on the history of the Texas oil industry were enhanced significantly in 1991 with the acquisition of the archives of the Texas Independent Producers and Royalty Owners Association (TIPRO) and with the TIPRO Foundation's funding of a CAH project to record the memories of key TIPRO leaders. This project has resulted in an outstanding oral history archive that supplements TIPRO's historically valuable organizational records. It is these two TIPRO collections—the oral history archive and the organizational records—that Lawrence Goodwyn has used so effectively in *Texas Oil, American Dreams*.

The oral history archive project that provided the source base for *Texas Oil, American Dreams* was made possible by financial sources administered by the Center for American History, primarily the TIPRO Endowment, the Sharp Fund for the History of the Texas Oil Industry, and the J. R. Parten Chair in the Archives of American History. I want to thank former TIPRO executive director Julian Martin and the TIPRO board of directors for their generous support and for their decision to place the TIPRO archive at CAH. Dr. Barbara Griffith, former head of the CAH Oral History Program, not only conducted oral history interviews for the TIPRO project but also served as CAH's ambassador to the TIPRO management and its board of directors. Her work was exemplary. Ron Tyler, director of the Texas State Historical Association, and George Ward, assistant director, were enthusiastically supportive of this project from its earliest stages. I thank them and TSHA's Executive Council for making the publication of *Texas Oil, American Dreams* possible.

DON E. CARLETON, Director
Center for American History

ACKNOWLEDGMENTS

This book would not have been possible without the cooperation of three institutions—the Center for American History at the University of Texas at Austin, the Texas State Historical Association, and the Texas Independent Producers and Royalty Owners Association (TIPRO). I first wish to acknowledge the work of Dr. Barbara Griffith, director of the Oral History Program at the Center for American History at the University of Texas. To Professor Griffith fell the task of traveling throughout Texas—and, indeed, beyond—to interview the enormous variety of people whose lives have given tangible meaning to the descriptive term "wildcatter." The immense diversity of approaches to oil and gas discovery, to politics and society, to technological innovation, and to the environment as well as the sheer complexity of the issues that have surrounded America's wildcatting community collectively represent a genuine challenge for the oral historian, one Dr. Griffith met with persistence and grace. I know she joins me in publicly acknowledging our deep appreciation to all the independent producers in Texas who gave so freely of their time and energy to make this project possible. All students of petroleum issues will benefit from the thousands of pages of transcripts now being processed and catalogued at the University of Texas. I am the first of many scholars to stand in her debt. The director of the Center for American History, Don Carleton, has cooperated at every stage of this archival and literary effort. I take this opportunity to thank him as well as Barbara Griffith for their unflagging assistance at every stage of this project.

In addition, Professor Griffith and I participated in joint interviews with John Hurd, Jerry O'Brien, Bruce Anderson, R. L. Foree Jr., and George Mitchell. Some interviews, including follow-up interviews by telephone, were conducted by the author with Bill Rutter, Irene Wischer, Tom Coffman, and John Hurd, wildcatters all, and with Julian Martin and Scott Anderson of TIPRO's staff. All other interviews cited in the text were conducted by Barbara Griffith. I also benefited from conversations with W. Earl Turner and R. L. Foree Sr., some of which dated back to the 1950s. Turner's death, at the very outset of this project, precluded his involvement, although his column, "ExTIPROaneous," in the *TIPRO Reporter* stands as an invaluable guide to the evolution of producer policy after World War II.

Julian Martin read every page of the manuscript and saved the author from factual errors and interpretive omissions, for which I wish to record my deep appreciation. His analysis of the pivotal relevance of the end of Texas reserve capacity in 1972 to the American crude supply crisis of 1973 is specifically recorded in Chapter 4. But beyond this, as all TIPRO intimates know, Julian Martin is something of an archive in himself; a lifetime of association with TIPRO's most active participants has equipped him with a sophisticated sense of petroleum issues and association policy as both have evolved over time. He has routinely been able to provide the kind of nuanced responses that scholars earnestly seek and do not always find. I thank him for his sustained attention to all of my requests, as well as for being what he is—a storehouse of information on the independent producing industry in America.

TIPRO's new executive vice-president, Scott Anderson, was also helpful on TIPRO's more recent initiatives, detailed in the latter part of Chapter 6 and for which I am most grateful. I also want to acknowledge the friendly and knowledgeable assistance of TIPRO's Austin staff, especially Paula Christian, Christy Coventry, Amy Carman, and Sandra Bloodworth.

In ways that extend far beyond the limits of oil and gas, the Texas State Historical Association has through many decades established itself as one of the cultural blessings of the Southwest. It has been a pleasure for me to rediscover this truth once again. I wish to acknowledge the gracious and professional cooperation of Ron Tyler, TSHA's director. In readying the manuscript for publication, George Ward, TSHA's assistant director, served as an invaluable shepherd. I am indebted as well to Alison Tartt for her commitment and intellectual rigor as a copyeditor and to David Timmons for his design of the book. I also thank my friend and associate, Scott Ellsworth, for his contribution to the title.

Finally, I wish to take special note of the work of Nell Goodwyn in the difficult task of assisting me in sorting through hundreds of pages of interview transcripts. With a keen eye for the symbolic story or the specific interpretation that helped to illuminate an intricate topic, she supplied notes on every transcript that proved to be an invaluable guide through a mountain of material. Additionally, and as always, I wish to acknowledge the consummate editorial and critical review the final manuscript received at her hands. This is the sixth time we have engaged in such a joint literary effort, and, as always, I am conscious that a mere public acknowledgment of her editorial discrimination, no matter how phrased, constitutes a wholly inadequate attempt to convey to others the centrality of her role. One fact is at least suggestive: she was instrumental in the naming of the book—as she was once before in our shared endeavors.

INTRODUCTION

First a Tradition,
Then a Method of Survival

Although the initial production of oil in America came in Pennsylvania in 1859 and soon gave rise to the world's first monopolistic "trust"—John D. Rockefeller's Standard Oil Company—the truly great petroleum discoveries did not come until two generations later. On a January morning in 1901 on the upper Gulf Coast of Texas, a great torrent of crude oil blew out of the ground, shattered the pipe that carried it, and drenched the surrounding countryside with what was later estimated as 100,000 barrels of oil. They called the phenomenon "Spindletop." In the   fullness of time, another great torrent surged out of the ground near the small Texas hamlet of Henderson, setting off an unprecedented drilling boom that reached into five counties. They called this phenomenon "the East Texas field."

Though separated by more than a generation, Spindletop and East Texas were intimately and historically linked. Both came in remote and wholly unleased terrain, far from the gaze of anyone in Mr. Rockefeller's oil empire. The people who thus got in on the ground floor were local residents and their neighbors from nearby Texas towns and cities. Spindletop generated thousands of citizens who of necessity learned the nascent language of the oil patch and who thereupon began to put their knowledge to work. They labored as "roustabouts" and as "roughnecks" on or around equipment called "drilling rigs" for other men who became known as "drilling contractors." Attendant commercial arrangements were made by landmen, who would pay farmers and ranchers for the right to drill on their property. These lease hounds were also called oil scouts because another of their duties was to keep their employers current on developments around other people's drilling rigs. Eventually, a number of college graduates trained in geology and engineering would come to be associated with this band of people who bored holes in the ground.

Because it all started in an out-of-the-way corner of Texas, these arrangements, jobs, professions, and undertakings were all quite informally achieved, an ad hoc assortment of craftsmen and seat-of-the-pants specialists who came together for a time, drilled a well, and then separated. Their little community was temporarily brought together by yet another member of their tribe, one who contracted with the drilling contractors who hired the roughnecks. In oil country, members of this last calling were known as independent operators. But in popular lore, a more vivid term was invented to describe them: "wildcatters." They looked for oil where it was not known to exist—in "wild" country.

These wildcatters had one quality that distinguished them from their tribal counterparts: they knew how, as they themselves would describe it, to "put together a drilling deal." The less capital they had, the more nuances of this art they had to master. Carefully managed, a drilling deal could be put together with very little capital—by selling off enough of its component pieces to pay the contractors and the pipe supply companies and by giving the landowner a bit more "royalty" than normal in lieu of paying hard cash. What was left over after these arrangements constituted the wildcatter's interest in his own well. It often was quite small, as little as one-fourth or even one-eighth of the total. As a wildcatter might explain, it was the only way, given his financial situation at the time, to "get the drilling bit to the pay sand."

Spindletop created these social types in America. The surrounding terrain in Texas, with its pools of oil here and there, nurtured them so that they grew in number. Twenty-nine years and ten months after Spindletop, one of these independent operators hit a prolific discovery well in a remote corner of the piney woods of East Texas. Others of his breed broadened the field and defined its remarkable dimensions: at the time, it was nothing less than the largest oil field in the history of the world. But the most striking fact was that all of it languished in unleased country, so there were soon literally thousands upon thousands of additional members of the oil-finding clan. If Spindletop brought them into being, East Texas consolidated their numbers and made them a permanent social fixture in Texas. Together, Spindletop and East Texas served as midwives to the emergence in America of a new kind of entrepreneur, the Texas independent oil producer, the prototypical American "wildcatter."

This book is about their social and economic origins and development, their discovery of the unbalanced and distorted commercial world in which they lived, and the political trajectory that, out of their own agonies, they gradually came to embody. It is, in the end, the story of the institution they created to advance their beliefs—the Texas Independent Producers and Royalty Owners Association.

This chronicle has meaning beyond its provincial origins because the needs of independent producers intersected with an organically American political belief first set in place by Thomas Jefferson: the American antimonopoly tradition. It is proper at the outset to explore this relationship because it provides the unifying thread that makes the elaborate tapestry of TIPRO comprehensible. Without a clear grasp of this essential relationship, the intricate and unusual history of TIPRO remains indecipherable.

The republican idea that brought coherence to the American struggle for independence was the deeply felt need for people to fashion for themselves some kind of effective protection against centralized power. This quest had its origins in antiquity when it was focused on emperors and kings and the "aristocracies" they fostered, but it was in the eighteenth century that a fully fleshed-out conception of republicanism gave the idea of popular "liberty" genuine political texture. However, concurrent with the republican breakthrough of the eighteenth century, with its targeted emphasis on political centralization, came the emergence of new forms of economic centralization. Within the very first generation after the creation of the American Constitution, this purely economic development became sufficiently advanced that the victorious revolutionary named Thomas Jefferson was moved to warn his countrymen, in an 1816 letter, of the power and subtlety of the new danger: "I hope we shall crush in its birth the aristocracy of our monied corporations which dare already to challenge our government to a trial of strength and bid defiance to the laws of our country." In thus giving expression to what would become the American antimonopoly tradition, the author of the Declaration of Independence was one of the first republican theorists to try to acquaint the entire citizenry with the fact that the historic seedbed of tyranny, centralized political power, also had a potent economic dimension. Excessive economic concentration was threatening to a republican form of government precisely because it created the opportunity for dangerous "defiance" of the republican ideal itself.

For all subsequent American generations down to the present, antimonopolism became a gigantic umbrella under which a vast panoply of citizens endeavored at one time or another to express their political philosophy. For political activists in all walks of life—on farms, in business, in factories—to be a good republican meant being an informed antimonopolist.

The word "informed" is the key adjective in this description. Throughout the nineteenth and twentieth centuries, corporate concentration grew in ways that were both highly visible and deeply troubling to most Americans. Indeed, so great was the civic unpopularity of the great turn-of-the-century trusts—led by the "granddaddy of trusts," the Standard Oil Company—that the essential debate on the subject was not about the threat to democracy that they represented, but rather about how best to cope with the threat. But while the economic reach of the trusts was plain, Americans were far less successful in informing themselves about the political reach of these giants. For reasons that have remained obscure, antitrust statutes were both heralded in public debate and passed into law by the Congress—only to prove utterly ineffective in halting the onward rush of economic concentration. Somehow and in some way, the fine print of the statutes seemed to allow a variety of loopholes. One had to be something of a legal scholar even to begin to understand precisely why this was so. Casual observers meanwhile lamented the fact that the American public was never really sufficiently informed on the subject to address the problem.

Convincing historical evidence gradually accumulated to show that neither Republican Teddy Roosevelt nor Democrat Woodrow Wilson proved effective on the issue, and the same fate routinely visited their sundry successors in both parties down to the present. While the overwhelming majority of Americans would have been offended by any suggestion that they were willing participants in a failed antimonopoly process, they also over time grew weary of the struggle and eventually gave up on the notion of "solutions."

But independent petroleum producers could never grow weary and could never give up because they lived in the very center of a universe dominated by giants. It is this fact that makes the history of TIPRO germane in contemporary America. While other Americans might complain over the breakfast table about recurring corporate excesses, independents were forced, by the very nature of their occupation, to try to survive in a realm dominated by the so-called Seven Sisters, each of them international in scope, each of them integrated through every stage of production, transportation, refining, and marketing, and each of them capable of showing up at the next moment right on one's doorstep.

Informed? There were no Americans anywhere—not in the cloistered confines of universities, not in the brokerage houses of Wall Street, not anywhere—who stayed as well informed about "the majors" as the independent oil and gas producers who populated the ranks and provided the leadership of TIPRO. Indeed, as the half-century of evidence they have generated makes strikingly clear, their understanding was not rooted in any variety of intermittently practiced ideology. Rather, the antimonopoly rhythms of independent producers grew out of the most intimate knowledge of the day-to-day operations of the major petroleum corporations and reflected deeply felt grievances that emerged from the oil and gas fields of Texas. And the same antimonopoly tradition explicitly shaped hundreds of stories and headlines in the *TIPRO Reporter* as it chronicled pipeline discrimination and price discrimination through a half-century of the independents' struggle for equity in all phases of petroleum exploration and production. Historically, the activities of the majors have impinged so massively and so relentlessly upon small producers that their struggle for survival can at all times be understood as a concerted search for breathing room.

Over TIPRO's span of fifty years, independents were forced to learn subtleties about the American political system that in a number of pivotal ways often went well beyond the insights gained by the rest of the populace. Indeed, these subtleties often outpaced the sophistication of self-appointed political pundits in the press or even a goodly number of scholars in the nation's universities. During more than a half-century of all-too-intimate association, independents came to know a great number of things about the majors that few other people in America knew.

None of which is to suggest, even for an instant, that independents brought to their endeavors some special endowment of political or intellectual skill otherwise denied their fellow Americans. To assume such would be to miss the essence of their effort. Rather, what can properly be called the "self-education" of the independents was a long and quite agonizing process. It worked its will first in the fields of the oil patch itself, then later in the halls of government in Austin and, after World War II, in the U.S. Congress and the federal agencies charged with administering energy policy. Throughout, it was a process suffused with a great many surprises. Quite often they were grim surprises. But while the process of self-education yielded a steady diet of disappointing news in the short run, it also provided instructive guidance for the future.

In short, what Texas independents gradually came to understand went beyond the economic imperatives of corporate concentration to the multiple forms of politics through which these imperatives were advanced in the public realm. There were moments when TIPRO's activists acquired rather more knowledge about the majors than they enjoyed having; it was the kind of wisdom that underscored the stark power of the very forces they were confronting. But it was precisely in this institutional capacity that TIPRO played a role that no individual producer could have hoped to play alone. Meetings of TIPRO's task forces and of its executive committee brought together men of different generations and different areas of specialization who had all been forced to participate in the necessary folkway of "living with the majors." As one TIPRO activist, later a TIPRO president, remembered his early days as a fledgling member, "I learned in TIPRO meetings what certain public statements by different industry spokesmen actually meant. I learned how things really worked in Washington, and in Austin, too. It was a real education. Sobering. But real. Very real."

Collectively, when independents shared with each other their experiences and their insights, they were helping over time to create, inside TIPRO itself, an institutional memory of the independent producer's struggle for breathing space. Lessons learned in the 1950s in the bizarre Washington struggles over natural gas and in similar battles throughout the 1950s and 1960s over oil imports were, as this study details, mobilized by independents in new ways in the 1970s—with an effect that surprised major company executives as much as it puzzled veteran Washington reporters of both conservative and liberal persuasion. In so doing, independents scored some unlikely victories.

For most of TIPRO's oldest veterans, these results verified the utility of all the hard lessons they had been forced to ponder since the very earliest days of their association. In the course of this intricate sequence of events, TIPRO's approach to American politics changed over time in ways that gave the organization a distinctive style among other associations of oil and gas people. Recurrently, TIPRO was understood by admirers and detractors alike as being in the vanguard in giving voice to the aspirations of independents. In new ways, it is still out front in the 1990s, though its effort is often now centered in areas of production that were themselves largely unexamined only a decade ago.

Viewing the saga of TIPRO from a historical perspective, it is now evident that both the achievements and the setbacks of independents have the particular shape they do because they reflect the direct experience of small producers forced by circumstance to labor in a world of commerce dominated by others. The range of political assumptions that independents brought with them when they joined TIPRO was, and remains, awesome in its diversity. It has inevitably produced the kind of volatile internal debates for which TIPRO itself became famous within the producing industry. But what held these partisans together, even when they argued passionately with one another, were two ingredients: their shared understanding of the most subtle implications of major company policies and, secondly, the shared language of the American antimonopoly tradition, which surfaced in the founding TIPRO meeting in 1946 and which served as the animated subtheme of the association ever after. The tradition itself, sweeping as it is and relevant to independents as it is, has always provided small producers with a way to articulate their aspirations and their grievances that is so supple and effective that it serves to mute the recurring contentions that have intermittently divided them from one another. In the particular style of assertion that TIPRO fashioned in its own behalf, and in the specific victories that verified the continuing vitality of this style, organized independents created a specific kind of substance for the American antimonopoly tradition that it had previously possessed only at very widely separated moments in the nation's history.

It is an intricate theme, full of sinew, assertion, defeat, and renewal. But it is also the central thread that runs through the analytical chronicle that follows. What ensues is an account, frequently in the words of

TIPRO's people themselves, of the search of Texas independents for a measure of autonomy within the realm of a global market. The continuing search itself became the substance of their effort to survive, as independent people, in a world inexorably becoming more centralized. In its implications about the driving imperatives of modern life, their story is not provincial. It speaks to everyone who respects the idea of autonomy and independence.

Chapter One

DEMOCRACY COMES TO THE WORLD OF OIL

The enduring descriptive word for the oil industry is "surprise." Oil fields are discovered in unexpected places, expand in unanticipated ways, and inevitably decline, often for unforeseen reasons. Survival for the independent producer has therefore depended on one quality: a highly creative ability to adapt to change. Those who have proven unable to do so have routinely found themselves pushed to the edge of extinction.

The first surprises came in the beginning, literally in antiquity: the curious black liquid that oozed up around swamps not only seemed to make wheels turn more easily, but it also burned in ways that could help people see after dark. Alchemists and healers in the Middle Ages tested the possibility that the greasy fluid might have medicinal qualities. It was tried as a cure for cattle diseases and, when the death rate did not soar, it was tried on humans. By the early Renaissance, the stuff had acquired enough of a reputation that it was sold at fairs and markets in fifteenth-century Europe. Its proven value was as an illuminant, especially after the first rudimentary oil lamps were invented. Thereafter the surprises came in the area of production: Scots made lamp oil from cannel coal while Scandinavians made it from wood tar. A Czech proved that shafts dug into the ground could yield oil. By 1840, a Romanian had built a primitive refinery that filtered out the uniquely offensive odor of Romanian crude.

But these efforts were pretty small potatoes—there simply was not enough available oil in the world to sustain anyone's attention for very long. All this changed when the first genuine oil well was drilled in Titusville, Pennsylvania, in 1859 and started the process that levered what had been a small-scale curiosity into a global enterprise. The one thing that did not change, however, was the constancy of surprise, especially in the price of oil. When the first fields sprang up around Titusville in 1859, oil was $20 a barrel. Two years later it was ten cents a barrel. By the wartime summer of 1864, the price had soared to $14, but it was back down to $4 by the following year. As financial speculators endeavored to estimate the shape of the post–Civil War economy, the quoted price for oil was $1.35 in December 1866, $5.75 in July 1868, $7.00 in January 1869, and $2.70 in August 1870.

With tactics that made him both renowned and hated within a single generation, John D. Rockefeller soon brought a measure of order to the world of oil through a series of ruthless organizing tactics that linked his name to a whole series of new trends: monopoly, pooling, rebates, and the first and largest trust of them all, the Standard Oil Company. The world's first robber baron wiped out competitors with such tenacious resolve that he seemingly put a permanent end to surprise in the oil business. Everywhere one looked, Standard Oil presided with iron serenity over a private empire of petroleum.[1]

And then, on the upper Gulf Coast of Texas, came Spindletop.

"It's Oil, Captain!"

The discovery of the great salt dome near Beaumont in 1901 is a saga so bizarre and so overwhelming in the sheer number of superlatives it generated that it is a story invariably told in a language of breathless hyperbole. A "colossal explosion" at the rig! A gusher of "absolutely unprecedented" and even "unimaginable" proportions! Huge . . . the largest . . . the biggest . . . . And so forth. Such accounts miss the mark.

For the people whose lives have been shaped by the social realities of oil production, the long-term qualities surrounding the discovery well at Spindletop turn not on the wildly sensational nature of the details, but on precisely the opposite phenomenon. For wildcatters, for drilling contractors and roughnecks, for rock hounds and lease hounds, for independent operators of every description, the one feature of Spindletop that rings true nearly a century later is the striking commonality of the very happenings that outsiders find so sensational. The details are so achingly familiar that they merge heartbreak and ecstasy into a routine rhythm. Indeed, it is hard to imagine a single modern oil producer who has not personally experienced one or more of the specific joys and disappointments associated with Spindletop.

The details of the great well are essential to an understanding of petroleum production, not only because Spindletop yielded the state's most famous early independent oilmen, but precisely because the ingredients of good sense, good science, and good luck that they embodied blended into the cold hard world of finance with a starkness that ever after was to define both the potentials and the limits of the world of the wildcatter. The ongoing truth is that Spindletop happened because ordinary human beings named Higgins, Lucas, Galey, and Hamill simply wouldn't quit when all sorts of representatives of sanctioned wisdom announced they should pack it in. They didn't quit because they had reason to believe they knew better.

Another familiar harbinger of things to come turned on the fact that the demands of the drilling site outstripped the technical capabilities of the industry as it then existed. These capabilities had to be transformed—and they were. The key to making sense of Spindletop is to see the discovery well as the product of a series of concentric circles that linked visionaries with engineers, and speculators with practical craftsmen. The end product was a mixture of seat-of-the-pants geology, drillhole engineering, and speculative financial improvisations that were able to overcome all obstacles. It is no surprise to oilmen to learn that the fruits of these many forms of labor were not fairly divided—they almost never are.

Spindletop got its name from a man named Patillo Higgins.[2] This is fitting, for he is the one who had the vision in the first place. Higgins was a jack-of-all-trades dreamer who eventually became transfixed by a particular geographical feature near his hometown—the "Big Hill" just south of Beaumont. The distinguishing feature of the place was not its size (the hill—its name to the contrary— did not at any point rise more than twelve feet above the surrounding coastal plain) but rather the rotten odor of sulfurous gas seeping near its crest. Though no surface oil could be found, Patillo Higgins was certain that significant crude deposits lurked beneath the mound.

He soon convinced a good cross section of the town's leading citizens that a veritable metropolitan boom merely awaited the drilling of the necessary initiating well. The resulting Gladys Oil Company was named after a girl in Higgins's Sunday school class. The new company bought and leased most of the land around Big Hill (a considerable hunk of acreage, as the mound was more than a half-mile in diameter), and drilling soon began. The year was 1893. The objective was a depth of 1,000 feet, but the first effort did not get below 400. The loose sands of the coastal plain did not respond to the light drilling equipment Higgins was able to mobilize. The hole ruined, he tried again—and again—failing each time even to reach the depth obtained on his original try. Three dry holes.

Years passed and Higgins, long since abandoned by his original backers, acquired a local reputation as a benign but thoroughly addled crackpot. To keep going, he sold off his lease holdings until he was down to a mere thirty-three acres. His efforts to drum up scientific support failed miserably. Oil was no longer alien to Texas (a water-drilling enterprise had inadvertently struck oil in Corsicana in 1894), but the Gulf Coast remained resistant. Three separate geological surveys produced resounding negative opinions. The information was scarcely private: one scientific judgment published in the local press soberly advised the citizenry "not to fritter away their dollars in the vain outlook for oil in the Beaumont area."

So Higgins carried his message elsewhere, advertising in an eastern trade journal. The effort was not entirely wasted; the circle of involvement widened, though just barely. The one response was from an immigrant engineer who, as Anthony Luchich, had once held a commission in the Austro-Hungarian navy. He came to America, kept the military title, anglicized his name, and thus responded to the ad as Captain Anthony Lucas. Higgins's florid description of the "great oil-bearing concession" near Beaumont undoubtedly carried little weight with Lucas, but the added description of a mound of gas and sulfur suggested the existence of a salt dome. It was a geographical feature about which Lucas had acquired firsthand knowledge as an engineer on a salt mine in the Louisiana bayou country. On two of these mining explorations, Lucas had encountered a measure of sulfur and oil associated with the salt.

Lucas traveled to Beaumont to look things over because he had come to believe that oil, gas, salt, sulfur, and mounds were somehow associated. He liked what he found at Big Hill and promptly leased 600 acres from the Gladys Oil Company for $11,000 in cash and $20,000 in notes. For his part, Higgins traded his thirty-three acres for a 10 percent interest in Lucas's larger holdings.

With the believers in Big Hill now doubled to two, drilling began in July 1900. Using rotary drilling equipment from Louisiana, Lucas expected to reach 1,000 feet within a matter of weeks, but the sandy soil foiled him as it had earlier foiled Higgins. Lucas and his stout-hearted Georgia wife saved money by living in a shack near the drill site, but after six months and 575 feet—punctuated by a few intriguing shows of oil—the equipment had reached its maximum capacity and Lucas was broke. The number of dry holes at Big Hill had climbed to four. Only one source for additional financing seemed possible—Standard Oil. Lucas wrote one of Rockefeller's top executives, Henry Fogler, and the latter dispatched the company's production chief, Calvin Payne, to Beaumont.

"Experts," then as now, quite naturally put great stock in precedents and in personal experience. Payne had looked at oil fields in Russia, Romania, Sumatra, and Borneo and had never seen a salt dome. He reported to his superiors that he had found "no indication whatever to warrant the expectation of an oil field on the prairies of southeastern Texas." Big Hill, he concluded, "has no analogy to any oil field known, as in fact there was not the slightest trace of even an oil escape."[3] Standard Oil said goodbye to Big Hill.

Lucas turned next to a renowned scientist, C. Willard Hays, soon to become chief of the U.S. Geological Survey. Hays couldn't find any surface oil seepage either, and that was good enough for him: he could see "no precedent for expecting to find oil in the great unconsolidated sands and clays of the Coastal Plain."

As every oil operator knows, the will to drill a specific site is a compound of three ingredients—capital, some measure of scientific encouragement, and intuition. Higgins and Lucas had a fair stock of the latter, but it was being warred against by the utter absence of the first two. After the expert from Standard left town, Lucas turned in desperation to a University of Texas field geologist named Dr. William Battle Phillips, director of the Texas State Mineral Survey. Phillips inspected the site, weighed the contradictory opinions of Hays and Payne on the one hand and Lucas on the other, and came down on Lucas's side. He thought the Lucas theory about oil in salt domes sounded sensible. The interlocking circles had acquired another ring: Phillips gave Lucas a letter of introduction to the Pennsylvania oil-prospecting firm of Guffey & Galey.

With Phillips, the Texas enterprise now had a bit of scientific support to array alongside the determination of Lucas and Higgins. Lucas went to Pittsburgh in search of the third ingredient—money. He had more than a modicum of hope because the Guffey & Galey firm had not only acquired an oil-finding reputation in Pennsylvania and later in Kansas, but in the process it had also proved its willingness to take a gamble.

The two Pennsylvania men were, in fact, quite a distinctive duo. Colonel James McClurg Guffey was a particular variety of circuit-riding salesman. He had no theories about finding oil and sense enough to engage in no pretenses that he did; he happily consigned that part of the business to the keen-minded John Galey. Guffey sold the particular deals Galey advised him to sell. He dressed his role with committed fervor—pleated shirts and shimmering vests, Prince Albert coats, an elegant white moustache and a broad-brimmed black hat atop a flowing shock of white hair. It was easy to surmise that Guffey was the kind of man who was ideally equipped to move with confidence and ease among the Irish pols who dominated the urban machines of the northern Democratic Party, and, indeed, his personal dossier was topped off by that very fact: in the administration of President Chester Arthur, James Guffey had served as Democratic National Chairman!

While Guffey pursued investors, Galey pursued oil with the passion of the committed prospector. Small, modest, and determinedly inconspicuous, Galey had fashioned his commercial style in Pennsylvania. His business strategy was well developed: find promising leases, drill them, find oil, put together a big package, sell it to the Standard Oil Company—and move on. John Galey did not enjoy selling oil; his passion was in finding it.

When they met in Pittsburgh, Galey found Lucas's story sufficiently interesting to warrant a trip to Beaumont. What he saw at Big Hill looked promising, and he left it to Guffey to browbeat a suitable deal out of the desperate Lucas.

Guffey's negotiating style was to counterpose a trickle of hope against a tidal wave of gloomy facts. The site, he moaned to Lucas, had much against it. The people at Standard, the richest and best-informed people in the business, thought Big Hill was hopeless. Three Texas surveys had reached the same conclusion. The outsider Hays concurred, extending his negative conclusion to the upper gulf plains as a whole. The four dry holes already drilled at Big Hill added practical verification to the thumbs-down chorus. Finally, Lucas's trifling 600-acre lease was too small to justify a major investment. In short, Guffey and Galey would play, but only under strict conditions. First, the deal must be kept totally secret to allow Lucas to increase the lease holdings on a massive scale. Guffey & Galey would invest $300,000, take possession of seven-eighths of the leases, and leave Lucas with a one-eighth stake in the overall play. A deep well would be drilled. If it failed to produce oil, the venture would be closed.

Lucas accepted these terms. He set about quietly leasing 15,000 acres surrounding Big Hill. In his turn, Higgins also accepted the deal—though this meant his holding was now reduced to a one-tenth portion of Lucas's one-eighth. For both Higgins and Lucas, what really counted was that the dream—at whatever cost—was kept alive.

Guffey, for his part, now needed $300,000. To get it, he turned to none other than the famed New York banker Andrew Mellon. The Mellon partners had a settled distrust of the flamboyant Guffey, but this was balanced by two facts: Andrew Mellon himself liked Guffey, and both he and his partners had respect for John Galey's "amazing power to scent a hidden pool of oil underground." After a good measure of internal discussion, the Mellon group provided the necessary funds.

The Mellon interests aside, the wildcatters who coalesced to sustain the possibilities of oil at Big Hill were an interesting study in variety. In fact, they formed a constellation of personalities that, singly or together, could easily find a home at a post–World War II TIPRO convention. A quick sketch of each illustrates the point. Patillo Higgins was a tall and angular East Texan, a logger, a carpenter, a browser of books, a campfire brawler, and, above all, a man of very large speculations. He had figured out that gas in contact with sand and shale would turn them to rock, which, in turn, would be impervious to oil and thus form a trap—traps that could hold oil! Higgins saw no reason why the town of Beaumont, buttressed by enough oil, might not become one of the great cities of the American West. After persuading enough local investors to get the well started, he went it alone for years when the early hopes were dashed. He endured through dry holes 2 and 3 and continued the vigil with Lucas through dry hole 4. Patillo Higgins adapted to each partition of his initial lease holdings necessary to finance a sustaining new endeavor. If he was a visionary, he was also a long-distance runner.

Anthony Lucas found the settled social rigidities and business habits of Central Europe to be much too confining for a man possessed of his tumultuous energy and ambition. A capable engineer, he focused on results rather than form, and he married a woman of similar outlook. Living in a shack near Big Hill seemed a sensible short-term expedient to preserve limited capital. When the capital ran out completely, he and his wife simply made the shack permanent by hauling in apple boxes and egg crates for furniture. The point was to get the drill bit to 1,000 feet; everything else was secondary.

Geologist Phillips added a measure of professorial independence. His personality was not flamboyant, and he derived no special joy from disagreeing with so much authoritative scientific nay-saying about the Beaumont site; rather, he simply thought Lucas's idea about oil in salt domes was reasonable. He knew a lot about minerals, particularly minerals in Texas, and he was quietly stubborn about what he knew.

But if Phillips brought a measure of down-home solemnity to the wildcatting team, the Pennsylvania duo of Galey and Guffey provided more than a swath of color to match Higgins and Lucas. Most of all, they brought the wherewithal to finish the well. Or so it appeared at the time. But before all the surprises had run their course, it became apparent that more than Andrew Mellon's money was needed to bring Spindletop onto the stage of history. The fifth and final wildcat at Big Hill turned out to be a saga of technical innovation. Though it was by no means clear to outside observers, the discovery well was the product of on-the-spot experimentation that proved absolutely essential to overcome a mountain of drilling problems. Since the soft soils of the coastal region were interspersed at varying depths with hard-rock formations, the drilling contractors were confronted by a sequence of hazards that were new to the fledgling industry.

A large rotary rig was brought in, operated by the Hamill brothers of Louisiana—Curt, J. G., and Al. The brothers had gained their initial oil-drilling experience in the Corsicana play and had learned to employ unusually large casings that allowed them to telescope four- to ten-inch pipe into the hole. On their rig—truly a big one for that era—the

Hamills kept the drilling bit cool by circulating water down the pipe. In a bit of on-the-job training at Big Hill, the brothers discovered that mud piped down the hole effectively plastered the hole against the cave-ins common to loose strata of sand. But where to get enough mud? And enough thick mud? The brothers drove a herd of cattle through the water pit, dug the mud out, drove the cattle back through, and dug some more out. It worked, and the world of petroleum had what all would soon recognize as an indispensable new invention: drilling mud.

It did, indeed, work but, in this case, only for a time. After 160 feet they encountered an assortment of loose gravel and sand that even their newly created high-tech mud failed to seal off. So they were forced to substitute what Al Hamill termed "a strong back": they drove eight-inch pipe downward by hand, rigging up a heavy block that, when lifted and then dropped, drove the beveled edge of the pipe into the strata—inches at a time. It was man-killing labor, and two men on the drilling crew quit. But the Hamills had caught a full-blown case of the Big Hill Disease and stayed the course—two backbreaking weeks before they were able to push through the 285-foot formation. After a spate of normal drilling, they then hit a pocket of natural gas that blew sand and mud up the pipe. The rig crew could not screw on additional lengths of pipe because when the counterpressure of the mud pump was halted, the pipe would stick. As with the four previous drilling attempts at Big Hill, the Hamill rig was stuck fast.

At this juncture, Captain Lucas took full possession of his role as one of the world's first petroleum engineers. After a sleepless night brooding about the problem (Galey had, after all, agreed to finance one well only), Lucas concluded that a back pressure valve could be fashioned in the pipe following the same principle that permitted water to be pumped into a steam boiler without allowing the steam to escape. He jury-rigged such a valve the very next day. The thing worked. Drilling again resumed. Anthony Lucas's invention of the back pressure valve became an essential part of all subsequent drilling rigs. It was Spindletop's second permanent technical contribution to the oil industry, following hard upon the Hamills' creation of drilling mud.

As the rotary bit proceeded downward, shows of oil and gas became intermittently—but increasingly—frequent. In the early morning hours of December 9, 1900, Al Hamill came on duty and soon noticed a change in the drilling rhythm. The previous shift had experienced slow going and almost a full length of pipe stood above the rotary table. Around three o'clock in the morning, the pipe began to go down at a quickening rate and Hamill detected oil in the ditch and slush pit. By the time breakfast arrived, the pit was full of oil. The brothers sent word to the Lucas shack little more than a mile away, and when the captain arrived he asked for an estimate of the potential productivity of the well.

Al Hamill's experience was restricted to the small Corsicana wells, producers of 10 to 25 barrels per day. He thought he had something larger, so he pulled a comparative figure out of the air: "easily 50 barrels a day." To Lucas and everyone else on the rig, it seemed golden news, perhaps too good to be true, but certainly a welcome estimate after so many disappointments. They added another joint of drill pipe and made an additional thirty-five feet through what everyone hoped was oil-bearing sand. They then hit hard rock once again and the pace abruptly slowed. It was time to summon John Galey from Pittsburgh.

For his part, the taciturn Galey had, in addition to his service as a conduit to Mellon capital, already played one other pivotal role: he had hand-picked the drill site. Upon his return to Big Hill in response to Lucas's summons, Galey decided they should drill down another 300 feet before trying to complete the well. They hit the 1,020-foot level by the first week of January 1901, when they pulled the pipe to change drilling bits. They had managed to lower only 700 feet of pipe back into the hole when the well suddenly began to spout mud—700 feet of mud and more! It surged with such force it washed over Curt Hamill, sitting high in the derrick. He hurriedly scrambled down.

All then watched in amazement and growing terror as tons of heavy pipe began to shoot up out of the hole, up, up, over the derrick, the joints breaking and crashing all around them. After a period of absolute chaos, an eerie quiet settled over the rig and the drilling crew cautiously approached the mud-wracked ruin that moments before had been an ultramodern drilling rig.

And then, suddenly, it happened. Without warning, a sudden roar could be heard, immediately followed by a volcano of mud, rocks, gas, and oil rocketing hundreds of feet into the air.

Absolutely no precedent existed for the scene that engulfed the Hamill brothers, and it took several minutes for its meaning to set in: an enormous, continuous surge of petroleum roaring out from the depths of the salt dome, cascading hundreds of feet into the air and drenching the

entire countryside in a black mist. Curt Hamill, covered in oil, suddenly came to his senses and remembered the fire in the boiler. "We've got
to get that fire out," he yelled, and all joined in throwing buckets of
water until the fire was safely doused. Captain Lucas arrived at a full gal-
lop and breathlessly shouted:

"Al, Al! What is it?"

"Oil, Captain. It's oil!"

"Thank God," Lucas sighed. It was hard to find anything else to say.

And oil it was, not fifty barrels a day as Al Hamill had forecast, or
even hundreds of barrels in an hour, but literally thousands of barrels
shooting skyward and raining down on equipment, animals, humans,
and miles of Texas prairie. It spewed somewhere between 75,000 to
100,000 barrels a day for nine days—the staggering total of 600,000 to
one million barrels—before a vastly expanded workforce and an increasingly frantic drilling crew could get the torrent capped. It was, indeed,
"the biggest" and the most "unimaginable" oil well in the history of the
world. Everything about it was "unprecedented," "beyond belief," "the
largest," and, clearly, "the most."

It was also a potential disaster—as soon became clear. The towering
gusher could be seen from a distance of ten to fifteen miles and people
by the thousands rode horses, walked, ran, took buggies, and pressed
close enough to feel the black mist rain into their faces. Many ended up
standing in the rapidly spreading pool of oil that radiated out from the
wellhead. Inevitably, someone threw down a lighted match and an
enormous fire started.

Hurrying back to Beaumont, Galey hired hundreds of men to build
a dike around the well and to spread sand outward from the site to protect against more fires. What followed next was part development, part
boom, and part madness. But first there was the matter of awarding credit for accomplishments already achieved.

In the vicinity of Beaumont, the new well was called "Captain
Lucas's amazing discovery." In New York papers it was "Colonel Guffey's
great gusher in Texas." But in the paneled boardrooms of Wall Street,
the word was quietly passed that "the Mellons have hit it big, very big,
in oil." In this casual labeling and accrediting process, John Galey's
name would occasionally find its way into print—if the story was long
enough—but the one person routinely overlooked in virtually all
accounts was Patillo Higgins.

Higgins had not been around on the big day, having left Beaumont early on the morning of the discovery to pursue a lumber deal he hoped would get him out of debt. But he had scarcely given up on Big Hill; indeed, when the Hamill rig first began drilling, Higgins took the precaution of buying thirty-three acres on the hill from a real estate company that called it Spindletop Heights. After the strike, the local papers took to the name. Thus it was that Patillo Higgins found the site, stayed with it for the greater part of a decade, provided the name for the discovery well—and then more or less disappeared from view. Forty years later, when townspeople erected a monument at Spindletop, Higgins's name would nowhere appear. The granite shaft honored "the first great oil well in the world—the Anthony F. Lucas gusher."

A curious fact, this—and one that calls forth all sorts of folk sayings familiar in oil country and elsewhere. As independent oil operators, along with a number of other knowledgeable citizens, are prone to say, "Some stay the course, and some don't; until you get some data, it's not always clear what to believe." In the oil business the matter of timing yields no hard and fast rules. The subsequent history of the Beaumont salt dome provided much specific evidence to add to the bare bones of this sort of popular wisdom.

What gradually became clear with Spindletop was that the oil patch had begun to develop an indigenous culture, one grounded in the startling tension between surprise and change. These were the counterrotating gears that generated among oilmen poise and panic, rigidity and adaptability. Through it all, few readily visible guidelines appeared that could be counted on to work over the long haul. "Staying power" did not necessarily mean hardheadedness. Producers could go broke being hardheaded. True, panic was never helpful, but, on the other hand, what some regarded as poise and prudence could also cause people to miss out completely on a promising oil play. All could agree that an oil operator needed to think things through, but, unfortunately, nobody could be sure just what this trustworthy adage meant in practical terms. In all events, the gains and losses were huge because, historically, it was the nature of oil production for the stakes to be high.

"History," of course, affords at least the appearance of a kind of after-the-fact certainty that events never have at the moment they occur. Spindletop was a great well, but it was by no means a foregone conclusion that it stood amid a great field. At least, that's the way matters appeared to Andrew Mellon. He was no plunger. Immediately after the discovery, Guffey pleaded for large sums to develop the field. Mellon opted instead to finance a few more wells. Others, of course, had the same idea, and in a matter of weeks the little mound outside Beaumont sprouted a good number of rigs. Every well drilled on the salt dome produced a flowing well. There could be no mistake: Spindletop was in fact a great field.

Nevertheless, Andrew Mellon did not feel any immediate affinity for the oil business. A huge problem existed in a central area—control. It was not only the fact that prices fluctuated far more than in other businesses, but there seemed to be too many players. In the case of Spindletop, the Mellons were yoked to Guffey, Galey, and Lucas, with subsidiary players like Patillo Higgins and also hundreds, perhaps thousands, of projected operators who owned tiny leases, or even pieces of leases, adjoining the drill site.

The negotiations between the Mellon interests and Colonel Guffey were a study in contrasts. The colorful Guffey had lived in a state of high anxiety virtually every moment since the original well had come in. Every sign of caution from the Mellons merely increased his insecurity. It was not until Guffey and Galey had drilled two more wells, both gushers, that the Mellon bank was willing to put up an additional $3 million for development. Nevertheless, from the Mellon standpoint, a considerable amount of administrative tidying up remained to be achieved. The Mellons shepherded into being the Guffey Petroleum Company with the understanding that Guffey would buy out both Galey and Lucas. This was done—although Guffey was able to take the $750,000 the Mellons thought he would be paying Galey and pare it down to half that sum, plus some extraneous stock in other ventures. Guffey knew his (ex-) partner's chief interest was in exploration rather than development, and he knew also that Galey did not always find it easy to pay sustained attention to the financial side of the business. Thus, as Guffey set about to flimflam his partner, only a minimal level of deception proved necessary.

Anthony Lucas proved a tougher bargainer. He did not yield up his one-eighth until Guffey paid him $400,000. The captain retreated from the scene, bought a modest home in Washington for himself and his Georgia bride, and lived comfortably ever after.

It did not take long for the Mellons to elbow Guffey to the sidelines, and he was shuffled out completely in 1907. A Mellon sat as president of Guffey Petroleum for a while, and then the enterprise was reorganized as Gulf Oil Company.

The institutional fallout from Spindletop was, indeed, a surprising tangle. Patillo Higgins's Gladys Oil Company had given way to a one-tenth interest in a wildcat drilled by Anthony Lucas, which had given way to a one-eightieth interest in a wildcat drilled by Guffey and Galey, which gave way to the Guffey Petroleum Company, which gave way to Gulf Oil Corporation. Along the way, all the principals had picked up and partially sold other leases around Big Hill so that in the end everybody got something. But it is the nature of humans, including those in the oil business, to exaggerate the importance of their own role. Anthony Lucas, for one, was so convinced of the absolute centrality of his own contribution to the Spindletop discovery that he had great difficulty finding the will to pay Patillo Higgins his one-tenth interest in their original partnership. Higgins had to sue to get it. He won. James Guffey had the same difficulty with Andrew Mellon. After years of frustration, Guffey also had to sue. A battery of Mellon lawyers parried and delayed, filed motions and appealed, as year after year passed. In the end, James Guffey did not win. By the time the case was over, Spindletop had given heft and substance to a number of major petroleum corporations that would figure prominently in the ensuing century of energy development: the Texas Company, Sun, Pure, and of course Gulf.

But in ways that included independents as well as major companies, the development of Spindletop established patterns—surprising and chaotic as they were—that became common in all the great fields that materialized during the discovery years. Indeed, the shadow of Spindletop came to fall across all parts of Texas because many of the discoveries of the next two generations were found by independents who had first gotten started in the course of developing the great salt dome on the upper Gulf Coast.

The key to understanding why Spindletop gave birth to such a large family of independent oil operators reposed in a simple fact—multiple royalty owners whose land remained unleased until after oil had been discovered. When Guffey and Galey originally told Anthony Lucas to increase his lease holdings as quickly and as massively as possible—and do so with profound secrecy—Lucas understandably set about to acquire large chunks of acreage. The 15,000 acres of lease holdings he soon acquired constituted a patchwork of plots, interspersed with many other unleased sections, small, smaller, and smallest. The value of these tiny holdings had nothing to do with previous economic guidelines—price was a function of what might be called "collective emotional mood." During the frantic days when the size of the Spindletop field first began to be grasped, a man who got off a train in Beaumont was offered a small lease for $1,000. He turned it down, only to see the passenger behind him accept. Within two hours, the new owner had sold the lease for $5,000—to a man who held it for even less time before trading it for $20,000.

The Spindletop boom quickly became so frenzied that even people who were in on the ground floor lost their bearings. Worried about the Mellon's long-term commitment, James Guffey temporarily lost his poise and sold fifteen acres on the Hill for $180,000 to a syndicate headed by former Texas governor James Hogg. The new owners carved out a two-and-one-half-acre section and promptly sold it for $200,000! They then "merrily chopped the rest" into enormously profitable pieces as small as one thirty-second of an acre. Guffey thus got a lesson in boom psychology. Nothing that had ever happened in Pennsylvania prepared him for the emotional effects Spindletop had on human beings, including himself.

It was the beginning of a way of life. The new breed of independents spawned by Spindletop spread out over Texas, fashioning jerry-built drilling deals to mobilize the necessary capital and then probing an increasing variety of subsurface formations. A marvelous plethora of dry holes resulted, but so did interesting discoveries—in places named Burkburnett, Ranger, and Electra and at Sour Lake and the Powell field. Today, all veteran oil operators know the tales of stupendous leasehold inflation embedded in the vivid old stories from the first two decades of the Texas fields that were developed in the aftermath of Spindletop. In oil country, the lore is rich: the pig pasture that went for $35,000; the downtown hotel lobby where traders carried $100,000 in suitcases; the great land syndicate created over a poker table; drilling sites on town lots so tiny they could barely contain a rig; a hamlet of 700 people that overnight bulged with a population of 50,000.

A sudden oil bonanza distorted everyone's sense of normal price levels, particularly when petroleum was compared with more familiar minerals. There were boomtowns where oil sold for three cents a barrel and water sold for five cents a glass. Across Texas in the first twenty years of the new century, the stories emerged from the coastal plains and from the prairies north of Dallas. Tales of triumph and heartbreak. Oil culture.

But the deeper truth, lurking beneath the bizarre and sensationalized stories, was a quiet social fact: thousands upon thousands of people across Texas were learning to participate in a new art form, one that embodied many crafts and diverse specialties—and one that rewarded those with an intimate knowledge of local terrain at the same time it rewarded those with a sense of a world market. It was an art form that involved technical excellence in engineering and expertise in geology, but just as centrally included nontechnical individuals who could recognize excellence in others.

Yet the culture of oil had still other dimensions. Good sense, yes, but also the kind of creative good sense that throughout Texas came to be described as "putting together a solid deal." In ways that were hard for outsiders to fathom, elements of character and integrity played integral roles in the way independent operators practiced the art of oil-finding. Over time, an oil operator found he liked the way a particular geologist "sat on a well." He learned to treasure a forthright engineer who "spoke English" rather than "all that technical jargon." Self-taught independents developed an eye for subsurface maps and an ear for the way landmen described leases. If one paid close attention, it was possible to develop a fairly keen sense of the commercial realities of the drilling contractor—a world of pipe and drilling bits, of "heaving holes" and drilling mud, and, near the moment of truth, a day when the tale told by an electric log brought in the ultimate verdict on a borderline venture. Every one of these ingredients, the people and the pipe and the mud, bore in some direct and crucial way on the particular hole in the ground on which everything else depended. Only oilmen knew the enormous variety of holes in the ground that were shaped by combinations of hard-rock, porous sands and—not least—by the depth of the well being drilled.

In the course of all this self-education, an oil operator learned how to save vital capital by putting other people into the deal. Geologists, landmen, drilling contractors, and, frequently, other independents all became at one time or another partners or employees, supporters or debtors, investors or creditors. It all depended on how one put together the deal to share the risk. The independent oil operator—that creator the world knew as "the wildcatter"—fashioned and lived in a web of social relationships that in its essential components was unlike any other in the nation.

The Graveyard of the Wildcatter

The scale of possibility suggested by Spindletop was most dramatically confirmed by the great discoveries in West Texas in the 1920s.[4] The discoveries themselves, and what followed from them, confirmed the permanence of oil culture in Texas. It is an interestingly symmetrical saga that runs from what old-timers called "glory-to-God wildcatting" to more modern, technologically informed chance-taking. The end result, in the 1950s, was a new kind of independent moving into the ranks of TIPRO. In all its guises, old-style and new-style, the story of the great West Texas discoveries is suffused with surprise and contradiction because it took place in areas where independents had drilled so many dry holes that the whole region had been written off. In popular lore, West Texas was "the graveyard of the wildcatter." So deeply entrenched was this folk wisdom that even after discoveries were made, the region's negative reputation continued to dominate thinking: each new find was termed "the last big one"—until strikes along the Canyon Reef after World War II finally silenced critics for good.

The discovery well in West Texas came in 1920. It was modest—a 50-barrel-a-day producer in Mitchell County. The big bonanza—one that was to transform the economic foundations of the University of Texas System—was the famed Santa Rita No. 1, drilled on university lands in 1923 in Reagan County. Under tremendous gas pressure, it ushered in the fabulous Big Lake field and also confirmed one of the great reputations in American wildcatting—Mike Benedum. The saga behind Santa Rita No. 1 contained the stuff of Sunday supplements, full of sensational and ironic detail etched onto a canvas of superlatives.

For one thing, Big Lake provided proof of the virtue of Mike Benedum's persistence in wildcatting. But contributing to the saga were five other men—Rupert T. Ricker, a Big Lake attorney and former army officer who leased (with money he did not have) 431,000 acres of University of Texas land for ten cents an acre; Frank Pickrell and Haymon Krupp, who handed Ricker a tidy profit by buying his lease, forming a drilling company, and promoting the money for a test well; Dr. Hugh Tucker, the geologist who selected the site near the old Kansas City, Mexico and Orient Railroad; and Dr. John Udden, whose optimistic oil report to the University of Texas board of regents was the first link in the chain of events that led to Ricker's getting the leases in the first place.

The test site itself was in lonely, forbidding country, far from any market and far from any pipeline. In the spring of 1923, Frank Pickrell junketed through the mesquite, cactus, and chaparral of Reagan County over the tracks of the Orient Railroad. On his flatcar he had his drilling equipment, his driller, and his workmen (roughnecks who were later to quit the lonely country and be replaced by cowboys). Fourteen miles west of the little hamlet of Big Lake, he unloaded by the tracks and began a race against time. His purchase agreement from Ricker had specified a test within eighteen months. To validate the 700 square miles of leases, he had to spud in by midnight. The original location had been staked three miles from the railroad, but because of the time element it was decided to drill along the track. (The original site, drilled later, proved dry.) Through the hours of sundown and into darkness, the little band of workers pushed desperately, and just before midnight the well was spudded in.

Then came another happening to add to the Big Lake legend. Among the investors promoted by Pickrell's firm had been a group of Catholics in New York. At the suggestion of their priest, they decided to christen the well Santa Rita—the saint of the impossible. They prevailed upon Pickrell to climb to the top of the drilling rig when the well was spudded and sprinkle dried rose petals blessed at a special mass, saying, "I christen thee Santa Rita."

But Santa Rita was to need even more than divine help before the discovery—a modest 100-barrel well—could be translated into the epochal Big Lake field. The successful wildcat generated crashing apathy within the oil industry. Neither nearby Texans nor major company officials in New York could be interested in the project. The well was too small, transport costs were too high from the remote desert location, and the price of crude had fallen again. Most decisive of all was the common wisdom: West Texas was the "graveyard of wildcatters." The convention was shored up by the knowledge that the original 1920 find in Mitchell County had made nobody a fortune and that the initial high prospects had been considerably reduced by subsequent production performances.

As Spindletop's Patillo Higgins had before him, Frank Pickrell began a futile tour of American financial circles in an effort to secure enough investment funds to prove or disprove his field. Besides his small well and huge acreage holdings, he had nothing—not even housing or drinking water. Most of all, he had no tankage, no pipeline, and no storage facilities. It was the same dilemma that would haunt Texas gas producers throughout the 1950s and 1960s.

It is possible that Frank Pickrell remembered the history of Spindletop and knew the name of the city where a similarly desperate Captain Anthony Lucas had found the backer of Spindletop, John Galey. Or perhaps Pickrell went to Pittsburgh simply because the John Galey of the 1920s, the famous wildcatter Mike Benedum, lived there. In any case, after a prolonged struggle, Pickrell won Benedum's agreement to drill eight wells to prove or condemn the field once and for all.

Benedum's initial hesitancy was grounded in the fact that his own Transcontinental firm was in such shaky condition that he had to raise drilling money in his native state of West Virginia. For this purpose he formed the Plymouth Oil Company and utilized his own reputation as the nation's most successful contemporary wildcatter to sell 300,000 shares of stock at $1.50 per share.

The testing of the Big Lake play started badly: Santa Rita No. 2 was just barely a well, not over 15 barrels on its best days. No. 3 was a dry hole. No. 4 was another weak well. All three were south and west of the discovery. Nos. 6, 7, and 8 continued the pattern: two dry holes and one tiny producer. They also continued the directional pattern—south and west of Santa Rita.

But Benedum ordered No. 5 drilled in a new direction—north of the discovery. It came in at 300 barrels a day, enough to renew everyone's flagging hopes and induce Benedum to ante up another $800,000 to keep the Big Lake crews busy. He staked No. 9 a bare 200 feet from the discovery well, but the direction was the important element: it was the first test drilled to the east. It roared in at 5,000 barrels a day. No. 11, completed next and still farther east, came in for 8,000. The thrust of the field was confirmed: Santa Rita No. 1 sat on the western edge of oil sands bearing great pressure. Glory lay to the east. The enormous gamble had paid off.

The Big Lake field immediately began to show huge profits. The price of crude rose, and in its first full year of operations, 1925, the Plymouth Oil Company was able to pay $1.50 a share in dividends, a 100 percent return on investment. The next year, it paid $5.25 a share.

Almost everyone connected with Big Lake got rich. Pickrell sold out for $4.5 million, went broke in the Depression, and made a later fortune. The University of Texas System began receiving the torrent of royalties that, in the 1930s, was to transform the Austin campus from a cluster of modest buildings into an $86 million plant. By 1995, the university system possessed a permanent endowment that exceeded $4.5 billion, a figure exceeded among American universities only by Harvard.

Mike Benedum had blessed his original Plymouth investors, but his own Transcontinental venture continued a precarious existence. He decided on a revolutionary move—to test the land west of the Pecos. As one observer put it, "The river was supposedly a geographical boundary, and certainly a psychological one, beyond which no wildcatter was disposed to venture. It was accepted belief that to drill west of the river was a sheer waste of money."[5]

But a rancher named Ira Yates had hounded Benedum's geologist, Levi Smith. In developing Big Lake, Smith had acquired a local reputation as a sound technician and a square shooter. In common with several million other Texas farmers and ranchers, Yates had an obsession about oil resting securely beneath his ranch. It was a theory that had long predated the Big Lake discovery some one hundred miles to the east. "Signs of oil are common along the Pecos River," he said. "You go down there and there'd be a spot twice the size of an ordinary desk oozing from the bank." Though Levi Smith was unimpressed, the sheer persistence of Yates's pleadings, fortified in repeated conversations with the geologist, finally won him over: "I'll tell you, Mr. Yates, I'll guarantee you myself that we'll drill a well." Benedum arranged with Mid-Kansas Oil and Gas Company to take a half interest in two blocks of leases, one of which included the Yates Ranch, in exchange for drilling four wells. But Mid-Kansas insisted on drilling all four (which were dry) outside the Yates Ranch. With still no test on Yates's land, Benedum and Smith determined to honor Levi's pledge and told Mid-Kansas that Transcontinental would drill the Yates test well if Mid-Kansas had had enough. Though officials of the latter company were reluctant, they finally agreed to come in for one more well.

The result was one of the most thunderous strikes in history. On October 28, 1926, at a depth of 1,000 feet, the well roared in. Around midnight, the driller walked to the ranch house and told Ira Yates he had a "big oil well." Before noon the next day, the rancher sold a very small part of his royalty for $185,000, which turned out to be a mere pittance compared with the gigantic royalties he would receive as the field reached full potential. The 4,000-barrel-a-day rate of the Yates No. 1 was also something of a trickle compared with the 71,000-barrel-per-day rate it attained after being drilled a mere 500 feet deeper. Over seventy wells were eventually sunk on the lease. One, the No. 30A, came in at the rate of 204,682 barrels per day—up to that day in 1929 the largest producing oil well anywhere in the world.

The myth of the West Texas graveyard died in county after county throughout the Permian Basin: the World-Powell field in Crockett County in 1925; the Upton-Crane field, developed from 1925 to 1929; the J. S. Cosden strike in Ector County; the prolific field on the Hendricks Ranch in Winkler County in 1926; and other fields in Loving, Howard, and Glasscock counties. The culture of the oil patch, spudded in at Spindletop and nurtured at Burkburnett, Electra, Ranger, and a host of other fields in the first thirty years of the twentieth century, began to acquire a permanent richness with the great discoveries west of the Pecos and, indeed, throughout the Permian Basin of West Texas.[6]

It was only because all these things had happened—because these crafts and sciences had been developed and these relationships had been fashioned and tested—that what happened next could have happened at all. The year was 1930. And what happened was more "unimaginable" than "unimaginable Spindletop" and larger than anything that had happened at Big Lake and in the Yates field. It was something so big it couldn't be described simply by calling it a well or even a field. Most of the time, it was just called "East Texas."

Many things grew out of East Texas—and one of them was TIPRO. Though the final organizational formalities would not unfold until well into the next decade, the origins of the Texas Independent Producers and Royalty Owners Association lay in the struggle to develop the East Texas field. For what the great woodbine pool proved to the people it most centrally touched was the existence of a very stark contradiction: the independent oil operator was here to stay in America, and yet independents had no effective voice of their own in the global realities of the petroleum industry. This was the ultimate lesson of East Texas and this was the historic reason TIPRO came into being.

The Slowest Well in Texas

But of course the saga of the immense pool under the eastern pine forests didn't start with grand flourishes.[7] Rather, it began as an idea in the head of one man, one obsessed old wildcatter, one hardheaded seventy-year-old veteran of the oil patch who had convinced himself that all the scientists of petroleum were wrong. His name was C. M. "Dad" Joiner and he was well aware that virtually all the major companies had leased far-flung sections of East Texas at one time or another. In its own good time each had given up all or most of their holdings—the most recent being the "local major," Humble Oil. Nobody but Dad Joiner was fixated on the piney woods. Mineral leases could be had for the asking, $5 to $10 an acre or even less.

Joiner had his eye on Rusk County, or, more precisely, on the woodbine sand some 3,600 feet underneath Henderson and nearby Overton. Indeed, he had spent the better part of three years trying to get a drill bit below 3,500 feet. The discovery well was called Daisy Bradford No. 3 because Daisy Bradford Nos. 1 and 2 had been abandoned long before their drilling bits punctured the woodbine. In ways that were all too familiar to many oil independents, Joiner had been forced to wage a mighty struggle to keep a roof over his head and bread on the table as he put together his successive drilling deals. In fact, on some of his ventures he sold five-eighths and then seven-eighths, leaving only the one-eighth royalty that the landowner retained. And as the needs of his stomach continued, Joiner could find ways to slice up his lease holdings to create even more salable shares. It could not be said that Dad Joiner's marketing achievements were wholly without precedent among wildcatters. It had all been done before.

But while Dad Joiner's unrelenting persistence created situations that encouraged glib or complacent observers to ridicule him, what was subsequently taken as his borderline marketing style has had the effect of concealing the essential social truth about the great East Texas discovery well.

Far from taking advantage of people, Dad Joiner ultimately was able to get his drilling bit to the woodbine sand precisely *because* of the freely given assistance of his neighbors. Around the towns of Henderson and Overton, Joiner initially convinced everyone how serious he was by leasing 5,000 acres of hardscrabble Rusk County farmland. But while that act gave people hope, what won their hearts was his absolute refusal to give up when the drilling bit on Daisy Bradford No. 1 permanently jammed at 1,098 feet and Daisy Bradford No. 2 expired at 2,000 feet with the pipe hopelessly hung in the hole. Though such news dashed hopes for miles around, they revived when word went out that Dad Joiner was still hard at work. In truth, the second well absorbed all his available capital and then some. In desperation, Joiner found an experienced Beaumont driller, Ed Laster, and brought him in (with a little bit of cash plus some lease interest) to save the second well. But after a thorough inspection, Laster said the well was gone. He advised Joiner to start over a third time. There was no way for Laster to know, at that early stage of his relationship with Joiner, that the old wildcatter had already thoroughly exhausted the ready reserves of the local economy. He learned this truth only when he discovered the extremes to which Joiner could go in "cutting up a deal." The old wildcatter had created $25 certificates to reach people with cash, but that turned out to be a fairly small platoon in Rusk County at the time. For the farmers, railroad workers, and retail clerks who made up the great bulk of the population, Dad Joiner fashioned tiny "interests" in the well that he could sell. The waitress who brought him coffee at the diner ended up with a 25/75,000 share of the test well plus a 1/500 interest in the syndicate that owned 500 acres offsetting the well. She was not alone. Even local government workers such as mailmen and policemen got their piece of the test on the Bradford place. If the old man wouldn't give up, neither would they: the thing to do was to get the drilling bit below 3,500 feet. After all, it had never been there. As Laster soon discovered, people gave what they could, even if it was only their labor—freely offered on credit. When Daisy Bradford No. 3 was spudded in May 1929, it was a community event.

It also was one of the slowest holes ever drilled in the state of Texas. Money for pipe was a problem, and how many lengths Joiner could get his hands on determined how far he could drill that week—with the additional requirement of finding a way to keep a crew on the rig. Joiner ranged as far as Dallas and Houston, bringing in potential investors on Sundays—the one day a week he made certain he had a working crew on the rig.

This procedure earned Dad Joiner the settled condescension of the major company oil fraternity. One major company scout made twenty separate trips to the rig without once finding it operating. As a proper nine-to-five man, the scout never checked the rig on Sundays. Even the sight of the forlorn, jerry-built drilling rig, running or not, was enough to inspire a certain amount of derision among the cognoscenti of the oil business. In any event, what was literally a month of Sundays passed and then another. A year after he began, Joiner was still drilling Daisy Bradford No. 3.

Meanwhile, the stock market had collapsed and the nation had plunged into a depression. The arteries of commerce dried up and choked even those tiny capillaries that reached into Rusk County. Everyone was strapped, so they just shared the poverty. Joiner kept a crew by feeding them. He got the food because the Overton grocer accepted Joiner's scrip against future production. So did other merchants. There was so much of Dad's promissory paper floating around Henderson and Overton that it traded as money. The fact provided as good an illustration as any other economic evidence of the crippling shortage of circulating currency that was at the time pervasive in the rural South in the 1930s.

The town banker in the nearby hamlet of Overton appeared regularly (after banking hours) to don overalls and go to work. His wife cooked for the crew. When the rig was shorthanded—a chronic condition—sympathetic cotton farmers would take a day off and lend a hand, often on the chance they might get something to eat. As the Depression summer of 1930 passed and winter loomed, Dad's well was about the only thing people had to look forward to. It was a favorite place for people to gather after church on Sundays.

At one alarming juncture, Joiner's lease on the Daisy Bradford property lapsed. But Daisy Bradford was a player, too. She gave him an extension, and when that didn't suffice, she gave him another one. It was, after all, the only prospect she had as well. No one else was drilling in Rusk County. Finally, in September 1930, sixteen months after it all began, the drill bit on Joiner's dilapidated rig passed the 3,500 mark and soon thereafter penetrated the top of the woodbine sand.

But there was to be one final drama before the great moment. Ed Laster had stayed on as Dad Joiner's unpaid (but shareholding) driller because he was among the many who had come to admire the sheer grit of the wraithlike old wildcatter. Laster quietly took a core sample, inspected it casually, waved the crew on, tossed the core in the back seat of his car, and drove away. As a veteran of the oil patch, he knew that if the well actually proved out, it was vital to acquire as much offset lease acreage as possible before the word got out and prices soared. Back in town, he inspected the core more closely and discovered, to his astonishment, that the bottom nine inches were soaked in woodbine oil. He immediately returned to recover the two buckets of cores he had left behind at the rig. Only one could be found. The next day, Laster discovered to his relief that none of the crowd of oil scouts at the rig had any hints about the core. Finally, late in the day, another scout arrived and sardonically told Laster, "I found your bait, Ed, but you didn't catch a fish." The scout thought Laster had seeded the core so that Joiner could sell more stock. He passed this news on to the other scouts. They had all long since convinced themselves not to take old Joiner seriously. No major company made a move in East Texas.[8]

Unfortunately, while the bit was functioning and the pipe was in fair-enough shape, the rig itself ceased to function. Joiner fashioned another one that was considerably more stable—with materials obtained on credit. By this time, the world's most democratically assembled crew of roughnecks had told their friends, neighbors, and fellow stockholders that things looked promising on Daisy Bradford No. 3. Laster had been forced to show some core samples to get the necessary credit. This was enough for the townspeople and the farmers: they were all oilmen now. Leases began trading—no less than two thousand transactions in the twelve days that had passed since the original core sample had been taken. "An oil boom without oil," as Ruth Sheldon Knowles later described it. Finally, the new rig was ready, and on October 1, 1930, Laster cemented a concrete plug in the bottom of the hole and set pipe to complete the well. The final step was to drill the plug and discover precisely what they had.

No less than 8,000 people, most of them plainly if not raggedly dressed, were on hand. The plug was drilled and a bailer sent down to bail the mud. Again and again, through the afternoon and the rest of the night, the bailer dipped in and out of the hole bringing up mud. No sign of oil. It went on for two days as people watched, went home to eat, and came back. Joiner and Laster were by now deeply concerned, for they both knew of many a Texas well that had produced a show of oil and nothing else. Laster decided to swab the hole, a process as drab and routine as bailing.

Finally, late in the afternoon of the second day, oil became visible in the mud being brought out of the hole. More and more visible. And then it came—a great black torrent roaring out of the woodbine, spewing through the casing, over the rig, over the surrounding pine trees. Daisy Bradford No. 3 was a gusher that seemed to cover a good part of the county with the blessed essence of 39 gravity crude. For the hard-pressed farmers and townspeople, Joiner's triumph meant not only that their land would be leased at considerably more than $10 an acre but that their tiny interests were now a negotiable piece of a flowing oil well. At the onset of America's worst depression, Dad Joiner had been a lifesaver.

Nevertheless, Daisy Bradford No. 3 did not set bells to ringing in far-off corporate headquarters around the world. Everybody had data on East Texas: it was generally considered to be "scenery." But to nearby Texas independents, Rusk County was not remote and Joiner's well seemed to provide tangible evidence that the piney woods could not be dismissed as scenery. Independents came to Rusk County and did some dealing. Leases passed $50 an acre, then $100. Offset wells began going down. Leases edged up to $200 per acre. On December 2, 1930, the Stroube & Stroube No. 1 Frederick roared in some 600 feet north of the Daisy Bradford, and prices soared past $500 per acre.

Independents were all over the region now, talking to farmers, speculating on trends, and probing around for any subsurface data that might exist. A sizable number of people acquired interesting chunks of acreage, and before the end of the year some had paid $1,000 an acre for it. Still, East Texas remained the province of independents, centered around the town of Henderson. The majors weren't playing—though they had begun to watch with sustained attention.

The No. 1 Della Crim changed all that. Drilled by a Fort Worth independent named Ed Bateman, the well was a full twelve miles north of Joiner's discovery—presumably in another geological world. Be that as it may, the Bateman well was just four miles south of a small hamlet of 900 souls called Kilgore. The place was big enough to have telephones, and on that day, December 27, oil scouts from major companies dialed corporate headquarters around the world to report that the Della Crim had blown in at 10,000 barrels a day.

In the woodbine sand.

Joiner in the woodbine; Stroube and Stroube in the woodbine; another well with enormous pressure and volume, the Deep Rock No. 1 Ashby, also in the woodbine. All were wells offset from the Daisy Bradford. But now the Della Crim—10,000 barrels a day from woodbine sands and located not two miles away but closer to two *counties* away! What was going on in East Texas?

To observers unfamiliar with the oil business—and this included journalists from nearby weekly newspapers and from the few East Texas dailies—the big story clearly was in Kilgore: the place had gone berserk. All manner of strange people had arrived, scouts and landmen and promoters of every stripe, along with an avalanche of craftsmen. As one observer reported, "I would judge there are between 1,500 and 2,000 carpenters at work in this little Gregg County town .... The sidings are filling with unloaded freight cars." The writer was so breathless that his hyperbole was redundant: Kilgore was "the most seething, wildly excited and booming oil boom town."[9]

But to oilmen, the word being passed over the long-distance lines not only contained more informed "news," it was highly competitive news. Oil scouts from Standard knew that other scouts from Gulf, Texaco, and the rest were sending identical messages to their home offices. Leases that had been traded among independents for three months in the range of $100 to $1,000 per acre now were traded again— at astronomical prices. The Della Crim lease went to Humble for $2.1 million. East Texas had blown wide open.

Still farther north, the businessmen of the city of Longview watched with envy the newfound prosperity that Dad Joiner had brought to Henderson and Ed Bateman to Kilgore. The Chamber of Commerce offered $10,000 to the operator of the first well in Longview's trade territory. In less than a month, the chamber was out its $10,000 and the boom had grown exponentially. The Farrel-Moncrief No. 1 Lathrop blasted in at a site no less than twenty-five miles north of the Joiner discovery and fourteen miles north of Kilgore. It, too, was a gusher. And it, too, was in the woodbine sand.

Still, no one quite grasped the unfolding reality, it being rather difficult for human beings to conceptualize something they haven't pre-viously imagined. It was clear that in some places in East Texas, quite a few places it seemed, the woodbine was an oil-bearing sand. But it took almost three more months for hard evidence to make visible what pre-viously was beyond everyone's mental horizons. In March the No. 1 Cook brought the woodbine boom to Smith County, and in May the No. 1 Richardson opened up Upshur County. Far to the south, the first producers edged into Cherokee County as well. At last, it was possible to think it through. East Texas was not three fields centered on the Joiner, Bateman, and Moncrief wells. It was one vast lake of oil forty-three miles long and three to ten miles wide. It was so big it was hard to think about.

Perhaps the most stunning fact was that for three amazing months of early development it had all happened in wide-open country. Literally thousands upon thousands of Texans had a personal stake in the magic of the woodbine sands beneath five counties in the piney woods. In America, the profession of oil production had been massive-ly democratized.

Thus it was that three separate factors coalesced to produce the ori-gins of TIPRO out of the unprecedented case history of the East Texas field. The first, of course, was its sheer size—quite simply, the largest oil discovery in the history of the world. The second factor was more pro-saic—the simple circumstance that the field existed in a part of the globe where the culture of oil had breached the boundaries of special-ists. Required for the discovery and development of the East Texas field was not some esoteric body of knowledge that only a private and espe-cially privileged platoon of experts possessed. It was something a Dad Joiner or an Ed Bateman could bring into the world. Indeed, Bateman, a former newspaperman whose adventurous spirit outpaced his capital reserves by a good margin, sold pieces of his wildcat as far away as Canada. For all who wished to follow in the footsteps of the Joiners and Batemans of East Texas, all that was required was the experiential knowledge of how to put together a drilling deal. A great many Texans now had that capacity; perhaps nowhere were they more densely con-gregated than in Rusk County, where Dad Joiner had instructed a good portion of the population in the nuts and bolts of financing a test well. The third and final factor was the status of land royalties at the moment of discovery: on that autumn day in 1930 when the Daisy Bradford No.

3 blew in, virtually all landowners in the five counties had possession of their subsurface mineral rights.

This latter happenstance was to have far-reaching repercussions. The fact that the major companies had to buy in at high prices meant that thousands of people had the opportunity to acquire a measure of capital that *they themselves* could utilize in making arrangements for the development of sizable portions of their own holdings. And this economic opportunity was not restricted to farmsteads; the sheer scope of the woodbine pool meant that populated areas by the dozens (whole hamlets of town lot owners!) were securely situated atop oil-bearing sands. Here was a democratic opportunity that pushed the economic frontiers of capitalism far beyond Adam Smith's wildest dreams!

Or did it? Could average citizens, in fact, hang on and develop their oil-bearing property? Indeed, could the average independent do so? Lease prices after the Moncrief discovery had become absolutely prohibitive except for the most well-heeled corporations and individuals; the problem for everyone else had become, not to get more acreage, but to hang on and develop what was already under lease.

Simple economics generated ominous imperatives: it cost roughly $10,000 to complete a well to the woodbine. In the throes of the Great Depression, it was an unattainable sum for most people in East Texas. To drill, then, meant debt. Money to pay off the debt came from producing and selling oil; and though production was no problem since the bottom hole pressure was so great that all the woodbine wells flowed, *selling* oil became a definite problem as production increased wildly. With the price plummeting, the cry went up that the majors were putting the squeeze on independent producers and royalty owners in an effort to acquire title to more acreage. But petroleum engineers had a cry of their own: unrestrained production raised long-term questions about bottom hole pressure and generated dire warnings that uncounted millions of barrels of production would be irretrievably lost. The East Texas field had to be put under production proration, they said.

A battle was joined. A mere eight days after the Moncrief strike, the East Texas Lease, Royalty, and Producers Association was formed in Tyler with proration as the seething topic. Their most vociferous spokesman was A. D. Lloyd, the geologist who had worked with Dad Joiner and Ed Laster to bring in the Daisy Bradford and who, like everybody else, had taken a piece of the wildcat well in lieu of money. In language that was to become conversational coin of the realm in the months and years that followed, Lloyd denounced proration schemes as "naked confiscation of private property" and a "device to force small operators to the wall."[10]

Meanwhile, production continued to skyrocket, bottom hole pressure continued to drop, and the limits of the field continued to spread. On March 1, an anxious Railroad Commission called a hearing that quickly turned into a riotous session, enlivened by the arrival of thirteen train cars full of piney woods oil operators and royalty owners. In an atmosphere of growing hysteria, the Railroad Commission's first proration order went out on May 1. The largely voluntary effort was a complete failure. When the commission set allowables at 70,000 barrels a day, the oil flow reached 150,000 barrels; when the allowable was raised to 90,000, production hit 300,000; the next allowable of 160,000 yielded a production response of 400,000 barrels daily.

A whole new world had come into being, but its particular shape and even its ultimate meaning was impossible to forecast. There had always been wildcatters in the oil business. In the popular wisdom, wildcatters were a separate breed of humankind: they were rampant individualists doomed, except for a tiny handful, to go broke. But now, with the amazing developments in East Texas, the evidence was mounting that a new name would have to be employed to describe the growing number of solitary entrepreneurs who obviously had come to the oil business to stay. They called themselves "independent oil operators" and that designation seemed fairly descriptive. The term stuck.

In the spring of 1931, the big question was how many of this new breed would be able to stick long enough to give the descriptive term long-term meaning. The fate of Dad Joiner was a case in point. Even before he was able to market a single barrel of oil, he was the object of lawsuits from investors in one or more of his Daisy Bradford tests who had become sufficiently aroused by their sheer numbers to enjoin him from any production until they were satisfied they were going to get their proper share of the profits. Their plea to place Joiner in receivership ran into the following judicial opinion from the presiding Rusk County judge: "I believe that when it takes a man three and a half years to find a baby, he should be allowed to nurse it for a while. Hearing postponed indefinitely."[11]

The old wildcatter thus got an immediate reprieve. But he clearly faced many future hurdles, some of his own making and others a product of the very bonanza he had been so instrumental in bringing to life. The larger question posed by the turmoil in East Texas went beyond Dad Joiner: how many small producers could survive in the corporate world of the twentieth century?

Chapter Two

"ANARCHY" VS "ORDER"

Independents and the Majors

The raw facts that rolled out of East Texas in 1931 seemed dangerous to major companies and deeply frustrating to independent
producers. But to everyone the chaotic situation proved conclusively that no system existed or if one did, it did not work. When the
Texas Railroad Commission, under intense public pressure, dramatically raised production allowables by 50 percent, production increased 100
percent. When allowables were doubled, production quadrupled. The
entire global market became saturated and then supersaturated with
woodbine oil from East Texas. The flood of what some people called
"extra-legal production" quickly acquired a name. It was "hot oil." East
Texas independents made certain there was plenty of it.

The Railroad Commission began issuing injunctions to restrict production by individual producers. Independents went to court to stop the
injunctions, and a number of judges came down on their side. In such a
climate, some people talked of anarchy and called for order while others talked of monopoly and warned of confiscation. Geographical location shaped how the tumult in East Texas was perceived. Viewed from
Kilgore, Henderson, or Longview, production had been nicely democratized. There were many small producers, many small refiners, many
small pipeline companies, and many truckers. But from the standpoint
of New York or London or Amsterdam, production in East Texas was
"fragmented."

As Daniel Yergin phrased it in his award-winning book, *The Prize: The Epic Quest for Oil, Money, and Power*, the great challenge of the 1930s lay in "bringing the East Texas field into harness." Yergin saw the world of oil through the eyes of major integrated companies, and from this perspective the international situation was "complicated by the fragmented nature of ownership in East Texas, and by the large share of production coming from the independents."[1]

This was putting things mildly. In the thirty years that linked Spindletop to Santa Rita to Daisy Bradford, Texas had come to number in its population thousands upon thousands of workaday people with a practical understanding of the jargon of the oil patch. Farmers in the East Texas countryside, ranchers in the far reaches of West Texas, and town-lot owners in places like Burkburnett and Kilgore had all learned what a royalty interest was. They also understood what had to happen to turn a test well into an oil property. This kind of experientially grounded knowledge transformed the way Texans thought about the woodbine sands underneath the piney woods. Throughout the region, people announced their determination to sell their production, pay off their debts, and retain title to their oil—no matter what. In everyday terms, this translated as "no matter what allowables those people in Austin set."

New grassroots oil refineries made their appearance, rough-hewn topping plants that funneled their stock into oil trucks equipped with powerful headlights and intricate backcountry road maps for night hauling. When the Railroad Commission sent agents into the field to turn off valves on flowing wells, a new technical innovation appeared—left-handed valves that turned oil flow on when state agents thought they were turning it off. And the hot oil ran . . . and ran . . . and ran.

And so did the passions of all participants. High principles were extolled on all sides, then violated and reaffirmed. Debates concerning "what to do about East Texas" took place at the level of a shout. The judicial dialogue was every bit as contentious. The Railroad Commission found its orders countermanded both in state courts and federal courts. On July 31, 1931, the federal circuit court in Houston handed down a far-reaching decision that countermanded the proration orders of the Railroad Commission restricting output in the East Texas field. Writing for a unanimous three-man panel, Circuit Judge Joseph C. Hutcheson said: "Certainly when a subordinate body like the Railroad

Commission of Texas undertakes as here to deal in a broadly restrictive way with the right of a citizen to produce the oil which under the laws of this state he owns, it must be prepared to answer his imperious query, 'Is it not lawful for me to do what I will with my own?' by pointing to a clear delegation of legislative power . . . . We have searched but we can not read in any legislative pronouncement support for what the commission has done here." Proration advocates promptly took the court up on its suggestion by pressing hard for legislation establishing market-demand proration. The measure received a full hearing in the Texas Senate within three days of the circuit court's decision. With the galleries packed with interested East Texans, the Senate rejected the market-demand provision by a vote of 16 to 9.[2]

In the summer of 1931, production hit 850,000 barrels daily. On August 15, 1931, Texas governor Ross Sterling, a former president of Humble Oil, declared martial law. The Texas National Guard, under the command of General Jacob F. Wolters, who in civilian life was the general counsel of the Texas Company, entered East Texas to enforce the famed General Order 4, closing down all wells in Rusk, Gregg, Smith, and Upshur counties. The Guard established a large military camp at "Proration Hill" near Kilgore and riflemen began patrolling the fields. More than once Railroad Commission officials were turned away from storage tanks by angry owners brandishing shotguns, and there was the oft-repeated story of the investigator who located a switch controlling a hot oil pipeline hidden behind a bathtub in the operator's home.

The truculence of operators could be explained by their awareness of the issues at stake: cries of conservation by major companies were answered with demands for an end to price discrimination as practiced in the way major company purchasers treated different kinds of sellers. It was a problem that would take TIPRO years of effort—years of sophisticated research coupled with relentless negotiations in state and national legislatures—before anything approaching equitable field rules acquired a measure of legal sanction.

Three generations after the turmoil, it is perhaps now possible to set down a summary of these times with something approaching historical detachment.[3] A good start would be to acknowledge that a measure of truth existed in the arguments of both sides, augmented by a generous dose of partisan propaganda from each as well. In addition, certain economic realities tended to undercut the righteousness of all participants and generate private actions that contradicted public statements. Both majors and independents were hip deep in these kinds of contradictions, as a simple recitation of events makes plain.

The evidence is overwhelming that the majors were not engaging in a systematic campaign artificially to reduce wellhead prices. On the contrary, in April of 1931, even before the dimensions of the field had been established, a consortium of four major companies posted prices of sixty-seven cents per barrel for 39 gravity East Texas crude—a figure markedly above the twenty-five-cent level to which prices had sunk earlier in the month. But as field development proceeded at breakneck speed— 1,000 wells in production by June 1—this effort collapsed. As the summer passed, East Texas crude went down to twenty-two cents a barrel, then thirteen cents and finally ten cents. In order to move their product in a glutted market, some desperate independents had even begun to take as little as three cents a barrel. The source of the downward pressure was not hard to find: by the end of the year, no less than 3,372 wells had punctured the woodbine sand where fifteen months earlier only Dad Joiner's lonely derrick intruded on the pastoral piney woods scene.

But evidence is also conclusive that while major companies were deeply concerned about the influence of cheap Texas crude on international oil prices, causing them to try to boost East Texas prices, it also became evident that they were quite willing to endure a two-price system: a prevailing price for East Texas crude and a much higher wellhead price everywhere else. This fact drove a goodly number of independents into a frenzy and caused them to doubt the intentions behind every single action the majors took. Nor was this an idle or temporary prejudice; price discrimination by major company purchasers was to be a recurring arena of controversy within the industry, one that brought large numbers of independent operators into the ranks of TIPRO in the postwar years.

Thus, in the early developmental years of the East Texas field, the prevailing contradictions were complex in their origins and stark in their long-term implications: none of the participants wanted to see oil at a ridiculous ten cents a barrel; in fact, a continuing struggle for control of the vast field was taking place.

Ironically, the nationwide depression placed the whole issue of prices in a new frame of reference, one that soon produced surprising spheres of agreement among people having wildly different economic and political priorities—oilmen big and small, regulators state and federal, and politicians left and right. Ardent New Dealers in Washington were driven by the frigid realities of the Depression to lobby within the Roosevelt administration for policies designed to bolster wellhead prices. What this meant, in the long run, was that the economic divisions in American society between consumers and producers did not inevitably preclude any and all kinds of broad approaches to price stability. Indeed, the very survival of the nation's economy, staggered to its knees by the severity of the Depression, weighed heavily in the balance.

There also existed two short-run imperatives that were not contradictory: the driving force behind declining prices transparently was traceable to unrestrained production; and unrestrained production was, in irrefutable scientific terms, depressing field pressure and threatening the permanent loss of hundreds of millions of barrels of otherwise recoverable oil. Conservation was not necessarily a code word for price gouging; elementary sanity required some kind of prorationing.

Here again the lessons of Spindletop (and a number of subsequent fields) proved the point. So many wells had been drilled in the first year of the play on the Beaumont salt dome, releasing gas as if a giant balloon had been punctured, that no less an engineering authority than Captain Anthony Lucas himself had been forced to conclude that "the cow had been milked too hard and moreover she was not milked intelligently."[4]

Here was the core problem: people with diverse interests—even opposed interests—had to find that elusive "intelligent" way. The Spindletop field never produced the oil its initial field pressure and reservoir data indicated it should have produced; the gap between "recoverable oil" and "recovered oil" was huge on the coastal salt dome. Indeed, this very fact was in the minds of a number of East Texas independents who proceeded to contribute to the general chaos by insisting on running hot oil even after they had paid off their drilling obligations. They did so either because they were caught up in the general hysteria and felt they might lose their production if they cut back while others did not, or they did it simply because they wanted to make more money in the short run, at whatever cost. Fortunately, unlike Spindletop, the quest for an intelligent way was not futile in East Texas. But it took considerable time.

The problem was a uniquely American one. The United States was the only major oil-producing country in the world that allowed private ownership of subsurface mineral rights or, in oil field parlance, "royalty interests." This legal fact, rooted in Jeffersonian conceptions of a nation of "freehold yeomen," offered the possibility of fundamentally democratizing oil production. Spindletop and its many successors across the state generated the Texas wildcatter as a social type, and the enormous size of the East Texas pool sitting beneath unleased land made the phenomenon of the independent oil operator a permanent fixture in the industry.

Nevertheless, the democratization of oil production was a process that could be denounced, sometimes with a measure of accuracy, as inefficient. A classic illustration is embedded in the oral tradition of the producing industry. When a future Arab oil minister, Abdul Tariki, first saw the East Texas field as a student at the University of Texas, he announced that, in light of Saudi Arabian precedents, the field could have been fully developed by drilling a total of five wells, each producing over 100,000 barrels daily. In purely engineering terms, his argument was incontrovertible.

Yet this technocratic analysis was not quite as sophisticated as it sounded. Simply stated, the issues were not simple. As a percentage of gross revenues accruing from full development of the East Texas field, the amount of waste involved in technologically unnecessary drilling costs was, in historic terms, not irrationally excessive. The real waste lay in the enormous loss in recoverable petroleum reserves that might take place if production continued at an unrestrained pace. Unfortunately, restraining production meant planning—and planning meant some sort of approach that considered the entire field as a unit. With thousands of owners, how to think in terms of "unitization" became the great challenge.

It was more than an economic question and much more than a transitory political controversy. The ultimate issues resonated with all sorts of long-term philosophical implications: how to conjoin community needs with individual interests—that is, how to collectivize in order to plan, yet proceed in a manner that respected individual rights—and how to balance all these competing dynamics in a manner that could pass some kind of reasonable definition of efficiency. Finally, and perhaps most agonizing of all, in a republic based on law, the ultimate solution had to be legal—and legal in a specific form that could survive as a constitutionally defensible statute. Though he doubtless did not fully recognize these competing considerations, Sheik Tariki's easy disdain and impatience with the "East Texas problem" was rooted in an unwittingly simplistic approach that passed over most of the difficult political achievements embedded in Anglo-Saxon jurisprudence since the Magna Carta.[5]

As is often the case in formal political struggles that mask deeper economic drives, the legal debate appeared to turn on a question of semantics. By law, the Texas Railroad Commission was specifically forbidden by the legislature from controlling production in the name of halting "economic waste." The commission's regulatory power, summarily restated by the circuit court in Houston and once again reaffirmed by the Texas legislature, was restricted to "physical waste." Exactly what this meant—amid the sea of woodbine oil—was anybody's guess.

For example, some very messy economic details testified to the uneven burdens generated by the Depression. While wellhead prices had plunged from $1.30 a barrel at the beginning of 1930 to thirteen cents in August of 1931 (actually as low as three cents in East Texas), the retail price of gasoline in the same period declined only slightly, from seventeen to thirteen cents a gallon. For independents, this yawning difference was known as "the refinery price squeeze" that pointed to the favored advantage integrated companies had over independent producers, over small East Texas independent refiners, and, for that matter, over all consumer interests.

The business of contriving workable definitions of "physical waste" and "economic waste" took place within this intricate maze of competing interests. The Railroad Commission started out by testing a new definition of the scope of its powers under the physical waste statute. The agency argued that low prices meant that all marginal wells—the so-called stripper wells that could produce only a few barrels a day—would be forced to shut down because it made no economic sense to stay in production. Such an arbitrary shutdown, the commission argued, constituted physical waste and thus armed the commission to prorate everyone's production so as to bring prices back up to a level that made stripper production practical. This was an ingenious reading of the law, but it did not weather the courts, which found, simply enough, that all such commission orders constituted undue restraint of trade.

The repercussions around the globe were unprecedented. East Texas production, soaring past the one-million-barrel-per-day mark, satisfied fully one-half of total U.S. domestic demand. As prices sank to thirteen

cents a barrel, Texas oil began to undersell Russian oil in European markets. The international price settled far below the cost of production—
which some industry officials placed at roughly eighty cents per barrel
for U.S. crude. Thanks to the Depression, global demand continued to
fall, despite rock-bottom prices.

But, as always, the burden was unevenly distributed throughout the
industry. Finally, in the second half of 1931, even independent producers began calling for some sort of voluntary proration as the only way to
create conditions that would allow small operators to escape bankruptcy court. But given the economic pressure everyone was under, no voluntary plan had the slightest chance of working.

For a brief moment, a blip of stability appeared—at a price level in
the seventy-cent range temporarily set by Texaco buyers—only to collapse under the continuing downward spiral of demand as the
Depression worsened throughout 1932. Governor Sterling called the
legislature into special session and secured passage of a new statute
authorizing the Railroad Commission to prorate to market demand. Yet
six months later the price of East Texas crude still hovered below twenty-five cents a barrel. As it became apparent that the crisis had reached
proportions beyond the reach of any individual state government, an
increasing chorus of voices (by no means restricted just to majors or just
to independents) called for some kind of federal intervention.
Meanwhile, the art of hot-oil running reached new levels of sophistication, not to mention wide acceptance within the population of East
Texas. There were underground flow lines, tenders obtained illegally on
truckloads of "water," forged purchase orders, perforated and gateless
valves, and elaborate pipeline bypasses.

The Cultural Politics of 'Hot Oil'

Into this desperate picture stepped the newly elected Franklin
Roosevelt, or more precisely, Roosevelt's secretary of the interior,
Harold Ickes. Ickes was called by many names, then and later, but as he
tried to sort though the competing arguments of economists, consumers,
independents, and major companies, he came to see the flood of petroleum out of East Texas and the ten-cent oil it generated as a driving peril
to the entire national economy. It threatened, he said, "disastrous results

to the oil industry and to the country."[6] Almost effortlessly, Ickes entered a quagmire that controlled him every bit as much as he controlled it.

In the 1930s, as in many eras before and since, American politics harbored an active antimonopolist sentiment, solidly rooted in popular culture and extending with bipartisan ease deep into both liberal and conservative traditions. There were Americans who believed that near-monopolies or oligopolies had to be regulated so that smaller entities could survive and prosper; and there were Americans who believed that monopolies could not be effectively constrained except through the government's stepping in and taking ownership. The nineteenth-century Populists, with deep roots in Texas, agitated for the first approach, and when that didn't work, opted for the second. But in mainstream circles, the first school of thought had much more popular support: regulation seemed preferable to the government's taking ownership. This belief held despite the fact that the experiment in regulation since the Teddy Roosevelt–Woodrow Wilson era had essentially confirmed what the Populists had already learned—namely that regulatory agencies inevitably came under the effective influence of the large corporations ostensibly being regulated. Neither school of thought, in short, had a historically verified track record of success.

For his part, Harold Ickes was a convinced believer in the second approach. Deeply skeptical of big business domination of any sector of the economy and correspondingly sympathetic to small producers and consumers, Ickes's problem at the policy level was that he had less faith in small producers and consumers than he did in his own personal capacity to serve as their protector. Ickes was a definite believer in big government, particularly in that sector of the government headed by himself.

The raw social facts of the Great Depression meanwhile severely truncated the policy options as Ickes saw them. The whole of the national economy was in shambles. For life to be pumped into the system, prices had to rise above the cost of production. For that to happen, production had to be constrained. And, as Ickes came to view the problems in petroleum, this meant that hot oil had to be reigned in. The federal government's authority to regulate interstate commerce had to be brought to bear, augmented by specific new legislation designed to prevent excessive oil production from entering interstate commerce. Since the Texas state government had been unable to bring order to the great field, federal agents had to be dispatched to East Texas to check on all the wondrous new devices fashioned by the creative traffickers in hot oil: underground storage tanks, off-the-books pipelines, left-handed valves, and night-hauling truckers.

Under Ickes's prodding, these initiatives were duly invoked. Soon federal agents began issuing "certificates of clearance" that were required to move petroleum into interstate commerce. The Connally Hot Oil Act of 1935 completed the regulatory edifice.

These structural alterations did not occur without a prolonged and passionate controversy that involved Texas independents at the highest level of national decision-making. By the time the Roosevelt adminis-tration took office in 1933, production beyond allowables set by the Railroad Commission did constitute, for the first time, the "running of hot oil" since the Texas legislature, acting late in 1932, had passed a bill empowering the commission to institute market-demand proration. In cultural terms, it seems germane to note that such production had become discredited as "hot oil" in the eyes of the American public before it became illegal. Most East Texas producers abided by the new rules, but some had become habituated to full production as a court-approved right; preferring to believe the Supreme Court would ultimately uphold it as a constitutionally protected privilege, they continued as before. It may be noted that this fact has induced many scholars and oil journal-ists to read back into the 1930–1932 period the "hot oil" criteria that, in fact, did not come into play until after November 1932. At the same time, it should also be noted that many producers, majors and indepen-dents alike, anxiously looked forward out of rational self-interest to the restoration of normality in East Texas and therefore opposed unre-strained production.

This dynamic was massively reinforced by the wholesale draining of oil, from independents and major companies' facilities alike, by people who can only be described as thieves. A number of such people, possi-bly as many as a hundred, simply tapped into pipelines and storage tanks and drained off huge quantities of oil, which they then sold. Some of the thieves became so bold and ingenious that they actually were able to hire oceangoing tankers to transport their stolen goods to both the east and west coasts. It is not too much to say that some fortunes, quite lit-erally, were made in this manner.[7]

The entire controversy over East Texas dramatically illustrates how conventional assumptions about ideology prove hopelessly inappropriate in predicting political conduct in the oil industry. One of the strongest proponents of federal intervention in the East Texas field was Bryan Payne of Tyler and one of the strongest opponents was J. R. Parten of Madisonville. Though both men were widely known independent operators, Payne was nominally conservative in politics while Parten was perhaps the best-known liberal in the ranks of wildcatters anywhere in America. But both men saw the long-term future of the producing industry as closely linked to cooperative efforts among independent operators: Parten had been instrumental in the formation of the immediate organizational precursor to TIPRO—the Independent Petroleum Association of Texas—and served as its president in 1933, while Payne would later serve as a TIPRO president. Additionally, both men were firm antimonopolists and both had faithfully followed the production guidelines laid down by the Texas Railroad Commission (i.e., neither ran hot oil). But the proliferation of oil theft in the East Texas field altered their priorities with respect to the role of the federal government. At a decisive Washington meeting of oil industry representatives in the spring of 1933, Parten stoutly opposed pending legislation giving Harold Ickes virtual dictatorial powers in East Texas. Indeed, speaking in his capacity not only as IPA president in Texas but as a national board member of the Independent Petroleum Association of America (IPAA), Parten publicly challenged IPAA president Wirt Franklin for exceeding his authority in attempting, without a vote of the IPAA's membership, to array the national independent association in support of a bill arming Ickes with vast regulatory powers over the East Texas field. Payne, on the other hand, testified before Sam Rayburn's House Interstate and Foreign Commerce Committee that "I want to make it plain that I am for federal control. There have been 50 to 100 million barrels of oil stolen out of East Texas. There are 100 hot oil thieves over there that should have their income tax records checked from 1929 to the present time. Those operators have stolen our oil and have turned around and bought surrounding properties." Across the industry, battle lines were drawn in such a way as to render an ideological interpretation impossible. According to one observer of the controversy, "Every oil lobbyist in Washington seemed to be working for [the Ickes bill]." The president of the Standard Oil Company, Walter Teagle, went so far in opposition to Parten as to propose that the entire field be taken over by the government and held as a national oil reserve. Meanwhile, huge numbers of independents supported Parten's position including, to his embarrassment, such high-silhouette producers as Clint Murchison of Dallas—whom Parten characterized as "a hot oiler in every respect." Conversely, other opponents of Ickes as an "oil czar"—such as the Superior Oil Company—could scarcely be depicted as classic independents. Further confusing the issue was the position of Railroad Commission chairman E. O. Thompson, who opposed the Ickes takeover, as did the state's New Dealing attorney general, James V. Allred. Prominent independents across the state were quite divided, with H. L. Hunt favoring the Ickes plan and Hugh Roy Cullen opposing. A careful student of East Texas, James Presley, offers a crucial distinction: "There were two kinds of hot oil: that produced over the allowable and that which was stolen. Some oil was both. In any case, it was difficult to build evidence and secure a conviction."[8]

With the passage of the Connally Act in 1935, it could finally be said that oil production in East Texas was "brought under control." The cultural campaign to discredit hot oil was the historic centerpiece of the entire drama. In legal terms, not a single barrel of hot oil had been produced throughout the tumultuous months of 1931–1932 when the East Texas field was in the headlines. During that time, all production was legal for the simple reason that the courts consistently struck down regulatory efforts to restrict it. Furthermore, among those who understood the essential economic issues at stake (a good part of the population of East Texas, for example), hot oil was not only legal, it seemed the only available defense against monopoly control. In this setting, major oil interests put their publicity departments to work generating an enormous amount of quasi-historical, quasi-political, and quasi-legal opinion about the scandalous behavior inherent in "the hot oil racket," a generalized term which commingled oil thieves with oil producers in a way that discredited both. Scarcely a major metropolitan daily could be found in oil country that had not editorially harrumphed about the "unrestrained conduct" of independent oil operators and the threat they posed to the orderly functioning of the republic. That this multifaceted campaign was successful in shaping public opinion cannot be doubted. Indeed, the U.S. senator from Texas, Tom Connally, would not have dared put his name to the Connally Hot Oil Act had the popular climate in Texas in 1931 persisted until 1935. He was able to do so only because the cultural campaign of the majors effectively shaped public opinion. It was not to be the last time that Texas independents would be the recipients of a vivid education as to precise dimensions of the cultural and political reach of the major oil companies.[9]

In any case, the wellhead price of oil began to rise. In this manner, a measure of order was restored in the mid-1930s through the combined (and often countervailing) efforts of state and federal courts, state and federal legislatures, major and independent producers, the Railroad Commission in Austin, and the Department of the Interior in Washington. Industry codes were for a time lodged under the National Industrial Recovery Act; when that practice was declared unconstitutional by the Supreme Court, an Interstate Oil Compact came into being. In the aggregate, the structure that fashioned oil prorationing was jerry-built, lobby-ridden, and internally contradictory on several levels. But it had the inarguable merit of functioning better than anything else that had materialized since Dad Joiner's magnificent wildcat had first spewed oil over the piney woods in 1930.

The proof lay in the arrival of price stability: from 1934 through 1940, the average price of oil varied between $1.00 and $1.18 per barrel—that is, at pre–Dad Joiner levels. Gradually the hysterical climate that characterized the early months of East Texas faded away. In the shakeout, a number of independent entrepreneurs also faded away. Among the more visible casualties were the lively breed of independent refiners, pipeliners, and truckers. But even within these highly vulnerable occupations, there could be found men who had taken significant parts of their payment not in cash or even in quantities of oil, but in interest in producing wells. In short, they fashioned a toehold for themselves as independent producers and, as such, survived.

As permanent legacies, East Texas offered some stark physical artifacts and one enduring technical achievement. Five years after Dad Joiner's discovery, the Daisy Bradford No. 3 had 17,650 companions spreading out over 120,000 acres and five counties. In Kilgore alone, 600 derricks dominated the scene—signaling the presence of almost as many wells as the town had people back in 1930.

The problem of field pressure was resolved as a long-term byproduct of a short-term problem—what to do with all the salt water. Woodbine wells on the west side of the field produced water from the very beginning—15,000 barrels daily by 1935, 100,000 daily by 1937, and a staggering 300,000 barrels by April 1941. Each barrel of water lifted from the water-driven woodbine formation produced the same effect as profligate oil runs had generated earlier: namely, it diminished bottom hole pressure and threatened the life of the entire field. Slowly, tentatively, the bold solution of injecting salt water back into the woodbine sand was explored. Aside from the engineering problems involved, the cooperation of many operators with conflicting economic interests had to be elicited. These hazards were surmounted, though not without tensions and controversies among operators, large and small, and also among different types of royalty owners. The East Texas Salt Water Disposal Company was, nevertheless, a successful enterprise. Within five years of the initial big push in 1942, seventy-eight injection wells were pumping almost 500,000 barrels of salt water daily back into the woodbine sand. The downward trend of bottom-hole pressure was not only halted but actually reversed. As a result, the one-billion-barrel potential for recoverable oil estimated for the field in 1931 was increased to over six billion barrels, of which 5.2 billion had been recovered by 1995.

In this fashion, the great pioneering years of the petroleum industry culminated in the decade of the thirties, with the unlocking of the great American field in East Texas and the discovery of even vaster pools underneath the Arabian deserts. In the oil patch, now a global oil patch, there were folkways and customs, and there were rules of procedure and laws. Situations recurred when some or all of them did not work, so normality became the constancy of change. It was the one folkway that did not change.

In the end, it could not be said that the development of the East Texas field was a model of democratic equity. Over the years, major companies found ways to manipulate field rules to their own advantage and did so with a relentless consistency that kept independents in a constant state of watchfulness and created a general skepticism about the merits of developing maximum efficient recovery field rules through "compulsory unitization." It can be said, therefore, that what made the giant woodbine pool the nursery of the Texas independent was not the largesse of international "big brothers" but the unparalleled experience that Texas wildcatters had acquired over the thirty volatile years between Spindletop and Daisy Bradford. This explained the long productive months in the early East Texas play when independents largely defined the range of the great field and secured for themselves an immense stake in its subsequent development.

As a breed, Texas independent oil operators had no neat profile, no easy biography. Some had an eye for terrain and had entered the business trading leases. Others worked their way in as roughnecks on rigs and, later, as drilling contractors. A handful of notable independents were trained geologists, and a few others were petroleum engineers. But down to World War II, a majority of operators, like most of their fellow Texans, had not graduated from college at all. What bound them together was a single trait without which they could not have become independents in the first place: each and every one of them could put together a deal. Excellence in this art was achieved only by mastering a number of subjects that required different combinations of skill and judgment. An independent contemplating a possible drilling site had to possess knowledge of potential mishaps and misreadings embedded in the relevant subsurface maps, he had to anticipate the drilling hazards endemic or possible in the region being considered, and he needed to make a delicate judgment concerning the number, direction, and cost of offset leases necessary to balance capital risks. Toward these ends, it was helpful if an independent could acquire an ability to read how other operators, large and small, were puzzling through the same questions. Perhaps most important of all was the little matter of character—the possession of an underlying fairness and integrity of a kind that encouraged potential prospects to sign onto one's oil play.

With the goodly percentage of casualties that one might expect in an occupation anchored in risk, the wildcatters of Texas developed individual ways to survive—literally thousands of individual ways. The experience of East Texas had been both liberating and traumatic. The lesson it taught was that if Texas independents were to emerge in the post–World War II era as individuals, they would serve themselves well if they got together and created some sort of collective presence that could give them a voice of their own in what had become a global oil business.

Not all future oil plays would materialize in unleased terrain like East Texas. Nor was it reasonable to expect that any future field would contain such a vast ocean of oil. Nor could sympathetic regional judges or intermittently cooperative federal courts be counted on to materialize in the future and take the side of the independent in complex controversies involving global economic interests. Independents had done more than prove how creative and tenacious they had learned to be in thirty years of wildcatting. They also had been forced to acknowledge that they had gotten some very fortunate breaks in East Texas. Rather than count exclusively on similar good fortune in the future, a number of producers decided they had better take some steps to protect themselves. As America emerged from World War II, the enduring legacy of the great woodbine pool under the piney woods was clear: to survive, Texas independent producers and royalty owners needed to create some institutional space they could call their own. In the very first year after the war, this idea was to acquire a name: TIPRO.

Chapter Three

CLOSING RANKS

For Americans, World War II changed everything. Vanished forever was a world where options were defined by what took place within the borders of one nation. In its place were new international developments that fostered both a global economy and a new kind of global Cold War politics.

By no means did the full scope of these sweeping new realities become instantly visible—particularly in the way they were to affect the petroleum industry. True, the old controversies over production proration that had transfixed oilmen in the 1930s disappeared in an instant with the first news of the Japanese attack on Pearl Harbor. No longer was the largesse of the East Texas field viewed as a threat to stability in petroleum. Since gasoline for planes and tanks was the absolute strategic starting point of modern warfare, it was obvious that none of the multiple tasks facing American industry would be more vital than the challenge of simultaneously fueling the enormous Allied war effort in both the Atlantic and the Pacific. Indeed, in the face of determined German U-boat attacks on American tankers off the East Coast, the demands of eastern refineries for crude quickly reached unprecedented levels. The order of the day, lasting throughout World War II, was emphatic: maximum efficient recovery at the wellhead. Nevertheless, for oil as for other industries, the transition to crash production schedules was viewed as a temporary phenomenon. All things being equal, some sort of postwar return to normalcy seemed fully predictable.

Yet even before the conflict moved into its climactic stages after the great Normandy invasion in 1944, persistent signs began to appear that the postwar shape of oil would carry Texas independents into the maw of international politics. These signs, variable and intermittent as they were, had a common source: they all turned on a hitherto unfamiliar part of the world—the Middle East.

A classic aura of déjà vu surrounded this subject: originally, major companies treated the prospect of oil on the Arabian peninsula with the same casual disdain that the Standard Oil Company had once visited upon the upper Gulf Coast of Texas in the pre-Spindletop days. The touted British mining engineer John Cadman, fated to become a prominent figure in the Anglo-Persian Oil Company, summarized geological reports on Arabia in the 1920s as offering "little room for optimism," and a company director seconded the verdict that Saudi Arabia seemed "devoid of all prospects" for oil. In short, the Middle Eastern jewel took years to polish. A small discovery appeared in Bahrain in 1932 and another in Kuwait in 1938, followed by a new find in Saudi Arabia. Although a small pipeline was built from the discovery well to the coast, a modest refinery erected in Bahrain, and, in 1939, the first tanker of oil dispatched to market, German field marshal Erwin Rommel's desert campaign in 1940 caused the frightened Allies to cement the region's wells against possible capture. One precaution had been taken: the early tests at around 4,000 feet had been supplemented by deeper probes to 10,000. Major company officials—both British and American— remained tightlipped, but word filtered out that oil prospects in the Middle East looked "promising." Insiders knew more than this; bottom hole pressure in widely scattered tests was both consistent and uniformly stunning. Although the information was closely guarded, the geological data confirmed that the lands adjacent to the Persian Gulf sat atop the most expansive oil deposits on the planet.[1]

The event that caused Texas oilmen to take notice was the public surfacing in 1943–1944 of something called the Anglo-American Petroleum Agreement, through which major companies took steps to establish an eight-member international petroleum commission. It was created, they said, to assess postwar global demand and allocate production quotas. The move was promptly recognized by independents as rais-

ing the very real prospect of international regulation of domestic oil production. One of the key conclusions of the agreement was that
"American security required restraint on the use of domestic reserves
and larger drafts on foreign oil supplies." It was not hard for independents to divine the slippery road down which this formula would carry
the country and the domestic industry as well. Glenn McCarthy, a
prominent Houston producer, quickly cobbled together a group of like-
minded independents to make certain the implications of the agreement were fully understood by U.S. senators charged with approving
what had become, in 1944, a full-fledged Anglo-American treaty.[2]

The subsequent fight over the treaty was a defining moment that
became the catalyst for the formation of TIPRO. The sheer audacity of
integrated companies in undertaking to control both global marketing
and global production levered petroleum issues out of the confines of
the industry itself into the much larger world of international politics.
For the founders of TIPRO, it was not a time to allow others in the
industry to have a free hand in framing the debate.

There is undoubtedly no more informed authority on these basic
causal relationships than one of the participants who was young enough
at the time, and persevering enough, to go on to play a major role for
independents over the next four decades—R. L. "Bob" Foree of Dallas.
"A group of would-be oil czars," Foree said, were "intent on making our
every business decision an international one for Washington officials
alone." The treaty they had in mind was, in his opinion, "catastrophic"
for independents.[3]

Indeed, as matters turned out, the major companies had serious
competition among the ranks of would-be "oil czars" and oil centraliz-
ers. Their most influential rival was none other than Secretary Harold
Ickes of the Interior. When representatives of the American oil companies Texaco and Standard of California lobbied in Washington for necessary government support for their postwar Middle Eastern plans, they
couched their appeal essentially in terms of the future national security
of the United States.

This gambit backfired. As Ickes saw the options, if the Saudi
Arabian fields were of such vital importance to the nation's security as
the international companies said they were, "why should not the
American government take over the Saudi Arabian concessions and
thus guarantee the necessary petroleum reserve?" Ickes got even more

explicit: "American participation in foreign oil development has been in the hands of American oil companies as private entrepreneurs. These operators have been in competition not only with themselves but with foreign companies in which foreign governments have exercised direct participating controls. In short, American private interests have had to compete with the sovereign interests of foreign companies, particularly Great Britain. Any realistic appraisal of the problem of acquiring foreign petroleum reserves for the benefit of the United States compels the conclusion that American participation must be of a sovereign character compatible with the strength of the competitive forces encountered in any such undertaking."[4]

In so writing, Ickes was putting into print the views of the top men in the wartime Roosevelt administration—Army Secretary Henry Stimson, Navy Secretary Frank Knox, and James Byrnes, director of the Office of War Mobilization. Alongside the liberal Democrat Ickes, the quartet counted two Republicans, Stimson and Knox, and the conservative South Carolina Democrat Byrnes. To guarantee America's needs for long-term oil reserves, they thought the government's interest in the Saudi Arabian concession should be no less than 100 percent! Lest anyone mistake the import of his words, Ickes soon thereafter explicitly proposed to the American oil companies that "the United States Government should have all of their stock interest."[5]

In appraising the effect of his suggestion, Ickes gleefully reported that the stunned oilmen "nearly fell out of their chairs, and it scared them quite a bit." For their part, the presidents of Texaco and Socal, W. S. S. Rodgers and Harry C. Collier, recorded the conversation as a "tremendous shock" that "literally took their breath away." As a bemused observer described the scene, the two major companies "had gone fishing for a cod, and caught a whale." Thereafter, as one oil historian rather inaccurately noted, "The industry demanded Ickes' head on a plate, since he was recognized as the brain behind all the interventionist efforts by the government." As it happened, Harold Ickes put his own head on a plate early in 1946 when he generated a bitter wrangle with President Truman over the latter's appointment of California oilman Edwin Pauley as undersecretary of the navy. As he had previously done so many times with Franklin Roosevelt, Ickes dispatched a six-page letter of resignation which, as Truman later said, "was the kind of letter sent by a man who is sure that he can have his way if he threatens to quit." It had always worked with FDR, but it did not work with Truman. He simply accepted the resignation. Harold Ickes, the chief sponsor of the Anglo-American Petroleum Agreement within the administration, was gone.[6]

It took a while, but the government's involvement became minimal in the final proposal that surfaced as the Anglo-American treaty. It was this version, sponsored by major international companies, not the Ickes proposal, that the domestic producing industry had to confront. It was designed, as some of its proponents indiscreetly conceded to concerned independents, to bring order to global oil production and marketing in a manner that would override prevailing antitrust statutes. Though Ickes was gone, it was clear that America suffered no shortage of potential oil czars.

In due course, the original two dozen men who gave voice to the independent cause (forcibly augmented by the intervention of Commissioner Olin Culberson) helped to round out a hastily assembled coalition of oil interests, large and small, which proved sufficient to ward off the treaty. But the magnitude of the issue itself served to underscore the need for independents to place themselves on a permanently organized footing. As San Antonio's Walter Henshaw subsequently wrote in an article in the *TIPRO Reporter*, "Much of the urgency for the formation of TIPRO was provided by the broad trend toward internationalizing the oil industry, as embodied in the Anglo-American treaty."[7]

Indeed, a very sobering discovery was embedded in the politics that led to the blockage of the treaty. At the outset, the handful of independents who went to Washington were, in Foree's words, "swallowed up" by the powerful and conflicting forces busily engaged in exerting their influence on the Roosevelt administration. True, the more sure-footed among the independent producers quickly found their sea legs and were able to play a useful role in sidelining the treaty. The most significant "convert" that the Texans were able to recruit was the Independent Petroleum Association of America, which had initially made gestures in support of the treaty. More relevant to antitreaty forces, however, were those major integrated companies that did not yet have a stake on the Persian Gulf. They provided the influence that defeated the treaty.

The introduction to global lobbying pressures was therefore a harrowing experience for the Texas independents: the lesson they took back home was that no clear, unalloyed voice of the independent industry existed anywhere in America. This was scarcely a generous appraisal of the previous work of the IPAA, which had performed honorable service on behalf of the nation's independents since its original founding in 1929. But Glenn McCarthy and his band of independents were put off by IPAA's early foot-dragging on the Anglo-American treaty, and they decided the times required a properly forceful case in Washington. Independent producers such as H. J. "Jack" Porter and Vernon Frost of Houston, Walter Henshaw and L. A. Douglas of San Antonio, Guy Warren and Maston Nixon of Corpus Christi, Bryan Payne of Tyler, Arch Rowan of Fort Worth, and Edward Kadane of Wichita Falls all shared with Bob Foree this sense of urgency. As they saw the options, if such an aggressive institutional forum were to come into being at all, Texans would have to fashion it: in no other region of the country did independent producers have the numerically significant presence necessary to carry through on such a project.

So it was that thirty-nine independent producers, led by Glenn McCarthy and Jack Porter, met in Austin in March of 1946 and formed TIPRO. Porter, elected as the organization's first president, typified as well as any one independent a central thread in the underlying philosophy of most of the organization's founders—namely, a distinctively vivid expression of the American antimonopoly tradition. Porter saw as symbolic a conversation he had in Washington at the time of the original struggle over the Anglo-American treaty. The dialogue, as he later recalled it, was with "a very good friend with Standard Oil Company of New York." The gentleman, said Porter, was for the treaty because he felt it would facilitate global marketing "without becoming involved in some of the anti-trust laws." Porter's cryptic response: "That's a good reason for me to continue to oppose it."[8]

This put the options starkly—which was precisely Porter's style. The credo of the founders was grounded in the belief that for monopoly centralization to be successfully resisted, it had to be addressed where the threat itself necessarily was centered—in Washington. Granted, the challenge was so enormous that the question it posed was downright daunting: could mere citizens, by the simple act of banding together, act effectively to defend their own interests as citizens? The American Constitution said so, the heritage of the nation emphasized the same theme, and politicians from left to right were forever endeavoring to associate their own election with the idea. But for people actually to stand up and act on the basis of the idea was considerably easier said than done. The founding meeting itself was a clear act of assertion, given the fact that many industry spokesmen advised producers that a loose and informal "liaison group" was all that was needed. Knowledgeable independents knew, however, that a diverse ad hoc committee would be a blueprint for endless and immobilizing wrangles over the organization's basic agenda. The conceptual breakthrough that TIPRO represented in the petroleum industry was the creation of a state institution primarily organized to address national as well as state issues—a citizen institution grounded in the intuition that the economic future of its members was necessarily involved at both state and national levels of political decision-making. This understanding distinguished TIPRO from all the other oil-producer associations—past, present and future—that came to be organized in the United States.

The founders of TIPRO resolved to create a formal structure of independents with a permanent staff, regional vice-presidents representing the thirteen production districts set up in Texas by the Railroad Commission, and, in due course, a mass membership of independent producers and royalty owners. An energetic full-time executive director was the first priority. Stepping into this post was E. I. "Tommy" Thompson, a man very much in the colorful and outspoken mold of his fellow Houstonians, McCarthy and Porter. An independent producer himself, Thompson had to face in two directions at once—toward the grassroots, where potential members were, and toward the centers of political power in Austin and Washington, where oil policies were made. He set about both tasks with resolve and also with the settled self-confidence that was his trademark.[9]

With this scaffolding in place, the pivotal task facing TIPRO was to recruit its own constituency. Bob Foree's sober characterization of independents as possessing such a fragile presence in Washington that their advocates were easily swallowed up by competing industry forces reminded one and all that the single indisputable asset that TIPRO could potentially muster was the sizable rank and file of independent operators scattered across the entire state. To this task the TIPRO pioneers turned with considerable organizing energy. They found some useful building blocks already in place in the early postwar period.

Wherever oil and gas fields had been developed in Texas, both producers and royalty owners had found it necessary to organize themselves in an effort to gain equity in field rules and marketing allocations. These smaller groups existed both as county organizations (the Sherman County Royalty Owners Association stood as a typical example) and as regional groups such as the one A. D. Lloyd helped to put together in the heyday of East Texas development, the East Texas Lease, Royalty, and Producers Association.

But materializing as well were even stronger groups like the West Central Texas Oil and Gas Association, the North Texas Oil and Gas Association, and the Panhandle Producers and Royalty Owners Association. In such local and regional groups reposed the real grassroots strength of the independent oil industry—not only the independent operators the outside world knew as wildcatters, or the independent geologists, landmen, and drilling contractors who had gotten a toehold in the industry, but the thousands of farmers, ranchers, and town-lot owners on whose land oil was being produced. A "Ten for TIPRO" program was launched, with each member charged with recruiting ten of his neighbors. Many of the most active members got their ten, and ten more, and ten more, led by independents like Houston's H. Merlyn Christie, Floyd L. Karsten, W. J. Goldston, and Mike Hunt, Beaumont's J. J. "Junker" Spencer and Bryan Beck, Abilene's Carl Shoults, Lamesa's Weldon Lindsey, San Antonio's Paul Henshaw, and, of course, Dallas's Bob Foree. No hamlet was too small, as Clifford Moers proved when he signed up his Ten for TIPRO in the hill country town of Boerne.[10]

A number of the founders became historically significant in the subsequent development of TIPRO. In addition to Porter's successor as president, Corpus Christi's Guy Warren, the association's third and fourth presidents, R. L. Foree of Dallas and Bryan Payne of Tyler, were original charter members, as were M. D. Bryant of San Angelo, who became president in 1953, and A. E. Herrmann of Amarillo, who assumed the reins in 1956. The initial regional leadership also included Walter Henshaw of San Antonio, Ed Kadane of Wichita Falls, and Arch Rowan of Fort Worth—all district vice-presidents and charter members.[11]

These independents embodied a rough consensus on two issues. As a function of the intraindustry dynamics they discovered to be at work in the struggle over the Anglo-American treaty, they felt the IPAA was not at the time representing small producers with sufficient aggressiveness. And, as a result of the prior lessons they had drawn from the early development of the East Texas field, they viewed compulsory unitization of fields with great skepticism. The second of these beliefs ensured their attention on the legislative scene in Austin, while the first emphasized the centrality of national issues.

TIPRO Debates Two Approaches

Precisely how to go about implementing these broad aims was, of course, an open question. Porter himself took the blunt position that "no good ever comes out of Washington." Others, including Guy Warren and Longview's Angus Wynne, thought well enough of the U.S. Congress to ally themselves very closely with Representative Wright Patman of Bonham who, as chairman of the House Small Business Committee, was one of the nation's leading antimonopolists. TIPRO worked closely with Patman's committee in a number of hearings in the late 1940s and early 1950s that focused on monopoly influences within the industry and praised him in the *TIPRO Reporter* as a man who had "kept the blood clot of monopoly from clogging the arteries and bringing paralysis upon us."[12]

It soon became even clearer that the broad array of founders were not in strategic agreement about how best to advance the cause of independents. The two most publicly visible TIPRO figures, Jack Porter and Tommy Thompson, fashioned a public manner that quickly stamped itself among oil journalists as a shoot-from-the-hip approach—a stance in marked contrast with the style that emerged in the formative years from TIPRO's executive committee. This second mode of advocacy, most tenaciously advanced by R. L. Foree, integrated the pressing needs of independents into a more carefully crafted strategic approach not only to intraindustry affairs but, even more tellingly, to national and state politics as well.[13]

Evidence gradually accumulated that TIPRO housed competing modes of advocacy. Porter and Thompson tended to see the political struggle essentially as one between the government and the industry, with the subsidiary qualification that, within the industry, producers had to be on their guard against monopoly. But both Porter and Thompson saw "socialism" as the greater threat. In contrast, the perspective to which Foree gave voice emphasized major company influence on the government rather than the other way around. Foree consistently concentrated upon monopolizing trends within the world of petroleum and focused his observations on the actions of major companies rather than criticizing individuals who might be associated with major companies. The differing emphases in the two modes of advocacy were real, but it would take a while for these distinctions, and the strategic nuances they housed, to become clear in terms of TIPRO policy. Individual producers would eventually sort out the subtleties of their differences in approach; they agreed at the outset that the important thing was to make the perspectives of independents publicly visible.[14]

Collectively, the independents who formed TIPRO and the producers and royalty owners they recruited were, in economic terms, the small businessmen of the world of oil. They were the ones who, in Guy Warren's words, saw congressmen like Wright Patman as "tireless defenders of small business." And independent operators were, as Foree was forever pointing out, the petroleum industry's only "political link to the small business community of the nation." It went without saying that the economic muscle of independents, by itself, was quite limited when compared to that of the major companies; but independents also possessed a certain political potential which, if wisely channeled, might fashion a measure of protection for small producers in an increasingly centralized world.

This was the message that TIPRO's early leaders decided the organization needed to carry to the state's producers: only a strong association of independents could keep up with legislative maneuverings and assert an influential independent position in Austin, where such issues as equity in production and field rules might be addressed, and in Washington, where the overall guidelines for postwar petroleum policy would be hammered out. If TIPRO could prove its relevance in these arenas, then oilmen in the state's local and regional groups would more easily see their way clear to join.

Much of the credit for the early growth of the organization went to the activist core of independent operators who spread the word of TIPRO not only in the major cities of Texas but throughout the eastern and western sections of the state where prewar oil plays had generated thousands of independent operators and royalty owners. By the time of the first annual meeting in Dallas in 1947, TIPRO could count 1,200 members. When Corpus Christi's Guy Warren took over as TIPRO's second president in a convention in his home city, membership had grown to over 2,500. It numbered almost 4,000 at the time of the third convention in Houston in 1949.[15]

As Thompson increasingly relied on the association's regional spokesmen to carry through on recruiting, he was forced by events to concentrate more and more on legislative matters. It quickly became evident that the battles fought on this terrain were remarkably technical and waged in legal language. Moreover, the intraindustry controversies, complex as they were, needed to be decoded and publicized in clear language so the facts could be made clear to the membership and the position of independents made comprehensible to the general public. Thus, Thompson soon augmented TIPRO's staff through the hiring of W. E. "Earl" Turner as staff writer and director of publicity and, later, Alvis Vandygrift as the association's general counsel. With the arrival of Turner in 1947, TIPRO began producing its own publication, the *Independent News*, which grew in the following year into a more muscular periodical, the *TIPRO Reporter*. And with the advent of Vandygrift in 1950, TIPRO began to explore the means through which it could try to hold its own in behind-the-scenes maneuvering over legislative language and in presentations before regulatory agencies.[16]

Prominent Texas civic leaders such as Vernon Frost of Houston, Walter Henshaw of San Antonio, Angus Wynne of Longview, M. D. Bryant of San Angelo. C. W. Brown of McCamey, and Maston Nixon of Corpus Christi, to name just a sample, brought to TIPRO's leadership a local-level prestige that was virtually unrivaled by any other group of voluntarily organized citizens in Texas. Within two years of its founding, TIPRO had shaped itself into a fledgling but increasingly genuine voice of the independent producing industry.

In TIPRO's earliest years, what would become the vast flood of Middle Eastern crude remained a comparative trickle in the American market. Through most of the first three years when TIPRO built its membership up to 4,000, the industry operated at more or less full production as the nations of Europe and Asia rebuilt themselves out of the carnage of World War II. The 26 million automobiles on America's roads in 1945 had swelled to 40 million by 1950, and oil had displaced coal as the nation's number one energy source. Though gasoline sales in the United States were fully 42 percent higher than they had been at war's end, the nation's proven reserves not only avoided depletion, they were actually 21 percent higher than they had been in 1946. The numbers testified to the professionalism of independents in finding and developing new domestic reserves.

This did not mean, of course, that the intrusion of international politics had somehow ended with the imbroglio over the Anglo-American treaty. On the contrary, the Middle East quickly reappeared as a rapacious consumer capable of absorbing a postwar commodity in short supply—oil field equipment. To protect the needs of the domestic producing industry, TIPRO was forced to intervene in Washington on the issue of allocations of pipe that major companies were buying and shipping to the Middle East as fast as they could. As the association's familiarity with the ways of the Washington bureaucracy increased, its ability to deal with oil equipment misallocations similarly increased. The needs of domestic producers were factored into the equation, and the problem got cleared up fairly quickly.[17]

If this result confirmed the merit of a national as well as a state focus for TIPRO, the question of tidelands oil soon reaffirmed it. Increasingly as the first postwar decade proceeded, ownership of the Texas-Louisiana tidelands gathered steam as a passionate economic and political issue that bore not only on potential tax revenues for affected states but on national presidential politics. Offshore drilling dated from as far back as 1896, when a pioneering venture was attempted from piers off the California coast. Along the Gulf Coast, the first efforts occurred in the 1920s from "islands" built in shallow water by dredges. In 1938, the Creole field was discovered in a salt dome drilled to 6,000 feet in 14 feet of water off the Louisiana coast. Others followed in Galveston Bay and Laguna Madre, in waters historically claimed by the state of Texas.[18]

On September 28, 1945, President Harry Truman issued an executive proclamation laying claim on behalf of the United States to the natural resources of the subsoil and the seabed of the continental shelf. For the states of the Gulf Coast, millions of dollars—and perhaps hundreds of millions—in leasing and tax revenues were at stake. The Louisiana legislature promptly enlarged the state's boundary to a distance of twenty-seven miles offshore. On firm historical grounds, effectively articulated by Senator Price Daniel, Texas claimed its boundary as three leagues or ten and one-half miles seaward, the dimensions of the Texas Republic at the time the state entered the Union in 1845. In a preliminary decision in 1947, the U.S. Supreme Court restricted California's offshore claim to three miles, a decision reaffirmed in 1950 with respect to both Texas and Louisiana. In a ringing dissent on the Texas case, Justice Felix Frankfurter wrote: "The submerged lands now in controversy were part of the domain of Texas when she was on her own. The Court now decides that when Texas entered the Union, she lost what she had and the United States acquired it. How that shift came to pass remains for me a puzzle."[19]

The tidelands issue was kept in the public eye, initially by TIPRO spokesmen and soon thereafter by state political leaders as well as a wide range of proponents for public education. The potential tax benefits for the Texas treasury seemed, for a time, to be boundless, particularly after public auctions for leases within the three-mile limit brought bids from major companies that soared above seven figures. The Magnolia Petroleum Corporation paid the state $3,180,960 for a 1,440-acre off-shore lease—over $2,200 per acre.

For a time, it seemed the Supreme Court might be overridden. So strong was the historic basis of the Texas claim that the U.S. Congress twice passed legislation extending the state's offshore boundaries. On both occasions, Truman vetoed the bills. The Republican Party, both in its 1952 platform and in the public addresses of its candidate, Dwight Eisenhower, supported the Texas position. The stand played a significant role in Ike's electoral victory in Texas that year. In the end, however, the Gulf tidelands fell far short of initial expectations as a source for petroleum, particularly off the Texas coast. Most of the oil deposits that were confirmed lay off Louisiana.[20]

Unitization: Threat or Panacea?

Though struggles at the national level seized most of the headlines, issues closer to home were also to prove of enduring significance. Indeed, even as the association was in its beginning years of self-organization, an issue surfaced that was to exercise producers for years to come: the recurring drive for a whole variety of unitization rules that—depending on the wording—impinged upon or threatened to impinge upon the rights of individual producers and royalty owners. In the very first postwar legislative session in Austin, various approaches to unitization were placed on the Senate's agenda. All those that went beyond "voluntary" procedures were opposed by a sizable majority of TIPRO's newly arrived membership. The memories of East Texas proved an enduring force within TIPRO's councils. When the association demonstrated it was equal to the task of explaining its opposition to a compulsory unitization statute, the proposal failed in the Texas legislature, only to reappear in 1949 with vastly increased lobbying pressure. Similar laws had been muscled though the legislatures of Oklahoma and Louisiana, where independents had not organized themselves on any firm statewide basis. Producer representatives in those states, functioning through the Interstate Oil Compact Commission (IOCC), routinely spoke out in favor of compulsory unitization.

In the words of an IOCC report, "If the full aims of conservation are to be accomplished, individual property or lease boundary lines will be disregarded in choosing wellhead locations. Individual wells will become channels through which oil is expelled from whole reservoirs or producing segments rather than from separate properties. Some form of unitization of fields will be necessary." Against this stepped-up campaign TIPRO began to display its organizational potential as independents from scores of legislative districts in Texas, armed with analyses generated by TIPRO, made the case for the independent industry. Despite the previous successes proponents had enjoyed in Oklahoma and Louisiana, the drive for compulsory unitization again failed.[21]

Two years later, unitization proponents tried once again and TIPRO president Bryan Payne once again raised the warning flag. But this time—unlike the early days before Earl Turner—the warning appeared in the *TIPRO Reporter*, which by 1951 was being circulated to 4,000 independents in every corner of the state. Whether in urban centers or rural areas, state senators and representatives quickly began hearing from the grassroots.

Yet it would be a mistake to portray TIPRO's membership as solidly arrayed against all concepts of unitized field rules. Indeed, opponents of unitization were often moved to employ some adroit internal politicking within TIPRO ranks to place their opponents in awkward company. For instance, the idea of compulsory unitization could be effectively discredited in the founding decade simply by demonstrating that its primary advocates were major companies. Price and pipeline discrimination by majors had been such a routine component of field development in

Texas that this fact alone made rank-and-file independents deeply skeptical of any ostensible "cooperative" plan that could be effectively controlled by major purchasers. TIPRO executive committeeman David Donoghue of Fort Worth scrutinized the evolution of unitization proposals since the 1920s, found the tracks of major companies promoting unitization in documents of the American Petroleum Institute, and reported his findings to the membership in the *TIPRO Reporter*. Donoghue was seconded by a number of other influential TIPRO activists, including Will Odum, a consulting engineer and a TIPRO director from Austin. Odum subjected to intense analysis the technical arguments advanced by engineering specialists on behalf of innovative unitization proposals and concluded: "Under the type of compulsion such planning necessarily entails, I see another business dominated by a handful of concerns . . . in which the shoe-string operator finds himself and his piddling production unwanted." Such arguments helped solidify producer opposition to all forms of compulsory field rules. Before the next legislature convened, proponents acknowledged that with TIPRO arrayed in opposition, compulsory unitization could not happen in Texas. So they backed off—and did not even introduce a new version of the bill. What Texas got, with TIPRO in the lead, was a well-crafted voluntary unitization statute.[22]

The word went out that TIPRO was "doing something" for the independents of the state—in both Austin and Washington. It was a message that gave a strong boost to ongoing membership drives. Indeed, successful recruiting campaigns would in time produce a membership so diverse that the ranks of TIPRO would itself divide on unitization controversies in various fields across the state. Michael Halbouty of Houston and Scott Hamon of Dallas emerged as the leading spokesmen for altering TIPRO's historic position while Tyler's Bryan Payne and San Angelo's M. D. Bryant reaffirmed the antiunitization stands each had taken during their tenure as TIPRO presidents. Fashioning rules that both protected individual rights and reservoir pressure would require technical expertise and political flexibility which, in the first postwar decade, neither TIPRO nor the major companies possessed.

In the meantime, however, the entire subject of price equity in natural gas production remained an open wound for producers. The wartime "Big Inch" pipeline from Texas to the East Coast—constructed to circumvent the German U-boat threat to tankers on the high seas—

had been sold to gas pipeline companies after the war, a development that was a significant factor in opening up eastern consumer markets for natural gas in the homes of America. As demand and retail prices of natural gas rose, the absurdly low, near-confiscatory prices that gas producers were saddled with under long-term prewar contracts became a central bone of contention within the industry. As producers knew (and they were virtually alone in America in understanding the fact), most natural gas in Texas had been sewn up by pipeline companies on long-term contracts at a time when gas was without a market and therefore virtually worthless. This condition dated back to the 1930s when the absence of consumer markets for natural gas generated the custom of flaring gas at the wellhead. Everyone understood that the markets would eventually come, but the problem had to do with the price in the short run. In the early days, a gas producer either sold his gas, often for the lifetime of the field, at giveaway prices or witnessed its drainage by a neighbor who would sell.

Down through the years of World War II, the absence of pipeline connections—a chronic condition throughout vast reaches of West Texas and visible elsewhere across the state—made the flaring of wells a universal practice. One oil scout traveling through West Texas in 1945 got the impression he was moving through a huge metropolitan area because of the thousands of gas flares piercing the darkness for miles in every direction. "So huge was the flare in Denver City," one native wrote, that "the town did not need street lights for many years after its establishment." And as a local Denver City journalist reported: "On cloudy nights, the torch light was reflected to such an extent that we seemed to be living beneath a flowing sea of flame, and during a heavy fog we floated in soft orange sherbet."[23]

The pioneering work of railroad commissioner William Murray proved crucial in setting in motion in 1947 the process that ended this reckless waste of natural gas. As a result of studies of casinghead gas (gas produced in conjunction with oil) conducted under Murray's direction, the commission implemented new regulations precluding flaring gas in the absence of special permits—which, it soon developed, were by no means easily obtainable. What this meant, in effect, was that flush oil wells could not be produced if gas was also being flared in the atmosphere. The practical effects were marvelous to behold.

Everyone who got shut down suddenly developed a frantic interest in fashioning markets for casinghead gas. Even the mere threat of Railroad Commission action, such as the eminent shutdown of the Seeligson field, galvanized people into action. The effect was visible across the state, especially in West Texas where a number of plants were constructed that either extracted products from natural gas or prepared it for public consumption.[24]

Under this sort of stimulus, natural gas markets gradually developed, though the prior intervention of long-term contracts yielded a crazy quilt of prices. The gross inequities were apparent to everyone. On the Gulf Coast, the range of prices paid by pipeline purchasers varied from 1.5 cents per thousand cubic feet in Kleberg County to 15 cents in Calhoun County. Meanwhile, prices in the Panhandle ranged from 2.5 cents to 9 cents. Virtually everyone in Texas suffered under this arrangement, not only independent operators and land and royalty owners but the state treasury as well—because inconsequential wellhead prices meant trifling state revenues from wellhead production taxes. As events were to reveal, TIPRO's labors in this area, both in Austin and in Washington, were protracted and arduous. There were many facets to this complex struggle, but TIPRO was eventually able to influence improvements in many of them—to the surprise and irritation of major sectors of the industry that nominally were more influential.

But to prove equal to the challenge, independents had to learn some subtle lessons in the world of economic politics. For starters, very few observers outside the ranks of producers had more than a shaky idea of the marginal relationship of wellhead gas prices to the retail cost charged consumers at the other end of the gas transmission corridor. The essential economic reality was patently clear to producers: through the miracle of transmitting gas from one place to another through a pipeline, the value of the commodity increased anywhere from 600 percent to 1,500 percent—and even beyond. Though industry insiders knew that the gas transmission companies were the real beneficiaries of the absurdly low long-term production contracts, it soon became apparent that the lobbying technique of gas purchasers was aimed at totally removing themselves from public view in all discussions about price equity. In their stead, the giants of the gas industry pushed forward "American consumers" as the interest that needed protection. TIPRO learned—painfully in the early going—that independents were being made to appear as "millionaire Texas oilmen" out to gouge "consumers." No political contest so framed, of course, offered any hope for an outcome that independents could endure.

For natural gas, as for oil, the real issue was monopolistic influence within the industry. But one had to know something of the functioning economics of gas production to see the common ground that both consumers and producers occupied with respect to the long-line transmission companies. As independents watched—and learned from—the politics of the major gas purchasers, there gradually developed within TIPRO a much more sophisticated political culture as a necessary precursor to successful advocacy on behalf of the independent sector of the industry.

TIPRO saw to it that the case of Mrs. Willie Lee Hill of Panola County came to the attention of metropolitan dailies in the state. Gas in a well on Mrs. Hill's land—located in the city limits of Carthage—was being produced by a company that then transported it to her Carthage home. For every thousand cubic feet she sold, she received 3.6 cents. For every thousand cubic feet she bought, she paid $1.33. The differential was no less than 3,700 percent! Producers and consumers, it could be seen, had a lot in common. There were powerful forces between them that somehow had to be made accountable.[25]

Persuasive as these economic facts might become if clearly orchestrated to members of Congress, they were even more relevant in hearings before the Federal Power Commission. Despite many actions to the contrary over the years, that New Deal agency positioned itself publicly as a guardian of consumer interests—which, on selective occasions, it was. And it could, again on selective occasions, make relevant distinctions within segments of a given industry, as it did when it finally exempted independent gas producers from utility-type regulation. But on many pertinent issues a clear trajectory for the agency's policies was very hard to discern. TIPRO's pleas for price equity could scarcely prevail on all occasions when producers could be portrayed as ruthless exploiters of hapless consumers.[26]

The challenge for independents, and for TIPRO as their advocate, was to become properly informed not merely on what politicians said on the stump but how they actually voted on key amendments in committees. The educational process, moreover, was a two-way street: independents had to teach Washington officials, both in Congress and in the bureaucracy, the operative economics underlying the processes through which oil and gas were discovered, transported, and marketed to consumers. The more TIPRO learned about the enormous cultural range of the major companies, particularly their demonstrated capacity to frame public issues in contexts favorable to themselves, the more daunting the political challenge facing independents seemed.

No issue dramatized the scope of the task more starkly than the matter of gas price equity at the wellhead. Early attempts to fashion minimum wellhead prices ran into a storm of industry-sponsored rhetoric that producers were promoting "socialistic intrusion" into the free enterprise system. Independents did not have a ready vocabulary that could express their dismay at this kind of gross political propaganda. Nothing could cause independents' teeth to gnash more than the spectacle of centralized pipeline purchasers using their quasi-monopolistic position to crush small producers and then justify the practice as the quintessence of "free enterprise."

Nevertheless, the experience that TIPRO gained in the formative years, while sobering, was also helpful. It took a while for all these lessons to sink in, but gradually the organization learned that its position in American politics and American culture was unique. On the one hand, successful independent producers were scarcely candidates for government-financed bread lines. They had won a stake for themselves in the economy. Yet the degree of insulation each operator possessed against short-run disaster varied widely: even relatively affluent producers could wreck the family business by staking everything on a wildcat well drilled below 15,000 feet in hard-rock country.

In short, while the rewards remained great, the risks fully kept pace. The independent producing industry flowered in Texas because of the unprecedentedly rich experience operators came to embody as a result of a half-century of wildcatting and field development. Gone were the riverboat gamblers of romantic lore who drilled "straight up" and made a million or went broke. Visible instead were producers who had learned how to move adventurously and at the same time prudently in a realm where large risks were absolutely a given. TIPRO's own membership roles verified that it could be done.

A New World of Politics

Yet in the global world of petroleum where the Seven Sisters could draw on capital reserves without parallel in corporate ranks, no one Texas independent could safely look upon himself as a central player. True, he was the entrepreneurial essence that validated the entire oil-finding enterprise: the wildcatters were the people who found new fields in America. And, in cultural terms, the independent producer provided evidence that the American dream was alive and well—that imagination and hard work could transform an individual's life from ordinary to a measure of genuine economic abundance. As such, the independent producer stood as a certifiable symbol of much that was rare and appealing about America, its economy, and the vibrant social relations of its people. The existence of the independent oil operator verified that "the little guy" could make it in America. But in the first postwar decades, independents were an endangered species because the nature of the oil business threw them into an integrated, international maelstrom where intimate and easy access to political authority was an ongoing capability for the Seven Sisters—but for no one else in petroleum. What the self-organized independent oilmen who created TIPRO learned in the association's first decade was that they had to think about politics and the economy in a new way. To prevail in political arenas where they were routinely outgunned, independents needed to search out and cultivate reliable allies—even if, in so doing, they had to assume the additional burden of teaching their allies enough rudimentary economics about oil and gas that their recruits could, in fact, be relied on.

This was a whole new world. It required a good measure of time and developed experience before independents could fashion a surefooted gait through this uncharted terrain. Nevertheless, such issues as price equity in natural gas, which threw producers into unmistakable conflict with long-lines transmission companies, taught one and all that TIPRO had to develop a broader political base and a much longer-term strategy if its members were to acquire the economic wherewithal to survive. For starters, systemic remedies for long-term grievances simply could not be obtained through one-shot legislative solutions. In natural gas the task was multiple: TIPRO needed to fashion a comprehensive program whereby it could gather case histories from the experiences of its own members, marshal these bits and pieces of information into the structured pattern of inequity that they actually represented, and then work out a sensible legislative solution that was principled, constitutional, and politically salable. It was a tall order—and it would take time to achieve.

Meanwhile, producers reasoned, one thing that might be accomplished with some speed concerned the maddening problem of gas measurement. The simple fact was that producers not only were being paid a pittance for their gas, but more of the product was being taken from their wellheads than was being measured and paid for by pipeline purchasers! As one disgusted producer put it, "Depending on which field and which pipeline company you're talking about, independents are being ripped off anywhere from two to 15 percent on every cubic foot of gas we sell. It's not only that the measuring devices are crude, or at least questionable, there really are no standards, no laws requiring standards or anything of that nature. It's a scandal." Speaking publicly, TIPRO's second president, Guy Warren, was scarcely less restrained in defining the issues: "The basis for the measurement of gas in the state of Texas is a disgrace. Gas pipelines over the entire period of the industry have represented that they were paying a certain price for gas yet, by virtue of the pressure factor used, have decreased their price to the royalty owner and to the producer as much as 25 percent."[27]

TIPRO raised the matter as a public issue, brought it to the attention of the state legislature, performed the necessary background research, developed the case histories, helped write a legislative bill, mobilized scores of independents across the state, and, after a three-year struggle with pipeline lobbyists in the Texas Senate, engineered passage of the Standard Gas Measurement Act of 1949. Though some bruises were publicly inflicted, particularly between TIPRO and Lone Star Gas Company, the problem itself promptly disappeared after the bill became law. A modicum of sanity had been fashioned in the realm of natural gas production.[28]

A clear sign of TIPRO's gradual evolution into a modestly influential voice in the American petroleum industry emerged following the outbreak of the Korean War in 1950. After the federal government reinstituted price controls and after some equipment shortages began to appear as a byproduct of the military's sudden appetite for steel production, the Truman administration charged the Petroleum Administration for Defense (PAD) with the responsibility of overseeing the emergency.

After some false starts in steel allocation that generated considerable alarm among independent producers, the administration decided the best way to ensure that producers possessed a permanent seat at the decision-making table was to name one of their own as the agency's production director—none other than TIPRO's 1950 president, Bob Foree. From the standpoint of independent producers, things went much better after that, at least on that one issue.[29]

By the time TIPRO's first decade had run its course, three other milestones had been passed—the discovery of major new oil finds in the Permian Basin, the Supreme Court decision in the Phillips case, and the appearance of inescapable factual evidence of the impact of imported oil on the domestic American market. The complex ramifications of both the Phillips case for gas producers and Middle Eastern imports for oil producers is a story that was to preoccupy TIPRO well into the 1970s. The initial phases of both are explored in the next chapter.

But the development of the Permian Basin put a crowning wreath on the first postwar decade of oil exploration by Texas independents, capping off as it did a dogged twenty-five-year adventure in West Texas wildcatting. The great discoveries at Big Lake and on the Yates Ranch had subsequently been augmented by wildcatting successes over wide regions of West Texas. As drilling technology improved, oil-bearing sands were discovered at a remarkable range of depths and in a wide variety of strata.

Called a "basin" because the rocks slope inward from all sides toward the middle, the area got its name from the thick permian deposits of organic sea life laid down before the Rocky Mountains were born. That monumental heaving of the earth warped the sea floor and the strata deposited below. As the eons passed, new sediments blown from the newly risen Rockies covered the older strata, producing with arid conditions the desertlike terrain of modern West Texas. The basin itself was huge, roughly 250 miles north to south and over 300 miles east to west.

The Jameson field of 1946 in Coke County gave prominence to the eastern shelf of the Permian Basin. But the biggest breakthrough came in the Canyon Reef, a prolific Pennsylvanian reservoir that began to produce high-gravity crude in 1948 in a belt 45 miles long, encompassing over 50,000 acres running through Scurry, Kent, Borden, and Howard counties. The Canyon boom brought flush times to areas thought by many geologists to have been previously condemned. As had happened in 1930 in East Texas to Humble Oil and Refining Company, the old Standard Oil subsidiary once again had possessed huge acreage holdings in the area of the Canyon Reef. Unfortunately, the company relinquished a considerable part of it in 1947 after drilling through the reef, neglecting to recover core samples, and hitting a dry hole at a greater depth. After the discovery well, another producer picked up the lease, reentered the hole, tested the reef, and completed a 1,500 barrel-per-day well.[30]

What appeared to be a second great bonanza soon followed in the Spraberry Trend. After initial discoveries in 1949, activity increased the next year, defining the contours of an immense reservoir, and development exploded in 1951. Some estimates placed potential recovery at four times the East Texas field! But despite successful tests over a wide area and promising subsurface data that led to conservative estimates of 1,000 to 3,000 barrels of recoverable oil per acre over an immense area, the Spraberry sands proved extremely tight and bottom-hole pressure declined at an almost unprecedented rate. Many producers and outside investors were badly burned. Eventually aided by improved secondary recovery techniques, Spraberry would later produce a substantial amount of oil, but nothing remotely approaching early predictions. Nevertheless, by the mid-1950s, the Permian Basin was blanketed with old and new fields in fifty counties. By 1956 in Howard County alone, discoveries had been made in eleven formations—the Fusselman, Silurian, Strawn, Canyon, Pennsylvania, Wolfcamp, Clear Fork, Glorieta, San Andreas, Yates, and Queen.[31]

With the development of the Permian Basin as a product of tests both by major companies and independents, tensions inevitably appeared over ratable take, pricing, and field rules—a continuing dynamic that added new members both to TIPRO and to the West Central Texas Oil and Gas Association and, after 1961, to the newly formed Permian Basin Petroleum Association. Indeed, the vivid play in the Permian Basin that exploded in the 1950s brought into TIPRO a new breed of independent operators—oilmen bearing professional training in geology, petroleum engineering, secondary recovery, and, it might be added, knowledge of the merits of taking core samples when drilling through the Canyon Reef. With university degrees in hand, some of these oil professionals went to work for independents, formed fledgling partnerships, or simply struck out on their own. Others worked for major companies for a time before following a similar route to becoming independents. As much as the old-time wildcatters, they learned the art of spreading the risk through putting together a drilling deal. And, like their predecessors, they sometimes went too far and suffered calamitous losses and at other times were too cautious and missed a promising play. They too, then, were classic independents.

But they simply could not pass as old-time seat-of-the-pants operators of the oil patch—because they weren't. They listened to men like Midland's Jim Russell, San Antonio's John Hurd, the partnership of Lester Clark and Bruce Street, Houston's Bruce Anderson and George Mitchell, and to adventurous wildcatters like Frank Pitts. It took a certain amount of intestinal fortitude to make the break and "go independent." This the young ones shared with the older generation. But whether old or new, independents had also discovered that it took a certain kind of political worldview to carry them successfully over the shoals that loomed in the immediate future.

In ways that would become clear in darker—and brighter—days ahead, TIPRO broadened its base in the 1950s through the influx of independent producers who had gotten a solid footing from their participation in plays in the Permian Basin. The struggle to survive in a global petroleum world dominated by giants would necessarily continue to be one waged against long odds. But, in their own style, independents were developing new techniques of their own. TIPRO's most effective days were still ahead.

Chapter Four

THE WARNING YEARS

T he postwar years had been a time of economic growth and consolidation for America, for the oil industry in general and for its
independent sector. Though inequities were strewn through the
entire process through which petroleum products were found, refined,
marketed, and taxed, the overall trajectory was upward. The old economic adage seemed to hold: a rising tide lifted all boats.

But early on, harbingers of trouble could be detected—bits and
pieces that cast a shadow over long-term prospects. In 1948 the United
States ceased to be a net oil-exporting nation. In that year, for the first
time, imports exceeded exports by a small margin. When many sectors
of the industry, by no means restricted to independent Texas producers,
gave voice to their unease about this basic structural change in the relationship of the U.S. economy to the international oil market, the subject became the center of interest in the National Petroleum Council.
In 1949 all of the major U.S. multinationals solemnly agreed to the
Petroleum Council's core policy statement that imported oil would
"supplement, not supplant" domestic production. Yet in each subsequent year the volume of imported crude increased to such an extent
that by 1953 the long-term dimensions of the threat seemed statistically incontrovertible: the domestic oil industry was gradually being
pushed toward the margins. In response to questionnaires tendered
by the Texas Railroad Commission to major purchasers, asking for

comment on the evolving import dilemma, the international companies uniformly downplayed the situation. There was one exception—the Standard Oil Company of Indiana, which had a substantial stake in domestic production. In an ironic reference to the National Petroleum Council's policy, Standard of Indiana offered the opinion that "imports are now supplanting rather than supplementing domestic crude production and should be reduced."[1]

The day before this 1953 Railroad Commission hearing, TIPRO's executive committee authorized President Bryan Payne to call for an immediate 250,000-barrel-per-day voluntary reduction in imports. Pleas of this kind had been made before—in response to the long-administered advice by major companies that the precondition for getting due consideration for independents was that they keep all contentions strictly "within the family." The difficulty with this advice was that, despite all demonstrations of conciliation, good manners, and forbearance by independents, "due consideration" was not forthcoming from the integrated companies. The ongoing reality was, quite simply, that producers were quietly and routinely ignored.

Therefore, in 1953, the TIPRO president distinguished his appeal from earlier ones. If, once again, the considered views of the independent sector of the industry were casually shunted aside, domestic producers would be driven, he said, "to appeal for help outside the industry." Such steps were inevitable, Payne explained, "whether we do so before the Railroad Commission, the Texas Legislature, the United States Congress or the bar of public opinion."[2]

In this manner Texas independents made an effort to keep the issue within the industry if at all possible. But what followed—month after month, year after year—gradually convinced every knowledgeable sector of the domestic producing industry that such an approach was hopeless. This was the great unwanted truth of the "warning years"—the period from the mid-1950s through the entire decade of the 1960s. To spell out these dynamics is no easy task, but it is impossible to make sense of the world of the American independent oil producer, or the actions of TIPRO as the voice of the independent, until the task is at least attempted, for the story—sobering as it is—nevertheless in the end is a liberating one.

The absolute starting point is to fix clearly and firmly the organic fact that TIPRO's gradual move toward autonomous action—toward a path free of the confines of "industry unity"—could never at any time be said to have been fashioned hastily. To suggest anything of the sort would be to oversimplify matters to the point of gross distortion. Indeed, the entire thrust of thought among producers was predicated on precisely the opposite objective: to try to find some way to live with the major companies. For independents, the operative reality undergirding this approach was grounded in the most elementary instinct for survival.

In ways that were far more subtle than the offhand analyses percolating through the nation's political community, independents possessed a richly textured understanding of the balance of forces within the world of petroleum. More fully than anyone else, independents knew that, in all the interstices of production and marketing, the integrated companies held the commanding economic heights. The very term "integration" described the coordinated links—from wellhead to pipeline to refinery to retail outlets—that could be summarized in one all-powerful word describing what the majors had that no one else possessed: connections. It was the major purchasers who connected the wellhead to the market, and it was their estimates of market demand that determined prorationing schedules. "Ratable take" was a term popularized by TIPRO as a basic ethical guide in determining that all wells be treated fairly, but it was never a term that described the functioning day-to-day reality of American oil production. The phrase had only relative meaning: independents were reduced to calling for "more ratable taking" than they were getting because the ongoing power relationships in the world of oil were such that the principle of ratable take itself was never more than a dream.

For most Americans—and this included those sundry sectors of informed opinion that liked to regard themselves as both knowledgeable and politically sophisticated—the multiple competitive advantages enjoyed by the majors were lost in what seemed to be the technical jargon of the industry itself. Judgments by independents on proration schedules or on ratable take were grounded in production realities that were simply beyond the ken of nonspecialists. It was much easier for onlookers to dismiss all such independent analyses as "special pleading" than it was to learn enough about oil production to understand what was being said. To outsiders, proration was nothing less than a subterfuge meant to achieve inflated crude prices, an elaborate masquerade in which major companies, independent producers, and the Texas Railroad

Commission all participated in covert harmony. For this underlying rea-son, the case for independents was maddeningly difficult to make, even by advocates who were intuitively diplomatic and instinctively concilia-tory toward all segments of the American population and to other oil-men, large and small. In the 1950s and 1960s, every TIPRO president and every task force chairman learned this truth firsthand.

Beyond this basic cultural reality, independents, like most Americans, proceeded from the basic premise that public dialogue was a level playing field in which verifiable facts were genuine components of the decision-making process. To acknowledge this belief is not to sug-gest that independents functioned under some romantic illusion that the self-interest of different players was somehow not an operative fac-tor in determining conduct. Far from it. Independents—again, like most Americans—acknowledged self-interest as a healthy dynamic within the free market system itself. And that meant that people tried to put the best possible face on the facts so that they squared up pretty well with one's self-interest. Thus, independents believed, for example, that legitimate debate could exist about precisely when imported oil was "supplanting" domestic production rather than "supplementing" it. It was a given that a legitimate disagreement with the majors could exist over precisely where this decisive juncture lurked.

But the lesson independents were forced to learn—against their deepest instincts and against their most settled hopes—was that such factually based junctures *might not exist at all* because the national deci-sion-making process might not turn merely on "facts." Rather, evidence accumulated that raw power was the determining ingredient in how vital petroleum issues were decided in Washington. Of all the connec-tions that vertical integration gave the major companies, the most pow-erful connection was political. But precisely how this connection worked was a puzzle not easily unraveled; Washington was a vast maze about which most Americans, including independent oilmen, had very little firsthand knowledge. Years after the fact, it is instructive to recount the independents' long rear-guard campaign to hang on by their fingernails to their U.S. market. This is so because the nature of the struggle reveals the precise reasons why small producers were driven to reassess their stance within the industry and within American society generally. And it reveals as well the actual lessons they learned that helped them chart a path toward autonomous action.

The first postwar discovery was that the economic shield erected against the spread of communism in Europe—the Marshall Plan—worked not only for the nations of Europe but also for the American economy and for virtually everyone in it. And it worked most specifically for independent oil producers. The one substantial force coping with the enormous appetite of exporters of Middle Eastern oil was the resurgent postwar European market. Through the 1950s and beyond, the rapidly expanding postwar economies of European nations, nurtured by Marshall Plan aid, increasingly absorbed an ever-mounting tide of Arabian crude. In lessening the need for the U.S. market to serve as the central focus of Middle Eastern production, it was the one trend in the global economy that softened the pressure on the domestic producing industry.

Yet the sheer size of the reserves held under concession in the Persian Gulf meant that the North American continent was a permanent beacon, whetting the thirst of marketing policymakers in every international company. And so it was that in major company offices far beyond the gaze of the American public the decision was reached that the U.S. market was simply too huge to leave to domestic production. Robust and expansive as the European market was, it nevertheless could not completely satisfy the appetite of the international companies. It was this underlying dynamic that became the driving force behind all crucial oil issues in the postwar years.

By 1957, it was evident that the rising volume of imported oil had begun to have long-term structural impact on the domestic industry. In the monthly allowable hearings before the Texas Railroad Commission, major purchasers dutifully reported lower and lower numbers for "current market demand." The United States, it was said, suffered from an overage of "stocks on hand." And so, month after month, production allowables declined—from thirty days a month to twenty, then to twelve, and, finally, to seven. In Texas, shut-in capacity soared. By mid-1957, the number of drilling rigs at work had declined by over 600. As every independent knew, fewer wildcats meant fewer discovered reserves. Under such conditions, domestic reserves inevitably would prove unable to keep pace with domestic reservoir depletion. Quite literally, the independent industry would die. Producers could read, they could count, and they could project the future: across the producing sector, voices calling for quotas on oil imports poured in upon Congress.[3]

The nation was now treated to an elaborate dance—a seventeen-year minuet of "voluntary" quotas followed by "mandatory" quotas, followed by necessary refinements to make quotas effective, followed by more refinements in light of continuing evidence that effectiveness had somehow proved elusive. Before each new dance step, major importers played out interminable public relations intermissions in which the old steps were defended as working or "nearly working" and observable signs of stress in the domestic industry labeled as "temporary." But however ingenious the reasoning, the bottom line was always the same: any new steps toward getting control of imports were "premature." The entire performance was orchestrated with such seemingly professional arm-waving that it succeeded, in Washington at least, in obscuring the demonstrable facts at hand. Inexorably, year after year throughout the 1950s, Middle Eastern crude became an increasing—and increasingly permanent—feature of the U.S. market.[4]

Reappraisal and a New Course

This fundamental sea change in global production and marketing forced TIPRO into an agonizing internal reappraisal of its style of advocacy in the same period in which its permanent staff in Austin was experiencing a similar sea change. Within a three-month period in 1954, TIPRO's original executive secretary, E. I. "Tommy" Thompson suffered a heart attack and went on extended leave, and the association's first general counsel, Alvis Vandygrift, resigned to return to private law practice. This was soon followed by the completion of Jack Woodward's bold and colorful tenure as TIPRO president.

The departure of the Woodward-Thompson team marked the end of what can properly be called the founding era of TIPRO, one that began when two Houstonians, Jack Porter and Glenn McCarthy, gathered a small group of producers in Austin in 1946 to form a statewide organization of independents. The original founders quickly earned a reputation in Austin's legislative circles as "swashbucklers." The flamboyant McCarthy neatly fit every cliché of the freewheeling wildcatter, even before he built the showy palace in Houston called the Shamrock Hotel. Indeed, he was so colorful, even by swashbuckler standards, that the gruff, outspoken Porter was deemed a less controversial choice as the group's first president. In sheer hard-hitting intensity, however, both Porter and McCarthy had to take a back seat to the third independent from Houston, Tommy Thompson, who had agreed to serve as TIPRO's first executive vice-president. No one in this trio was loath to voice provocative opinions, either in TIPRO meetings or to political and petroleum journalists. Among those who watched this early TIPRO style unfold firsthand was Frank Pitts, who subsequently characterized the Porter-Thompson team as "hard-headed, hard-driving people, unaccustomed to compromise." They would, said Pitts, "argue with a sign post." The founders performed, at some cost, the necessary role of demonstrating to more cautious souls that there was a new group in town called TIPRO that intended to be heard, come what may. They knew they were called "swashbucklers" and it suited them just fine.[5]

The original organizers nevertheless experienced great difficulty placing their personal stamp on producer policy. Throughout the first decade of TIPRO's existence, policy increasingly emerged from a broad democratic forum that was grounded in an internal dialogue among the activists who made up TIPRO's executive committee. This working group embodied an enormous range of political opinion as well as personal style, but it gradually became the moving force in TIPRO because of a quality its members held in common—the willingness to hear each other out. In ways that oil editors and other petroleum journalists could not easily observe, men like Vance Foster, Lester Clark, Vernon Frost, John Hurd, Frank Pitts, Bruce Street, Jerry O'Brien, Bill Rutter, Thornton Huddle, Edward Kadane, Malcolm Abel, and Bob Foree quietly set TIPRO on a course of broad-based producer advocacy. They were not yet in a position to routinely speak officially for TIPRO—only Foree had at that point served a term as president—but they increasingly played such a central role in Austin and Washington hearings on a variety of key oil and gas issues that they were, in effect, gradually defining the position of independents.

But what the Porter-Thompson tandem, and later the Woodward-Thompson team, could not effortlessly achieve in policy was in fact achieved in terms of image. Their public style went a good distance toward confirming the popular notion of oil independents as a colorful band who reveled in making flamboyant remarks for public consumption. They were "good copy" and most reporters loved them. One detractor among statehouse correspondents, however, characterized their style as "absolutist," adding by way of explanation that "they loved to seize what they believed was the moral high ground, reduce it to a pithy phrase or two, and then step back and let the chips fall where they may." In the same vein, the oil editor of the *Houston Post*, Billy Thompson, described the widespread industry and journalistic reaction to the early founders: "They were looked upon as loudmouths." Similarly, Jay Hall, oil editor of the *Dallas Morning News*, wrote in the TIPRO Reporter that the association's leadership indulged in "overstatement" in ways that hurt their cause with journalists. Thompson and Hall, both of whom came to be admirers of TIPRO, traced the rise of the organization's stature to the alteration of TIPRO's public style of advocacy.[6]

In the first heady postwar years of full production, the swashbuckling approach caused no special harm, but as the tide of imports and escalating price and pipeline discrimination began to reach alarming proportions in the 1950s, flamboyant advocacy began to appear increasingly counterproductive. There was a celebrated presentation in Washington late in 1954 when Jack Woodward, speaking officially as TIPRO's president, stunned a Federal Power Commission (FPC) hearing by observing that no amount of price discrimination by pipeline companies could justify any corrective federal action. When FPC commissioner Claude Draper inquired, in an incredulous tone, whether small producers and royalty owners would not be pleased to see the commission help end pipeline price discrimination against them, Woodward replied, "Thanks a lot but no thanks." Woodward went on to explain that however serious the problem of discrimination might be, it was no proper concern of the FPC. He emphasized he feared any FPC jurisdiction over independent production "as splitting the industry to the point that corrective legislation might not be obtained." Woodward concluded: "Lest there remain any doubt in your minds, gentlemen of the Commission, we of the Texas Independent Producers and Royalty Owners Association are unalterably opposed to federal regulation."[7]

For his part, Tommy Thompson, while also "unalterably" opposing federal jurisdiction "in any way, shape or form," had learned a great deal in eight years as executive vice-president about the monopolistic thrust of the industry and the threat it posed to producers. Not only did he know independents were losing ground, he could illustrate the extent of the danger through postwar statistics revealing that independents had discovered only 48 percent of new postwar reserves compared to their prewar performance of 77 percent. And Thompson could document that major company actions, unhampered by legislative statutes, lay behind these ominous numbers. But he, like Woodward, rested his strategic approach on the hope that remedial legislation would be achieved in Congress rather than through the FPC. On this basis, Thompson easily marched with Woodward in condemning any federal involvement in the gas industry. It was a stance that had become quite distinct from the growing consensus among TIPRO activists that producers needed to focus on their own interests rather than those of the industry. Even one of TIPRO's original founders, Tyler's Bryan Payne, had moved to this position. "Industry unity" was no longer an all-weather flag.[8]

Replacing Thompson as executive vice-president was W. Earl Turner, editor of the association's prize-winning journal, the *TIPRO Reporter*. Turner also dated from the earliest days when the founders discovered that in order to acquire needed members, TIPRO had to generate a conscious public presence. Toward this end, Turner was hired as publicity director, a position he soon restructured by becoming the association's foremost conduit of internal information. Turner initiated a monthly *Independent News* to keep producers abreast of events, and as developments got more intricate, he broadened the newsletter's scope in 1948 by creating the *TIPRO Reporter*. Turner's editorial duties forced him to study the politics of advocacy as practiced by the integrated majors and disseminated through a wide variety of organizational forums and industry journals. Such research proved a sobering training school, for it revealed to him the multiple ways major companies had developed a sophisticated "macro politics" that could, as the occasion demanded, variously play upon business and consumer constituencies and, indeed, extend even to trade associations created by independent producers. Under such conditions, Texas independents were routinely over-matched.[9]

In 1955 TIPRO's approach to Washington changed course. In that year, Foree, as TIPRO's most experienced Washington hand, moved to lay before the House Ways and Means Committee TIPRO's research data on the extent of the invasion of the U.S. market by major importers. The total figures for 1954 showed a 9.2 percent production hike in the Middle East compared to a 1.9 percent decline in domestic production. The shut-in capacity in Texas approximated a stunning two million barrels daily![10]

The enormous comparative advantages enjoyed by importers extended even into the realm of taxes: as income for the majors went up, their taxes went down—thanks to a congressionally sanctioned innovation that permitted importing companies to count the totality of the Arab share in revenues as "taxes" incurred by American companies. By this extraordinary bit of fiscal legerdemain, the contractual concessions paid to producing nations was looked upon as money paid into the U.S. Treasury. While international companies paid "taxes" that thus vanished into the air, domestic producers paid in genuine coin of the realm—no less than seventy-five cents in local, state, and federal taxes on every barrel of domestic oil produced. It was not only domestic producers who suffered from this arrangement; every American taxpayer was effectively involved in subsidizing the integrated companies. But though the House Ways and Means Committee listened to Bob Foree with courtesy and sometimes with considerable interest, no policy changes ensued. Clearly there was more to the business of educating Congress and the people than simply mobilizing germane factual information.

TIPRO thereupon began to expand its budget and beef up its staff. John Davenport, a former Texas assistant attorney general, came on board to fill Vandygrift's position as general counsel. Additionally, a new post, research director, was upgraded and Julian Martin brought in to systematize the association's knowledge of current and future industry trends and to buttress TIPRO's capacity to interpret the fine print in legislative initiatives sponsored by various sectors of the industry.[11]

As TIPRO prepared itself to explore new ways to serve independents, the Voluntary Import Program was finally set in place in 1957. It soon produced such stark evidence of its nonfunctioning that it was replaced in 1959 with a "mandatory" system. But results in the early 1960s verified conclusively that the Mandatory Program was not very mandatory. Nevertheless, the industry's elaborate public dance continued as if all were well. In the words of TIPRO's new research director, Julian Martin, who mobilized the numbers to prove it, the domestic market was guarded by what could only be described as a "sieve that does what sieves are supposed to do: leak."[12]

What made the economic fine print so ominous was the fact that long-term inflationary pressures within the global economy had produced a steadily rising level of drilling costs, borne by independent producers, at the same time the price of crude oil remained eerily becalmed. The Mandatory Program stood revealed as a form of elaborate window dressing that produced an amazing degree of stasis in global crude pricing. Detailed figures compiled by IPAA showed a per-barrel crude price of $2.88 for 1960 and $2.94 for 1968, while comparable per-well drilling costs went up almost 50 percent—from $50,806 in 1960 to $72,280 in 1968. In ways that outsiders could not fathom, these were utterly decisive numbers for independent producers. Drilling costs were the absolute anchor of all production deals on wildcat wells. If costs grew exponentially while crude prices remained static, the number of wildcats worth the risk declined toward the vanishing point. And exploration was the unconditional raison d'etre for independents: producers who weren't drilling were no longer effectively in the oil business. In short, the cost-price squeeze was choking the independent to death. At TIPRO meetings, veteran wildcatters mumbled to each other nervously: was the string being played out? was it all over for the independent operator?[13]

The Warning Years. No sector of the independent producing industry remained untouched. While a vast tide of accumulating bad news engulfed independent oil producers, similar brackish waters began to inundate natural gas producers. Here, too, the labors of independents took on all the aspects of a desperate rear-guard campaign waged against overwhelming forces that commanded the economic heights of the production and marketing process. And here, too, ironies reached new levels of public relations refinement as the titans of the industry pushed themselves forward as defenders of the American consumer in all matters surrounding simple equity in field rules, ratable take, and taxation— that is to say, in all matters in which the American consumer was not a relevant player.

In natural gas, too, a tortuously long and complex story can, with a bit of care, be summarized fairly swiftly. The essential requirement is to put aside sloganeering about "federal control" and focus on the real issues that were being decided. In the 1950s, the two great preoccupations of the U.S. natural gas industry became the Phillips decision and the Harris bills. The former was a judicial quagmire and the latter a legislative thicket. Both had the effect of increasing the comparative advantage of centralizing forces within the industry, thus exacerbating long-term monopolizing trends.

This is not to say that any such centralizing momentum was readily visible to the American population. In the aggregate, whole brass bands of mystification deafened public understanding of natural gas issues. Despite cursory press coverage through many rounds of public hearings and legislative debate on the succession of Harris bills, and court appeals in the Phillips case, the interests of consumers was but a minor tinkle of a piano amid a vast orchestration by major gas purchasers comfortably settled within the ranks of long-line gas transmission companies.[14]

Phillips Petroleum Company, a variously integrated producer, refiner, and seller of both natural gas and crude products, was defined in a 1954 Supreme Court case as a natural gas company subject to utility regulation. The Federal Power Commission's subsequent definition of the scope of utility regulation—ostensibly grounded in the Phillips decision—was expanded to include independent producers. Since all congressional bills on natural gas—and there had been many since the Kerr bill of 1949—variously impacted the industry's many producing, processing, and marketing segments (whether they were integrated under one corporate roof or not), "definitions" of each of the segments was a critical component of any piece of legislation. After the Phillips decision and the FPC's bizarre redefinition of independent gas producers as valid subjects for utility-type regulation, the subsequent history of natural gas legislation became a testament to the lobbying power of industry giants and a veritable treatise on how public relations spins on the lobbying process could create a legislative context that was baffling to the general public.

Through the entire process, all natural gas bills had a common public cover: congressional sponsors habitually announced that their measure was designed "to free independent producers from federal regulation." The original version, known as the Harris-Fulbright bill, was so loaded in favor of the industry's leading sectors that independents came to regard the entire legislative history of the bill as an absolutely dismaying example of the democratic process gone awry. As matters finally developed, lobbying excesses became sufficiently public to range into the area of national scandal, and President Eisenhower found himself forced to veto the complex, irrational, and retrogressive measure that eventually had limped through Congress.

The next version, the Harris-O'Hara bill, was even worse from the producer standpoint. In fact, it was so prejudicial against the long-term equity requirements of independents that a succession of TIPRO Gas Committee chairmen—indeed, whole committee memberships—were hard put to craft sufficient amendments which, even if adopted in Congress, would permit producers to support any gas bill at all.[15]

Goodbye to "Industry Unity"

These legislative gyrations gave independents an entirely new perspective on the American political system. The heavy hand of gas pipeline companies could be seen in every piece of legislation subsequent to the original Kerr bill of 1949. Indeed, that measure was the simplest of all the postwar efforts to integrate a new product, natural gas, into the American economic structure. In retrospect, independents could see that the original bill to clarify the status of independents was "too clean" because it incurred the wrath of the pipeline companies. In the midst of the Harris muddle, TIPRO was able for the first time to sort through the maze of postwar intraindustry moralizing and reach some startling new conclusions.

In June 1957, TIPRO signaled that it was reappraising the role of the American independent producer and his "wild and dizzy ride on the merry-go-round called industry unity." In its annual convention of 1957, TIPRO's membership voted to participate in an early test case to determine whether the Supreme Court intended what the FPC said it intended in the Phillips case. Lest anyone have trouble understanding the difference between the status of an independent gas producer and the status of "the Phillips operation," TIPRO reminded one and all that Phillips "purchases about 50 percent of its gas from producers and sells it to five interstate pipelines, which in turn sell it in 14 states." In essence, the FPC "allowed itself somehow to be persuaded" to take Phillips as a norm through which it could assert jurisdiction over independents. The precise nature of this "somehow" was a matter about which TIPRO had fashioned a sober new conclusion based on what insiders among producers had discovered during the long Washington struggles over natural gas regulation.[16]

For the first time, TIPRO made public this behind-the-scenes knowledge. While the FPC publicly said it did not believe independent gas producers should be regulated as utilities, it also was willing to "assert the most extreme interpretation of jurisdiction" in the belief that Congress would "immediately rectify an obvious error." But in proceeding down this road, FPC commissioners were following the trajectory of major company legislative strategists who, argued TIPRO, not only "preached that doctrine with a vengeance," but also privately "admonished" independents to stay on the industry team. Such producer deference would serve, it was said, as an appropriate preface for independents to "unite" with the industry in a "march" toward the needed remedy—namely "corrective legislation in Congress." In sum, TIPRO regarded the FPC interpretation as the central pivot in an elaborate game to coerce independents into supporting the next gas deregulation bill.

A similar FPC motive to regulate independents was detectable in its new proposed order for submission of elaborate field production data by independent producers, a completely unanticipated intervention that drove TIPRO onlookers to distraction: "This fantastic proposal would compel all independents to submit impossible data" and in so doing "served admirably to frighten some independents into accepting pending legislation which was—to say the least—a far cry from the original intent" of producer decontrol. In short, said TIPRO, the FPC had chosen "this particular time to rattle some bones and force independent producers back into line when they begin finding fault with the Harris-O'Hara bills in Congress." The industry custom of playing fast and loose with independents had reached a new plateau of ingenuity: "Nobody doubts that the FPC can ruin independent producers, and this proposed order serves as a well-timed reminder" to all independents "who fail to show enthusiasm for a bill which restores so little of their freedom while doing so much for pipeline companies and distributors."[17]

TIPRO's indignation was measured but clear: "Independents, it seems, are supposed to 'stand up and fight' only so long as they aren't hurting anybody. . . . When the long-line companies fail to agree on something, nobody assumes they should go along just to promote 'unity.'" Indeed, as TIPRO members searched their collective memory with a newfound intensity, they were able to recall it was "the bitter opposition" of pipeline companies to the original Kerr bill, "the only true independent producer bill," that proved decisive in persuading President Truman to veto it back in 1949.

But most of all was the alarming clarity of the FPC's priorities, so evident in its disdain for independents when they acted independently of pipeline companies. The accumulated evidence pointed to an unwanted conclusion: on natural gas, as on the taxability of the Arabian oil concessions, the Eisenhower administration was responding to the giants of the oil and gas industry. Accordingly, the call for industry unity was seen simply as a cynical ploy to let the majors harness for their own narrow self-interest the authentic social capital of independent producers. The fact that the majors were doing so through specific legislative devices that undermined the very survival of the independent producer added the final irony to the entire stratagem.[18]

The ironies were, indeed, everywhere. What TIPRO began to tell the public (but perhaps even more important, to tell itself) was that the future path of producer advocacy had to be much more organically independent than anything that had yet been achieved. In the Texas oil patch, if not yet anywhere else, the term "industry unity" was a dead letter.

TIPRO now launched a long-term strategic program that was to govern producer policy throughout the remainder of the 1950s and beyond—namely, the formulation of autonomous programs of advocacy on behalf of independents, with or without the approval of the industry's leading segments. Late in 1957, TIPRO called on all the nation's independent associations to join it in a direct intervention with the FPC to exempt true independents from its new reporting requirements. In its call, TIPRO reported that its own independent research had indicated compliance with the new reporting requirements constituted "a mountain of paper" that would cost each producer upwards of $4,000 annually for the rest of his life.

To TIPRO's dismay, the short-run response of other state-level producer associations across the country was to agree privately but to hold back from any public identification with the TIPRO initiative and its implications—opposing the major oil companies. Undeterred, Texas producers rallied all their own available resources. In oral and written arguments before the Federal Power Commission, TIPRO's new general counsel, John Davenport, spoke on behalf of the West Central Texas Oil and Gas Association, the North Texas Oil and Gas Association, and the Panhandle Producers and Royalty Owners Association. The elaborate documentation presented by Davenport, underscoring the sheer logic of the case for independents, carried the day: the FPC backed off from implementing its far-reaching proposed order.[19]

This TIPRO success, and the producer politics that surrounded it, revealed both the pitfalls and the promise inherent in the task of crafting a national coalition of independent producers. On the evidence, the rest of the nation's independent associations still had a distance to travel before they could routinely be counted upon—on all the relevant issues in both oil and gas—to act in their own self-interest. On the other hand, the immediate victory at the FPC level provided tangible proof that straightforward action by independents could produce positive results.

How to rally independents in other states? Obviously, the first step had already been demonstrated: TIPRO's own autonomous action could serve as a clear role model for the rest of the domestic producing industry. But other prerequisites for cooperation were not so easily put in place. It turned out that a considerable gap existed between genuine self-interest and perceived self-interest when it came to independents operating in different regions of the country.

The reason was traceable to the differentiated impact of imported oil on different groups of independents, a development that underscored in yet another new way the long-term structural implications of Middle East production on the realm of the domestic producer. The relevant fact was that the major importing companies played a far larger role in wellhead production in the rest of the nation than they did in Texas. Because of the impact of Spindletop and East Texas in bringing into being thousands of independent producers, creating in the process a vibrant and knowledgeable subculture of small operators who subsequently brought in a number of the large West Texas, Panhandle, and North Texas fields, the ranks of independents in Texas had no numerical counterpart anywhere else in the nation. While the risks were great and many a small producer had been driven to the wall, the continuing discoveries kept augmenting the ranks of independents, as TIPRO's own expanding membership rolls proved conclusively. What these realities meant, in terms of major company policy, was this: in order to make more room in the U.S. market for imported crude, the most efficient—and also most profitable—place for domestic cutbacks was in Texas. Thanks to the predominant position of Texas production on the national scene, cutbacks there could also be made with much less organizational and administrative reshuffling of marketing schedules than would be the case if cutbacks were spread proportionally across a dozen or more states.

A second factor contributing to major company preoccupation with Texas lay in the unique and historically verified prorationing role of the Texas Railroad Commission. As a direct product of the flagrant waste of reservoir pressure in the Spindletop salt dome as well as threatened waste of the woodbine pool in East Texas, the commission had developed logical and effective conservation policies that allowed it to govern wellhead production to prevent "physical waste." It was in the name of this conservation necessity that market-demand proration came into being in the 1930s, proved to be workable, and thereafter stood the test of time.

An Unwanted Umbrella

Thus as a sanctioned tradition (and here the ironies were, indeed, profound), the Texas Railroad Commission could be made to serve the interests of major importers in a way the commission itself could not influence. Majors merely had to take note of their own expanding imports and announce at the Railroad Commission's monthly allowable hearings that domestic stocks-on-hand were in such oversupply that market demand for Texas crude had "declined." In the jargon of commission hearings, the major purchasers "nominated" for purchase a steadily declining number of barrels of crude—and did so on a downward trajectory month after month. For this reason, the Railroad Commission's monthly allowables for crude production continued to drop in the decade of the 1950s—from twenty-one days of allowable production per month, to eighteen, and then, in November 1957, to twelve days per month. By 1962, monthly allowables had shrunk to seven days. As TIPRO put it, "Texas is taking a diminishing cut of a diminishing market." Shut-in capacity in Texas was stuck at a very high level—well beyond two million barrels daily.[20]

In effect, the major purchasers, acting through accepted Railroad Commission procedures, had constructed for themselves a "Texas umbrella" that was held over the entire domestic producing industry. By controlling Texas production, the majors could slowly but steadily depress overall U.S. oil production, creating in the process an ever-expanding market for their Middle Eastern concessions.

Gradually, elements of fantasy began creeping into the monthly nominations by the major companies to the Railroad Commission. Not only were nominations on a permanent downward trend, but evidence accumulated that the nominations themselves did not reflect the actual purchases the majors intended to make. By 1965, TIPRO was reduced to recommending to the commission that the reporting form used in allowable nominations during commission hearings be amended to require each company to tell whether it actually bought all the Texas crude it nominated each month. The "Texas umbrella" had so many dimensions that the editors of the *TIPRO Reporter* decided a 1965 story on allowables merited the headline "Fair Play—A Vanishing Tradition." As TIPRO summarized the situation in the 1960s, "With monotonous regularity, crude purchasers are precipitating situations with which present state conservation laws cannot deal adequately."[21]

All such prorationing developments within the domestic market, structurally controlled as so many of them were by major companies, made interstate cooperation among producers much more difficult to achieve. Independents in other states simply did not come under the constantly expanding pressure that was so heavily focused upon Texas producers.

This reality impacted heavily within the national producer organization, the Independent Petroleum Association of America, whose members in many states had not felt the severity of imports as dramatically as Texas producers. In its relations with IPAA, TIPRO had always thought of itself as a utility infielder, or "gap filler," capable of taking on national or IPAA-type issues only when the older association failed for one reason or another to do so. Some of the leading TIPRO activists were as a matter of course also IPAA participants, sometimes playing very prominent roles in both. In general, the two associations were able to work together because sophisticated participants in each realized that outgunned independents across the nation needed to make every effort to labor in harness with one another. Experienced activists easily grasped TIPRO's role both as a gap-filler and sometimes also as a goad in creating an appropriate climate among the nation's producing sectors that would encourage IPAA participation.[22]

In its relations with other state-level associations, TIPRO had a more complex history. The producer associations in Kansas, Ohio, and West Virginia, for example, were both well organized and generally quite active. A number of other state associations simply possessed too small a contingent of independents to be serious factors. Still others had more producers but were somewhat underorganized. But whether well constructed or not, state associations outside Texas simply could not mobilize the raw strength available in TIPRO and, for this reason, had never really developed an internal institutional tradition of active assertion that merited comparison with the TIPRO heritage.

Accordingly, during the ten-year period between 1955 and 1965, TIPRO was very much out in front of other independent associations in its persistent and detailed analyses of both the Voluntary Imports Program and the Mandatory Program that came on line after 1959. So much so, in fact, that a number of Texas independents cast about for some means of shoring up the smaller producer associations in other states. Toward this end, one of TIPRO's most energetic early activists, Lester Clark of Breckenridge, led a group of Texans to a meeting in Wichita, Kansas, in 1958 out of which emerged the Liaison Committee of Cooperating Associations, fashioned as a vehicle for producer cooperation across state boundaries. Clark was elected first chairman of the Liaison Committee. Soon, the group's internal structure was regularized with regional vice-presidents representing the California Independent Producers and Royalty Owners Association, the Rocky Mountain Oil and Gas Association, the Tri-State Oil and Gas Association (based in Indiana), the Kansas Independent Oil and Gas Association, and the Mississippi-Louisiana Oil and Gas Association. Internal communications were fashioned and rank-and-file members of cooperating state associations began receiving detailed analyses of oil industry developments of a kind TIPRO participants had long enjoyed through the *TIPRO Reporter*. Additionally, TIPRO's research director, Julian Martin, moved in to serve a number of successive terms as secretary-treasurer in the course of helping to mobilize the liaison group for coordinated action on national issues.[23]

Thus began a fifteen-year effort by independents to find a way to cope with oil imports, a campaign that over time would develop a number of different approaches. A cornerstone of many of them was embedded in principles first enunciated by the international oil consultant Bernard Darbyshire, who began a long association with Texas independents at TIPRO's 1958 convention. Under what became known as the Darbyshire Plan, each barrel of oil produced from U.S. reserves would earn for its producer the right to import a comparable volume from foreign reserves. Darbyshire proved quite open to all suggestions that the ratio of domestic-to-foreign crude should be adjusted in accordance with market realities; it was the principle he was after.[24]

The great merit of the Darbyshire Plan, needless to say, was that it went right to the heart of the relationship between foreign and domestic oil production. The plan became the conceptual centerpiece of a long series of comparable efforts to reform the nation's import programs through fees, tariffs, and charges on tanker tonnage. One of the more innovative attempts came with the proposal to initiate a quota bidding system, which required the government to auction the right to bid on import certificates of 1,000 barrels a day. The short-lived fate of bills introduced to this effect in Congress quickly caused independents to look for other ways to soften the devastating impact of imported oil.

For this reason, independents explored different methods designed to take advantage of a national security principle promulgated by Senator Lyndon Johnson and first incorporated as a clause in the Trade Expansion Act of 1955. The clause called upon the executive branch of the government to conduct, on request, investigations of oil imports to determine whether they posed a threat to national security insofar as they made domestic production uneconomic. Over the next fifteen years, such investigations were launched no less than eight times, and the resulting report on each occasion determined that a national security threat did, in fact, exist. Since the law required the president to do whatever he deemed necessary should such findings materialize, some marginal improvements were achieved as a product of subsequent executive orders. The most promising came in 1977 when President Carter initiated an oil import fee that, unfortunately, was promptly shot down in Congress. President Nixon had earlier fashioned a modest series of import fees which also had a rather short administrative life.[25]

But the hearings and executive orders themselves helped to publicize the plight of domestic independents. They also served as sites of advocacy to which TIPRO could attempt to rally other independent associations throughout the country. This continuing effort, dating from Lester Clark's initiatives in 1958, began to bear fruit in the 1960s. By the middle of the decade, both the Liaison Committee and IPAA had begun to augment TIPRO initiatives targeting the Mandatory Import Program. IPAA benefited in this regard from the energy and skill of Dallas's Tom Medders, who eventually rose to the IPAA presidency. A beneficiary of considerable experience on key TIPRO committees, Medders proved adept in helping to forge a common front of producers. Medders was, in Martin's view, "a key figure" in overcoming parochial regional concerns among independent associations and "shepherding them toward united action."[26]

A Lesson in Lobbying

Most of these efforts, of course, were directed at Washington. But TIPRO also learned some other lessons during the warning years that were much closer to home: most of them turned on the audacious lobbying techniques of major companies within the confines of the Texas legislature. In these encounters right on their doorstep, Texas producers took in a storehouse of information that, as events later revealed, were to pay off down the road—though the short-run lessons were quite sobering.

As the population of Texas expanded and the pressure on public education sharpened the search for revenue sources, the petroleum industry was, quite naturally, a constant source of legislative interest. Major oil and gas purchasers, habituated to speaking for the industry, had historically cast the subject of taxation in terms of levels of "production taxes." But early in the 1950s, the legislature explored, and eventually passed, a new type of revenue bill—a "gas gathering" tax that fell not on producers but on the long-line companies. The first effort in this direction taxed pipelines directly so that it was a clear unconstitutional intervention into interstate commerce. TIPRO's Alvis Vandygriff played a role in helping to craft a second effort, one more legally surefooted, that was introduced by the Amarillo conservative and state senator Grady Hazlewood. The measure came under heavy lobbying pressure and was distorted through a series of amendments that weakened the constitutionality of the statute. Warnings to this effect offered on the floor of the legislature soon proved to be well founded. The courts did, in fact, subsequently rule the Hazlewood bill unconstitutional. The effect of the decision was to leave the producing sector as the sole source of state revenue from the petroleum industry.[27]

But in the 1959 session, an entirely new approach to gas taxation was unveiled. Styled the "severance beneficiary tax," this economically sophisticated piece of legislation had the further merit of being judicially innovative in a manner that seemed to insulate it from constitutional questions. The striking feature of the severance beneficiary tax, independents discovered, was that the burden fell exclusively on precisely those gas purchasers who benefited most scandalously from the confiscatory life-of-field contracts forced on producers in the 1930s. Since major purchasers who possessed such contracts were the heaviest "beneficiaries" of gas severance, they paid the most: the tax was on the difference between the benchmark wellhead price of fifteen cents per thousand cubic feet and the actual price paid to producers by gas purchasers. The bill thus rewarded equity at the wellhead: any long-line purchaser who paid his producers the benchmark price or above paid no tax at all! On the other hand, so-called confiscatory purchasers who paid producers as low as three cents per thousand cubic feet were the ones who faced the brunt of the tax obligations. As written, the severance beneficiary tax went a long way toward removing the grotesque incentives pipeline companies derived from the scandalous life-of-field contracts that had so long disfigured natural gas production in Texas. In so doing, the measure provided a concrete economic incentive weighted in terms of fairness to the small producer. Just as relevant were the legal implications: the point of pipeline taxation was at the wellhead—clearly untainted by "interstate commerce."[28]

TIPRO had played no role in the formulation of the new gas gathering levy, but producers watched the ensuing legislative struggle with rapt attention. As might be expected, the long-line companies waged a multifaceted attack that came close to matching the lobbying pressures unveiled in Washington on the succession of Harris bills. Nevertheless, the severance beneficiary approach possessed so much tangible economic merit, and authentic political appeal, that it garnered a wide base of support. Originally conceived by Representative Robert Eckhardt of Houston, the bill also gathered the behind-the-scenes support of Governor Price Daniel as well as a remarkable coalition of liberal, moderate, and conservative members of the Texas legislature. As one veteran Austin correspondent confided to his colleagues in the press corps, "This bill makes too much sense to be easily demagogued against."[29]

As with the previous Hazlewood bill, the severance beneficiary tax came under a barrage of amendments that threatened the logic, not to mention the constitutionality, of the statute. Many of these amendments were so transparently unconstitutional on their face that they were beaten back, though the voting margin was narrow enough to underscore the potency of interstate pipeline lobbyists in the Texas legislature. Indeed, it soon developed that a series of new amendments, less transparently unconstitutional, were added to the legislation over the objections of its sponsors. In this form, the measure passed. In the end, after a long court fight, the severance beneficiary tax was deemed unconstitutional by the Texas Supreme Court, and Attorney General Waggoner Carr declined to carry the case to the U.S. Supreme Court. The issue passed from the legislative scene. Once again, producers were left alone as the industry's sole taxable targets of revenue-seeking legislators.

The lobbying processes that proliferated during the legislative struggles over the gas gathering tax and the subsequent severance beneficiary levy illustrated in subtle new ways the power of integrated companies to create legislative circumstances wherein the real fight took place offstage beyond public understanding—even, in many instances, beyond the gaze of capitol reporters for the state's major dailies. The complex process by which the Hazlewood and Eckhardt bills were rendered unconstitutional transpired in this manner—essentially beyond public view.

These unexpected twists and turns were all quite educational for independent producers. In ways that were to reap huge dividends in later years, independents learned some instructive lessons from the legislative politics of 1959. The decisive ingredient that officeholders like Representative Eckhardt and Governor Daniel brought to the issue of industry taxation was not ideology per se. This was quite evident in the fact that "conservative" Daniel and "liberal" Eckhardt had been at loggerheads with one another during the constant intraparty struggles that characterized the Texas Democratic Party in that era. If traditional political allegiances had proved controlling, their cooperation on the severance beneficiary tax could not possibly have occurred. What turned out to be critical was the on-the-ground understanding that both men came to have of the subtleties of major company lobbying as it impacted on the political needs of Texas constituencies, extending to revenues for the public schools. The latter, of course, was a subject in which both Daniel and Eckhardt had an interested stake. But beyond these obvious interests, both men knew what an independent producer was, they knew what an integrated company was, and they understood the resulting realities of ratable take, pipeline connections, and life-of-field contracts. In ways not at all common among politicians, they knew the internal political terrain of petroleum—as the industry's diverse segments defined themselves by their actions.

Herein lurked certain related political dynamics that TIPRO came to appreciate. The essential discovery was that truly informed legislative leadership, one capable of crafting sophisticated petroleum legislation, could translate into broad-based coalitions of support for independent oil and gas producers. To fashion such an effective coalition, however, any producer-oriented legislative helmsman absolutely had to possess two specific qualities: a subtle knowledge of the structural equities and inequities functioning between the various sectors of the petroleum industry and—equally important—a personal status within the community of elected officeholders. The latter was important in order for a given piece of legislation to escape a parochial political label—be it "conservative" or "liberal"—and thus facilitate the recruiting of a broad-based coalition of support. As it turned out, these were precisely the political qualities that—some fifteen years later—Lloyd Bentsen would bring to the decisive struggle over depletion. In short, what the pipeline tax issue brought into view in the late 1950s was some general truths about the dynamics of the legislative process that went quite beyond the personalities of Price Daniel and Robert Eckhardt.[30]

But there was a final prerequisite, one that TIPRO itself would have to provide—namely, highly engaged participation in the legislative process itself. In the Texas legislative struggles over gas pipeline taxation in the 1950s, TIPRO's role was essentially defensive and not deeply influential on the outcome. As time would show, the role of TIPRO in the 1970s—and in Washington rather than Austin—would be considerably more central. It fact, it would be decisive.

In the actual course of events, it took a while for all these political relationships, and TIPRO's stance within them, to become clear enough to guide association policy. But after all the turmoil surrounding the Harris bills in Washington and the sophisticated and alarming politics that effectively ended all discussion of gas gathering taxes on pipelines within the Texas legislature, enough was in place by the beginning of the 1960s for TIPRO's treasurer, Vance Foster, to offer a distinctive new appraisal of what independent producer politics was all about. As Foster put it, oil and gas producers needed to "junk 1920 thinking" and face the postwar world as it really was. "Traditionally," he said, "but for no good reasons that I know, producers have shied away from consumer groups and consumer-oriented congressmen. As a result, we are thought of as hidebound conservatives always out to elect the candidates with the most moss on their backs." This did not mean that TIPRO's treasurer was calling on the rank and file to pledge permanent loyalty to the Democratic Party. It did mean, however, that many in TIPRO's leadership were getting a much surer sense of how outgunned independents were within the industry, within the Eisenhower administration, and within the overall American political framework as it routinely functioned.[31]

There were proven perils all around—from the Harold Ickeses of this world who championed centralized control as well as from the advocates of industry unity who likewise had their own version of centralized authority and who, by their very size, represented a powerful form of centralization. Clearly, the task of trying to be independent in a world of both big government and big business was not one that lent itself to easy slogans. Most of the news for producers in the 1950s and 1960s was bad news, but for this very reason it contained instructive guidelines for future conduct. Thus it was that, in the very midst of the darkest postwar days for the Texas independents, they began learning the hard lessons and developing the sophisticated skills necessary to becoming significant actors in their own self-defense.

It had to be immediately conceded, however, that in the dark era itself, these rays of silver lining were often very difficult to detect. By and large, developments in oil and gas throughout the 1950s and 1960s constituted one long litany of ominous happenings. Indeed, TIPRO conducted a study in the late 1950s that showed the alarming extent to which integrated oil companies had expanded pipeline discrimination in the field. Over the twenty-year period between 1935 and 1955, oil reserves had increased 233 percent, producing wells had also increased 233 percent, and overall production had grown 257 percent. But in the period's closing eight years alone (1948–1955), production without pipeline connections had soared 738 percent! Increasingly, small producers were being forced to undergo the additional competitive expense of trucking their oil to markets. TIPRO observed: "Arbitrary refusal to connect new wells and even to buy oil trucked to market creates monopoly conditions which make it impossible for the small producer to live side by side with the big ones." Once again, the motive for this pattern of discriminatory behavior was traceable to the basic structural change that Middle Eastern oil had imposed on relationships within the domestic market between independent producers and major integrated companies. Stating the matter as simply as possible, TIPRO reported that the integrated companies were "using their pipeline subsidiaries to choke off Texas production in favor of more profitable foreign oil." The problem was exacerbated because of structural imperatives: "The discrimination that can be practiced against wells in a field through the operation of gathering systems can be practiced against whole fields or areas through ownership of trunk lines."[32]

As TIPRO waged its rear-guard struggle against imported crude, the gas pipelines continued their long campaign to free their affiliated producing companies from federal regulation. This objective, of course, threw the long-line companies into direct conflict with independents in a manner that occasionally produced some very heated pipeline rhetoric. In 1964, TIPRO president Malcolm Abel testified before the FPC that any decision by the agency to accord pipeline production the same treatment as that of independent producers "would constitute an invitation to monopoly concentration by driving the small businessmen out of the gas producing business through unfair competition." The Midland independent took exception to the testimony by pipeline representatives that because independent producers were fast dropping out of the gas business, it had become necessary for the FPC to take steps to encourage production by pipelines. "When natural gas pipelines engage in the producing end of the business," explained Abel, "they have an enormous natural advantage over independent producers. If they are permitted to abuse this advantage under the guise of 'equal treatment' the result can be catastrophic to the free enterprise structure of the natural gas industry." The TIPRO president's statement, of course, emphasized a simple reality which every independent gas producer in Texas knew in his bones but which, in bygone days, could not be articulated by those in the grip of "industry unity."[33]

The reply of the pipeline companies was offered by George Garver, president of the Independent Natural Gas Association of America. He announced he was "amazed and distressed" by an argument "so biased, illogical and unsupportable," and added that TIPRO's testimony "reflects no desire to reach a mutual understanding of our problems and casts the entire natural gas industry in the worst possible light for all to observe and for our opposition to make the most of." In short, Garver repeated the traditional injunction that independents were violating the elementary precepts of "unity." The pipeline spokesman thus provided no hint he grasped the depth of irritation among independents. In a subsequent address before the 1964 TIPRO convention, Garver offered additional views that left the assembled independents transfixed in disbelief: "I assure you that the pipeline companies are most sympathetic to the regulatory problems of the producers and recognize the frustrating ordeal that you have been subjected to in the matter of price regulation." For producers who had for years been subjected to near-confiscatory life-of-field contracts by the long-line gas transmission companies and who had additionally been ignored on basic issues of ratable take, the "sympathy" of pipelines was, to say the least, a bit difficult to credit. Garver was on somewhat better ground when he added that "nearly everyone, including the regulators themselves, is now convinced that the utility cost of service approach is completely unworkable for regulation of individual producer prices." But he largely vitiated the merit of this observation by going on to say that the producer-sponsored concept of area pricing was nothing more than "wallowing in a morass of untested theories." In natural gas, as in imported crude oil, the warning years provided small producers with a variety of examples of the negative consequences of "industry unity."[34]

It was therefore not surprising that the good news, when it came at all, emanated not from anything that resembled industrywide harmony but rather grew directly from the initiatives of independents. These, too, sometimes had the rear-guard quality of mitigating basic inequities while leaving the core inequity as a subject for future contention. A typical example came in 1962 when TIPRO's research director, Julian Martin, devised a new formula—percentage allowables—to replace the imprecise and cumbersome "allowable days" through which monthly prorationing schedules had been shaped for thirty years by the Railroad Commission. When the commission applied the formula in its November hearing of that year, the new procedure resulted in an immediate increase of

350,000 barrels per day in Texas production at a time when allowables had sunk to a dismal seven-day pattern. It was a temporary reprieve that helped save some embattled independents from extinction. But this creative refinement, helpful as it was in arming the commission with greater flexibility in setting proration rates, nevertheless could not address the basic problem of imported oil, which produced the problem in the first place. In the fullness of time, advantages accruing from the percentage-allowable formula were undermined by ever-increasing oil imports and the shrunken "nominations" they inevitably yielded from major purchasers at commission hearings.[35]

Of longer-term import was another TIPRO initiative—the Mineral Interests Pooling Bill, a product of the continuing evolution of TIPRO's approach to the larger question of compulsory unitization. To the delight of some onlookers and the dismay of others, the controversy over unitization within TIPRO in the founding decade could on occasion lead to a bit of passionate table-pounding. Yet even when routine civility came to characterize TIPRO's intramural dialogues, genuine tension remained because the stakes were often quite high for individual operators. Contributing to the tone of the discussions was the ongoing fact that arguments available to each side could invoke both high principles and raw facts that everyone had to acknowledge as being centrally relevant. Though TIPRO had formally reiterated its opposition to compulsory unitization in 1952 and again in 1956, the issue was not, in fact, settled and everyone knew it. Ever since the success of the East Texas Salt Water Disposal Company had demonstrated in the 1940s how cooperative field practices could dramatically increase recovery rates, unitization ideas carried a good deal of appeal for many producers.

It remained hard to come to grips with the issue, however. In 1960 a TIPRO task force headed by Midland's John Hostetler conducted an exhaustive study "on the whole unitization-pooling-spacing front" and concluded that "progress may have to await clearing up some substantial misunderstandings within the industry itself." Hostetler offered the thought that "a gentle mist of confusion still hovers over not only the economic and political implications but even the very terms most commonly used." Indeed, committee members suggested that some rhetorical descriptions employed by both sides needed henceforth to be avoided—such as assertions that the law of capture is an "archaic jungle law" or a "license to steal" because it operates to guarantee each tract owner "the right to drill as many wells as he pleases without restraint." The task force also suggested that it was unhelpful for people to characterize all pooling proposals as "forced pooling" or to imply that unitization plans are improper because of "compulsion" per se. The task force took a crack at writing a description that emphasized the weakness of both positions: "The application of the allocation rule to wells drilled on small tracts so that the operator is permitted to recover a disproportionately large share of the reserves amounts to confiscation of property just as surely as though that operator had been denied the opportunity to recover any of the reserves." Soon, TIPRO's unitization committee began to have co-chairmen, as in 1961, with Austin's Walter Koch representing the "antis" and San Antonio's J. Ed Kendall speaking for the "pros."[36]

Against this backdrop, the Mineral Interest Pooling Bill was conceived by TIPRO in response to the Normanna and Port Acres cases generated by the town-lot drilling of Stanley Woods in the early 1960s. A product of extended debate in TIPRO committees, a forum that produced the very language of the legislation, the measure protected the rights of small royalty owners who had previously had no defense against having their property drained other than by undergoing the expense of drilling themselves. As such, the Mineral Interests Pooling Bill settled some (though by no means all) of the issues surrounding unitization, leaving more difficult questions for another time. Less tractable was the celebrated Crown case, a notorious example of nonratable taking, one that kept TIPRO members and the association's legal counsel in a protracted court battle for years. Though the ultimate decision brought a measure of redress to the initial producer plaintiff in the case, the language of the decision did little to improve the climate of nonratable take under which independents generally continued to function. Lack of structural progress in this area was partially counterbalanced by the 1963 Kennedy tax bill, which, in the words of one TIPRO spokesman, was "one of the best things that ever happened to producers in terms of strengthening incentives for independents to go and find new reserves."[37]

In these multiple ways it gradually became apparent during the late 1960s and early 1970s that shifting new constituencies had begun to appear in a number of areas of historic contention within the industry— and, indeed, within the ranks of independents. One classic example was the attitude of some major producers toward production in the East Texas field. Historically, the sheer volume of production controlled by independents caused majors to make extraordinary efforts to maximize prorationing controls. But the complex pattern of reservoir depletion in the giant woodbine pool in East Texas, yielding as it did the phenomena of marginal wells in a flowing field, caused a reevaluation of priorities among integrated purchasers. In the fall of 1970, Mobil Oil Corporation, which had a stake in production in the field, went before the Railroad Commission and asked for an increase in the field's overall recovery rate from 268,000 barrels daily to 400,000. The move represented a 180-degree turn in Mobil's approach to East Texas production. It also involved a change in field engineering that, unless monitored with extreme care, would shorten the life of a number of other producing wells in the field, thus disturbing hard-won and long-established equities for these producers. Mobil's intervention did not change the commission's policy, but it did verify that not all "historic" positions in the oil industry were set in concrete.[38]

However, as the decade of the 1970s opened, all such matters were vastly overshadowed by another action that emerged from the very same Railroad Commission session that heard Mobil Oil's unexpected change in policy toward East Texas. In September 1970 the commission raised the state's crude oil allowable ceiling to the highest level in nineteen years. This development pointed to something much more fundamental that had, some three years earlier, begun to transform the general industry climate in which independent producers functioned.

Signal from the Middle East

This "something" was the 1967 Arab-Israeli War. Overnight, global crude shortages traceable to the conflict raised Texas production dramatically. A temporary price bounce also resulted, but the Railroad Commission utilized its time-honored proration formulas to authorize full utilization of the state's reserve production capacity, and the resulting flow of Texas crude soon brought both markets and prices back into stability.

But all was not as it seemed. The ease with which the supply shortage suddenly appeared and then was routinely contained constituted a self-constructed set of blinders that masked from view the exhaustion of domestic reserve production capacity. During the years prior to the 1967 war, the commission, operating under its TIPRO-inspired percentage-allowable formula, prorated Texas production at a 30 percent ratio. The temporary oil crisis generated by the war caused the commission to crank up the ratio to a 67 percent level. It was then quickly noted that the increase in allowables did not translate into a corresponding rise in production for a large number of old wells. As the months passed and more and more mature wells proved incapable of making their allowables, it became apparent to technically trained observers of prorationing that the state's vaunted reserve capacity might be in some sort of aggregate decline. To what extent was unknown. What appeared to be clear was this: independents somehow were no longer serving the historic role they had always played in bringing new production on line through wildcat discoveries. Monthly production totals in the late 1960s indicated that declines in the productivity of mature wells were consistently outrunning new production.

This was the situation in 1970 when former railroad commissioner William J. Murray, in the midst of a three-year term as TIPRO president, first suggested publicly his conclusion that "there is essentially no net spare efficient producing capacity in this entire nation." If true, the fact was at least as alarming to independents as to anyone else in the country. In an article entitled, "Tell It As It Is," Murray went on to say that he had for years felt that estimates of national reserves by both government and industry were "overstated by a considerable magnitude." It was not at the time "particularly alarming" since "the overstated supply was far in excess of what was needed or could be transported." But now, Murray said, things had changed. "Today, the reported spare capacity has been greatly reduced from the figures of the past, but these reported figures are still quite large—and in my judgment excessive by about the same margin."[39]

There was a resonant political subtext to this seemingly technical argument, even when couched in the understated language of a trained engineer. For years, Washington officials administering the import program had a ready answer to Texas producers pleading for relief. As Julian Martin summarized this dialogue, "Washington would say, 'Well, you don't need any help down in Texas, you are only producing one out of three days (or later, two out of three days) and you don't need any incentives for exploration because the country still has all this excess.'" The response of independents was grounded in an inarguable contemporary social fact that carried an implicit future consequence—namely, the absolute decline in numbers of independent producers traceable to the twenty-year cost-price squeeze; since wildcatters were the ones who found new reserves, their numerical decline moved forward the day when the nation's overall reserve capacity would necessarily vanish. The import of Bill Murray's announcement was, simply enough, that the ominous moment had in fact arrived. But in Washington the general analysis by independents and the specific declaration by Murray were both discounted as special pleading. Import officials were saying, in effect, "Prove it to us."[40]

TIPRO talked it over with specialists and administrators at the Railroad Commission, and it was decided to run some proration experiments that would test the system. The first thing tried, in 1971, was to go to 100 percent allowables on new production; and then—if the sky did not fall—to try the whole system. The initial experiment boosted the first month's production some 200,000 barrels a day, a bearable figure since production from old wells continued to decline in the ensuing months. The vaunted two-million-barrel-a-day Texas reserve had proven to be, on this preliminary test, a mere one-tenth that figure. This ominous result seemed to confirm the analysis put forward by Murray, indicating that the long years of Texas shut-in capacity had not only driven uncounted numbers of independents to the wall but also hidden from view a permanent decline in the state's producible reserve.

Armed with this evidence, the Railroad Commission gathered in El Paso for its monthly hearing in March 1972. The decision to go to 100 percent statewide was made. April was to be the test month. "We weren't quite as nervous the second time around as we had been the first time," TIPRO's Martin later recalled, "because we felt that if production hadn't jumped much at 100 percent on the best wells, then why should giving full allowables to older and weaker wells do much? Sure enough, total daily production in April went up only a few thousand barrels." The numbers had genuine historic significance: as a vehicle for balancing the collective needs of the nation and the individual rights of oil producers, market-demand proration had come to an end in America. "It was," said Martin, "a desolate truth to be proved right on this—in that we had to admit in the United States that we were suddenly beholden to foreign sources for oil that we had resisted so hard, so futilely, for so many years."[41]

It was, indeed, a somber moment in the history of wildcatting in America. It was also a turning point that could have been delayed by a number of years. Given the expanding world demand for crude and the finite limitations of reserves on the North American continent, the arrival of diminished productive capacity for the nation was historically inevitable in any case; but it came prematurely because of more than a generation of constraints on exploration that had been the inevitable byproduct of all the forces, within the industry and without, that had diminished incentives and depleted the ranks of the people who had historically found America's new reserves—the independent producers. The warning years had run their course and no one had heard the warning.

The American oil industry had come full circle. The twenty-five years after World War II produced a series of events that had a common theme: the forces of monopoly and centralization proceeded to work their will on petroleum policy in all of the decisive arenas of American democracy. This trajectory, visible through the entire period from 1945 to 1972, helped explain why basic structural problems continued to exist for producers of both crude oil and natural gas—irrespective of whatever else happened that bore on the status of American reserves.

Taking stock, independents who survived the warning years were leaner, more politically astute, and more experienced in the lobby-ridden process that governed established customs of decision-making in both Austin and Washington. As an independent association, TIPRO had withstood all attacks from better-positioned and better-financed forces within the industry and had, in addition, made great strides in rallying independents across the nation to present a united front on organic issues of survival. It was to be presumed that these preparations would stand producers in good stead in the years ahead. But in April 1972, an awesome and unexpected truth had been revealed. The days of shut-in capacity in Texas were gone forever.

For producers, the moment marked an interesting conjunction of professional belief with a certain patriotic faith. Because independents were the ones who found America's new reserves, they had long argued that their own well-being was intimately linked to the nation's self-sufficiency in energy. Though the assertion was transparently self-serving, producers also believed passionately that it was literally true. Now independents had been forced to discover that they were newly vulnerable—and vulnerable in what appeared to be a long-term context. It remained to be seen just how vulnerable this reality left the nation.

One thing was clear—though perhaps it was initially evident only to a handful of proration specialists who happened to be located far from the citadels of decision-making in international petroleum. In the offices of the Texas Railroad Commission in Austin, a certain institutional memory now seemed uneasily relevant: the Arab-Israeli War of 1967 had generated a temporary shortage of oil. It had not been noticed by the millions of American consumers because the commission had promptly opened the spigot on the state's heralded reserve productive capacity and the resultant stream of Texas crude had kept the global market stable. After a mere blip of a price bounce, things quickly returned to normal. Americans felt no sudden and unexpected jolt in their pocketbooks when they pulled into their neighborhood service stations. But as of April 1972, the reserve capacity for the whole of the nation stood revealed as a thing of the past. If anything now happened to global petroleum supplies, there would no longer be an infinite cushion of Texas crude to absorb the shock. The Texas umbrella had snapped shut and the whole of the nation, unaware though it might be, was exposed to whatever storms might come.[42]

As the rhythms of historical fate would have it, neither independents nor the nation had long to wait. In October 1973, a mere eighteen months after 100 percent production in Texas had effectively put a permanent period to the era of market-demand proration, the Middle East erupted in war once again. Within days, a worldwide Arab oil embargo had produced interminable lines of impatient motorists at America's gasoline pumps. This stunning development was made even more shocking when motorists finished their long wait only to discover that the price of a gallon of gasoline had taken an immediate leap—literally an instantaneous leap—from one day to the next.

Patently obvious to everyone, of course, was the fact that the precipitous explosion in prices occurred on crude oil acquired routinely by importing companies, routinely transported to the United States, and then routinely refined—all under pre-embargo conditions and at pre-embargo prices. In the immediate dislocation caused by the war, every gallon of gasoline being sold in the United States had been in the pipeline at conventional price levels before a single bullet had shattered the desert silence. People across the country were left understandably puzzled as to why the price of gasoline had instantly doubled—and in some places doubled again—at service stations across the country. When the major companies' explanations for this transparent price gouging proved something less than convincing to the American people, the enormous public outcry that promptly ensued guaranteed that the U.S. Congress would be involved in "windfall profits" legislation for much of the foreseeable future. Overnight, oil had become a passionate social issue of national proportions.

The warning years were over. America discovered it had an energy crisis.

Chapter Five

TRANSFORMATION

The oil industry turned upside down in October 1973, altering political customs in scores of countries and remodeling national economies around the globe. The unanticipated closure of the flow of Middle Eastern crude endangered industrial production throughout the technologically advanced world, undermining long established transportation priorities and dismaying hundreds of millions of motorists on every continent.

Looking back, it is possible to find a number of the signs foretelling the drastic changes that rocked the global economy in the 1970s. Indeed, some of these signs, blithely ignored as they were, had been put in place by independent Texas producers who for years had issued warnings about the perils of inadequate incentives for finding America's oil reserves. Other portents were faintly visible through public complaints of heretofore obscure oil ministers named Alfonzo and Tariki who labored in so-called Third World countries such as Venezuela and Saudi Arabia. These complaints covered a variety of subjects but had a common thread: the haughty attitude of major company executives made an authentic dialogue with them almost impossible on any of the basic issues affecting oil production and marketing. At one early juncture (later understood as a decisive juncture), a knowledgeable oil journalist named Wanda Jablonski, who took the complaints of Tariki and Alfonzo seriously, admonished the chairman of Standard Oil of New

Jersey, Monroe "Jack" Rathbone, that he had better start paying closer attention to the depth of resentment boiling up in the oil-producing nations. She offered this advice in the early 1960s, at the same time Texas independents were sending up similar signals of distress about major company domination of global petroleum issues. But Jablonski, too, was ignored. The major companies showed themselves fully as capable of condescending to Third World producing nations as they had long proven themselves to be in their response to American independents.[1]

But other omens of things to come did not emerge from matters centrally relevant to petroleum. They turned, rather, on national ambitions of whole nations and the personal styles of men who had come to power in them—nations such as Syria, Israel, Egypt, Vietnam, Iran, and the United States. Still another piece of prognostication touched on a subject that seemed, at the time, to be far removed from issues of international petroleum; it came from an American political scientist who in 1971 finished a book on "presidential character" which predicted that the incumbent occupant of the White House, Richard Nixon, possessed personality traits and a political style that would lead to his self-destruction. The book got a bit of notice when it was published in 1972—before becoming a best-seller after Watergate erupted as a national issue in the very midst of the 1973 global oil crisis.[2]

Yet the catalyst that pumped volatile political life into all these scattered forecasts was not American-made. It was the October war in the Middle East which produced the strikingly successful Arab oil embargo. In a remarkable conjunction of domestic and international crises, the embargo came at the precise moment of the "Saturday-Night Massacre"—Nixon's firing of the special Watergate prosecutor. The immediate impact was $6-per-barrel crude and consumer turmoil at the nation's gasoline pumps; a subsequent effect was the departure of Nixon in disgrace and the resulting 1974 Democratic sweep in Congress.

Overnight, it seemed, what came to be understood as "old-style politics" had been discredited—from influence peddling on behalf of leading corporate sectors down to and including special favors for individual presidential campaign contributors. As incoming freshmen members of Congress announced in no uncertain terms in 1974, reform was coming to Washington. It would come, they promised, in all matters of governance that touched upon fairness. The windfall profits of the major importing companies had cast a pall over the entire industry, generating an intense public interest in overhauling the nation's tax codes—all of which brought into view that lifeblood of the wildcatter, the oil depletion allowance. The spring of 1975 was truly a dramatic juncture for the nation, for its citizens generally and for its independent petroleum producers.

Interestingly, at no other previous moment in its relatively brief history had TIPRO been better prepared to act in a time of real and potential change than it was in the mid-1970s. All of the painful instructions that independents had been forced to undergo through the twenty-five years of TIPRO, preconditioned by the patterns set in the many decades before then, now came into play. In their elected leadership and in the supportive ranks of veteran activists who staffed TIPRO's key committees, organized producers were experientially armed to a degree that they had never before attained.

At the outset of this chronicle of the industry's most turbulent decade, it is useful to take careful note of some of the key individuals who were thrown into the breach to speak and act for the nation's independents. One of the most visible and, as events were to demonstrate, one of the most active was Houston's George Mitchell, who in 1972 succeeded to the presidency of TIPRO. An enormously successful independent, Mitchell had endured more than his share of prolonged struggles with gas pipeline companies and with other integrated players in the world of petroleum. Against very long odds he had succeeded in developing, as far away as the city of Chicago, retail outlets for his prolific natural gas production in Texas; in so doing, he had weathered all the impediments—financial, bureaucratic, and otherwise—that the integrated character of the industry normally imposed on producers who sought their own marketing connections. In a manner that went a good distance beyond the experience of some of his predecessors at the helm of TIPRO (who had also learned the ways of the majors), George Mitchell had gone to school on the ways of Washington as well. He brought great energy to the decade-long campaign in Washington that was to refashion the rules of petroleum exploration and development in the United States.

In a protracted struggle in which persistent and sophisticated advocacy was an absolute precondition if independents were to have a genuine impact on national energy policy, Mitchell's efforts were enhanced by the work of two able independents who headed the key TIPRO task forces in charge of national and state issues. They were Dallas's Frank Pitts, chairman of TIPRO's National Energy Policy Committee, and Houston's Bruce Anderson, chairman of the State Petroleum Issues Committee. Both men not only had spent their productive lives as independent oil and gas finders but had gained intimate familiarity with industry issues through long years of active participation in TIPRO's internal deliberations. As a result of these experiences, they, like Mitchell, had a proven grasp of all the subtle and not-so-subtle areas of contention between independents and the integrated companies.

The input of both Pitts and Anderson proved vital to the steadiness of Mitchell's elaborately orchestrated approach, but to focus on any of the three men unduly would distort the dynamics that produced TIPRO's breakthrough effort in the 1970s. An absolutely central ingredient was the depth of knowledge about petroleum issues that a wide assortment of activists had gained through a generation of work on the TIPRO committees that shaped producer policy. This accumulated experience dated all the way back to the earliest days when Bryan Payne debated Jack Woodward about the prerogatives independents could invoke to chart a course of action distinct from the majors. Among the original TIPRO founders, the veteran who remained most visibly in harness was Bob Foree. But he could draw on an experienced band of activists from TIPRO's first decade: Hamilton Rogers, J. Ed Kendall, Jerry O'Brien, John Hurd, Malcolm Abel, Thornton Huddle, Netum Steed, Jim Russell, A. W. Rutter, and Chester Upham. Each of these independents had become involved in the 1950s and had remained involved ever since. Indeed, so useful were the continuing contributions of Pitts and Anderson, along with those of Russell and Upham, that all four men would be elevated to TIPRO's presidency in the years after Mitchell's adroit tenure. (O'Brien, Hurd, Abel, and Steed had already served in the association's top post.) Within TIPRO, all of these future presidents, some Democrats and some Republicans, stood in the Foree tradition of broad-based producer advocacy.[3]

The new era began on a depressingly familiar note—namely, the spectacle of the nation's president backing off from previously expressed concerns for the independent producer in order to announce policies in harmony with the major companies. Instead of implementing a promised tariff system that would have eliminated the economic advantage of imported crude, President Nixon handed importers a windfall—and TIPRO a bitter disappointment—by dropping the existing import duties altogether. An appearance of sugar-coating appeared with a presidential promise to phase in, ever so slowly, a new fee structure.

In this sober setting, George Mitchell provided independents with a lengthy overview of both the international and domestic issues in oil and gas that would dominate the politics of petroleum in the 1970s. In so doing, he charted during the early months of 1973 a course of action that, in light of subsequent events, can in retrospect be described as almost uncanny in its predictive subtlety.

Mitchell's first strategic concern was that independents formulate a broad understanding of who their potential allies might be. While acknowledging that independents knew a great deal about the conflicting oil-policy advice Washington insiders were receiving from various industry groups, he stressed that most producers "don't fully realize how many contradictory forces are at work from within the government itself." After noting the sustained attention to energy issues by both consumer and environmental groups, he emphasized that "it is literally true that everybody has a stake in the energy policy of this nation." This thought set the stage for one otherwise alarming fact that had come hard on the heels of the Railroad Commission's move to full allowables in Texas—namely, that the state's production had peaked in 1972 and had subsequently begun to decline. Since this downward trajectory would inevitably accelerate if something were not done about exploration incentives for producers, the attack on depletion—insofar as it applied to independents—was organically counterproductive to the national interest.[4]

The only way to dramatize this heretofore unrecognized relationship between incentives, drilling, and reserves was to educate Washington policymakers as to precisely how the new technological advances in petroleum recovery intersected with simple economics in a way that could at least partially address the crisis in domestic reserves. As Mitchell put it, "I have attempted to point out that a nominal cent per gallon crude price increase would have both an immediate and long-range effect upon producibility. We all know about the three-to-five-year lag in getting the big increase from domestic exploration. But too little realized is the fact that a great many existing properties could be rendered capable of increased output in relatively short order—through the remedial work which can take place only if crude prices justify it."[5]

TIPRO Develops a National Strategy

This, of course, was simply a routine analysis of the economics of reservoir recovery. The challenge was to find a way to turn an analysis into public policy. With an eye to the past tendencies of some early TIPRO leaders toward swashbuckling in Washington, Mitchell said, "I don't believe in being more militant than necessary to get this job done." This word of caution did not mean, however, that he was advising a passive course; as a matter of fact, Mitchell made clear he was proposing just the opposite. Without going off half-cocked, Texas independents actually needed to step up their involvement because of late they had become "less militant than those in other states, notably Kansas and Oklahoma." There, said Mitchell, "independents are working actively toward combining area production into something like co-ops in order to bargain more effectively with the purchasing companies."

The outlines of producer approaches, soon confirmed by TIPRO's actions in 1974, were already visible in this sketch that Mitchell offered at the beginning of 1973. The levers of producer strategy turned on three separate fulcrums: close involvement with the Liaison Committee of Cooperating Associations to determine whether all producer groups in the nation were on the same page, a protracted educational campaign with consumer-oriented and environmental-oriented congressional representatives and senators, and, finally, outright avoidance of "industry unity" when it was signaled by major companies as a cover for their own agendas. In the short run, this coordinated approach also applied to the natural gas industry, where dramatic changes in governmental price regulations presaged the probability of a significant measure of decontrol.

The TIPRO president stressed that independents needed to keep their own position clear of contaminating influences. Should decontrol move far along on the agenda of Congress, said Mitchell, "I very much hope it is on the initiative of concerned consumers and the Administration. I'd hate to see 'the industry' try to battle this through Congress again, being accused of seeking windfall profits." In short, if all the old and harsh lessons of gas legislation in the Harris era were fully remembered by producers, bills sponsored by "the industry" would cost independents far more than they could possibly gain. Too many people now understood that gas was seriously underpriced for independents, in Mitchell's words, "to have to carry the load alone."

Here was a course change of genuinely strategic dimensions: TIPRO's president was advising independents to seek allies not in "the industry," but among consumer groups that could be taught the equity requirements necessary for producers to get low-cost household energy. The approach mobilized all the evidence that independents had accumulated throughout more than a generation of postwar politics. Stock clichés about what American "conservatives" or American "liberals" were supposed to believe constituted an extraordinarily uncertain guide as to what individual Republicans and Democrats in Congress understood about energy exploration and development—or about what an independent producer was and was not.

Independents were by no means fishing in untested waters. Producers now possessed some truly striking examples of profound Washington innocence about the most elementary facts of petroleum exploration. It extended deeply into the ranks of liberals and conservatives alike. There was, for example, the celebrated comment attributed to that classic liberal advocate, Senator Paul Douglas of Illinois, who favored "some requirements that companies stop drilling so many dry holes," which he understood as "adding to consumer costs of oil and gas which is found." There were the equally eccentric comments once offered at a Federal Power Commission hearing by another liberal, Senator Warren Magnuson of the state of Washington. Magnuson announced he had "heard" that "oil companies" were "dragging their heels" on exploration and development and, on the strength of that, expressed his willingness to consider "legislation to make companies shape up and look for more supplies." The thought that distinctions might exist among the priorities of different kinds of "oil companies" (such as, for example, large importers and independent producers) required a knowledge of the industry that the good senator clearly did not have.

A conservative equivalent to this kind of political nonsense also had wide currency in Washington. It most commonly took the form of rhetorical flourishes by self-described "staunch conservatives" who prided themselves on their defense of the "free enterprise" system by defending the monopolistic practices of "the oil industry," while ostensibly remaining unaware that their actions were systematically driving independent producers to the wall. Examples of this kind of Washington ingenuousness abounded in the 1970s, perhaps nowhere more starkly than in the congressional decision (achieved by a nice coalition of Republicans and Democrats) to remove all existing tariffs on oil imports, thereby handing an annual windfall of over a quarter of a billion dollars to importers without benefiting consumers a single penny.[6]

For TIPRO, there were two immediate tasks: to specify a clear position for independents not only on imports but on all matters of contention between majors and independents and, as a necessary supporting corollary, to rally the nation's producers in all states in support of this new and more assertive stance. In the summer of 1973, TIPRO sent Bob Foree to Washington to articulate the producer position at a fuels allocation hearing of the Oil Policy Committee. Supporting Foree was an old TIPRO colleague, Tom Medders, now serving as president of the Independent Petroleum Association of America, and Tom Schwinn, president of the Kansas Independent Oil and Gas Association. Foree made the necessary interpretations for the assembled policymakers: "It would be a major step in the direction of monopoly control were the allocation system to be employed in a manner to protect the privileges of major companies to acquire crude in all areas from which they had a history of purchases—at the direct expense of competition from independent refiners in the areas who are dependent upon that crude to operate their refineries at optimum levels." Foree then reminded the committee of the basic economic fact of life for independent producers—namely, that "the price of crude today for the nation as a whole, measured in constant dollars, is some two cents per gallon below the price received by producers in the mid-50s." The tripling of drilling costs in the same period landed wildcatters in the squeeze that yielded radically less drilling and, inevitably, a decline in American reserves. Ending the depletion allowance for wildcatters was less an exercise in reform than it was an example of a nation busily engaged in shooting itself in the foot.[7]

The new course was set. By the fall of the year, TIPRO could speak of working "in almost total harmony" with both IPAA and with the independent producer associations which comprised the Liaison

Committee. Long years of hard labor among regional producer associations—dating back to the late 1950s with Lester Clark's pioneering initiatives in setting up the Liaison Committee of Cooperating Associations—had begun to pay off.

Given the profound alterations in petroleum marketing engendered by the 1973 war in the Middle East, this TIPRO achievement was timely indeed. As the world learned that the OPEC producing nations, rather than the Seven Sisters, had moved into the defining role on international oil prices, consuming nations scrambled to adjust as crude prices went to $6 per barrel and then to $9. In Pennsylvania, wellhead prices soared past $12 per barrel in 1975. The years of transformation had begun.

But even before the long-term effects of this sea change could begin to be felt, evidence quickly accumulated that old habits of the major companies were dying hard. TIPRO almost immediately found it necessary to clarify the intricate maze of "posted" and unposted prices through which the major importers computed their profits and their tax obligations to the U.S. Treasury. In the interests of what might be called elementary education, TIPRO reminded everyone that IRS tax rulings dating back to the 1940s permitted importers to use royalties paid to the Arabs as "dollar-for-dollar offsets" against their U.S. tax obligations. When the principal petroleum-producing companies in the Persian Gulf raised the per-barrel basis for royalties and taxes from $3.00 to $7.00 per barrel, the "posted" price (an artificial figure used as a basis for computing royalties and taxes) increased to $11.65 from the $3.01 level prevailing at the outbreak of the Arab-Israeli War. By this mathematical device, TIPRO said, "the international oil companies are getting multi-billion-dollar tax breaks as a result of the unexpected sharp increases in the price of foreign oil."[8]

This was no mere rear-guard action to remind consumers and producers alike of battles lost to integrated companies in the distant past. The real meaning of these figures lay in their bearing on the outdated preoccupations still at work in the minds of Washington officials who once again were debating new ground rules for a transformed industry. The past was centrally relevant given the fact that consumer-oriented congressmen, when confronted with the enormous crude price hikes achieved by OPEC, automatically turned first and foremost to the oil depletion allowance as the target through which to express their indignation. Unless some rapid education took place, this blunderbuss attack on what they took to be the major companies would doom the independent producer.

As the new post-Watergate Congress convened early in 1975, what was imprecisely described as "the Washington lobby" became the center of public criticism; and the most loudly broadcast reform was, in the words of one New England congressman, "the once and forever end to the oil depletion windfall." This soon became what old Washington hands called "inside-the-Beltway wisdom." Its reach was so inclusive that even Texas congressmen who had long stood with independent producers had come to believe that any preventative action on depletion had suddenly become a totally lost cause.

One such representative was Charles Wilson, the East Texas Democrat from Lufkin. His account of what happened next provides an instructive picture of the role TIPRO began to play in the 1970s. "I got into it almost by accident," recalled Wilson. "A couple of guys from Houston, who were independent operators, came to a little fund raiser we had down there. I told them the depletion situation was hopeless, but they said, 'We want to go to work; we want to try to do some research; we have got to save the depletion for the independents.' And I said, 'Well, fellows, I'm sympathetic. I'll hope along with you and do a reasonable amount of work, but I still think it's a hopeless situation, and I don't think it is anything I want to waste a year and a half on.' Well, they talked me into thinking maybe we had a chance and they agreed we had to delineate seriously between the majors and the independents. About the same time this was going on, Senator Lloyd Bentsen reached the same conclusion."[9]

The "couple of guys from Houston" who rallied Wilson to the cause were George Mitchell and John Watson, one current and one future president of TIPRO. Meanwhile, Lloyd Bentsen reached "the same conclusion" after consulting with TIPRO's Julian Martin and other interested parties who pledged to perform the necessary background research and come to Washington to assist in crafting appropriate legislation. Bentsen's chief aide, Gary Bushell, reorganized his priorities and did the intensive research necessary to become current on matters relevant to oil-industry economics and the function of the depletion allowance for independents. Indeed, Bushell became a genuine authority.

Throughout the subsequent tax struggle, the role of Wilson in the

House and, most tellingly, Bentsen in the Senate underscored the centrality of the autonomous course of action charted by TIPRO and followed by the nation's other producer associations. Indeed, the intimate cooperation between the staffs of TIPRO and Senator Bentsen, personalized in the work of TIPRO's research director with the senator's chief administrative aide, marked out a new plateau of political involvement for independents that surpassed anything they had previously achieved.

But it was a long and tortuous struggle, one that proved once and for all the centrality of a hands-on approach to politics. Throughout the long months of committee hearings, floor votes, and final conference committee compromises, the long arm of the major companies was everywhere to be seen. When it was all over and the depletion allowance was gone for the majors but intact for independents, a somewhat dazed major-company spokesman experienced great difficulty coming to terms with what had happened in front of his eyes. Indeed, his postmortem on the struggle—fixing blame on the renegade actions of "certain large integrated petroleum companies"—reflected the age-old industry assumption that anything bearing on petroleum legislation happened the way it did because major companies caused it to happen that way.[10]

It is appropriate to return in due course to this aspect of the legislative wars of the 1970s, but it is first necessary to track the struggle in the sequential order in which it actually occurred. The starting point, of course, was a wry insider joke within the oil industry that independents knew all too well. The historic justification for the depletion allowance rested on the stark but elementary fact that eight out of every nine wildcats resulted in a dry hole. A drilling depth was a drilling depth—it cost just as much to get there and hit a dry hole as it did to get there and find oil. The ominous mathematics of this equation doomed the very idea of wildcatting by small operators unless some special incentive was created that could keep them afloat through a life of 90 percent failure. Yet small producers were relevant in America because—as major companies knew better than anyone else in the nation—small producers were the ones who did the wildcatting. When independents weren't drilling, U.S. reserves began to decline.

The reasons behind this ongoing reality in oil exploration were beyond the ken of most outside observers—including congressmen. Simply stated, these reasons had to do with raw economic power. To the untrained observer, the visible bonanza in oil discoveries seemed symbolized by the wondrous gusher that turned a Dad Joiner or a Captain Lucas from an impoverished gambler into a man of riches. But as any petroleum engineer could document, the real payoff was not in discovery wells per se, but in field development, a circumstance that turned on who owned the hundreds, thousands, and sometimes hundreds of thousands of acres of leases that surrounded the initial discovery. Once the contours of a field were established, no wells were wildcats—they were all producers.

As an essential dynamic of comparative resources, major companies put their speculative funds in leases and in sophisticated subsurface testing projects, not in wildcats. In any likely oil play, the majors held most of the aggregate lease acreage. As a routine procedure in the oil patch, the majors kept their leases until wildcats either "proved them up" or "turned them to dust." Even when a promising discovery further blossomed into a modest oil play, the majors might engage in additional lease acquisition, but they often continued to stand aside on exploratory drilling. The resulting process of testing the play occurred either through independently financed wildcats or through "farmouts," in which majors let a small operator drill on major company-owned leases in exchange for some acreage concessions, drilling cost participation, or some combination of these incentives. In whatever manner they negotiated the terms of farmouts, major companies normally eschewed rank wildcats, preferring to let independents take all the risks. In general, the majors turned themselves to drilling only when field contours had become defined. They wanted their depletion allowance on proven wells, not on risky wildcats.

It took an enormous amount of capital for majors to operate this way; it also required patience—precisely the kind of patience that large capital could effectively underwrite. Majors employed oil scouts to follow the play of independents as well as lease hounds to follow up on tips from their scouts. Indeed, most major company landmen wore both hats. When something showed early promise, majors demonstrated time and again their capacity to move with great speed to acquire leases before prices went up. As many a Texas farmer and rancher learned to his chagrin, majors could buy up whole counties before the public became aware of the dimensions of the oil play that was in the works. All it took was enough money and enough landmen.

The wildcatter became a permanent social type in America because the major companies made early errors of great magnitude in the nation's richest oil-producing region: Texas. The majors were uninterested in the Texas Gulf Coast prior to Spindletop, and they had given up on East Texas prior to Dad Joiner's Daisy Bradford No. 3. The integrated companies thus had to buy into these plays, paying large sums for proven acreage—a circumstance that provided thousands of small producers with a stake in oil country. TIPRO's very existence was historically traceable to this fact.

Independents proved how much they had learned about the art of oil finding—at Burkburnett and Ranger, in the Yates field and the Canyon Reef, along the Spraberry Trend and in the Austin Chalk, and across scores of counties in the Panhandle, in the Big Bend, and throughout the Permian Basin. Indeed, as the membership roles of TIPRO eloquently testified, not a region of the state failed to generate, at greater or lesser depths, oil and gas deposits of significant commercial value. And virtually every new field added new squads and platoons of small producers—and new members for TIPRO.

In the boardrooms of the integrated companies, Texas independents came to be regarded as a constant source of irritation. Producers wanted their oil taken at the same rate as oil owned by the majors and, for that matter, their natural gas, too. They accused the majors of selective development when pipelines connected to their own wellheads but not to those of independents. Small producers even developed the irritating capability of mobilizing technical data on reservoir pressure to bring the conservation practices of the Railroad Commission down on their side in hearings on ratable take. (The very term "ratable take," popularized by TIPRO, was simply another irritant.) Above all, independents could substantiate their carpings about monopolistic practices with elaborate data from ongoing activities in existing fields in a manner that put their criticisms in a maddeningly explicit category and distinguished them from more general ideological critiques periodically offered by industry outsiders. From a major company's standpoint, the most distasteful irritant of all was that the informed critiques of independents kept the whole issue of monopoly in public view where, they repeatedly reminded producers, it could not possibly do "the industry" any good.

Who Drills the Wildcats?

Balancing all this, for the major companies, was the unmistakable fact that independents, by merely existing, had definite uses. The social capital of independents—the quintessential small American entrepreneur—could be pushed into the public limelight whenever the major companies had agendas of their own to lay before Congress. The multiple Harris bills of the 1950s, conceptualized by gas pipelines but orchestrated as "freeing independent producers from federal regulation," were classic cases in point. Not that classic cases were needed; the whole public relations history of the major companies illustrated the same reality, in large and small ways. But however useful independents could be in serving as convenient shields behind which to advance other and more complex designs, the industry's integrated giants found the greatest utility of producers to lay not only in one very central area of politics—taxation—but in an absolutely central area of petroleum-industry taxation. That annoted area was, of course, the oil depletion allowance.

All of this set the stage for the politics of 1974–1975. Only one additional fact needs to be put in place to help make comprehensible the legislative netherworld of "tax reform" during the mid-1970s. Veteran Washington lobbyists had long since discovered that it was ineffective (because unseemly) to function solely through palpably direct influence on members of Congress. Granted that these elected representatives had the votes and therefore had to be kept fully "informed," it proved a far more persuasive tactic to have basic information bearing on legislation conveyed to wavering congressmen and senators not by paid lobbyists but by government officials with nominal expertise in the issues being debated. To this end, analysis on the depletion allowance was not always conveyed to the House and Senate through registered lobbyists but also through officials of the U.S. Department of the Treasury. Perhaps needless to add, the minions at the Treasury had received an earlier briefing on the relevant facts from the majors' specialists in production, marketing, and taxation.

Against this background, the case for depletion for independents was both brief and straightforward: depletion deductions were incentives for hazardous oil-finding; independents were America's hazardous oil-finders; case closed.

The dialogue between the Treasury and Congress was not so simple, of course, as Charles Wilson's pithy postmortem revealed. Treasury officials explained to congressmen like Wilson that independents "did not really drill the wells." TIPRO's figures pointed in the opposite direction: of 2,125 wells drilled in the United States in 1974 in the range of 5,500 feet, the majors drilled 359 and the independents drilled 1,766. As Wilson recalled the dialogue, "The Treasury then said, 'Okay, but the majors are the only ones to drill any deep ones.'" Again, drilling data presented another picture. In the 17,000- to 25,000-foot range, the majors drilled 23 wells and independents 25. Treasury then said, "Okay, the independents drill some wells, but they don't find any oil; only the majors find the oil." The well-armed Wilson had some relevant figures of his own, the most striking from Louisiana, where, in the 10,000- to 12,000-foot range, 112 wells had been drilled in 1974—97 by independents and 15 by majors. Of these, independents had 10 successful wells for every one for the majors. Indeed, of the 50 successful wells drilled at all depths in Louisiana in 1974, the breakdown was 48 for the independents versus 2 for the majors. The relevant general fact was quite straightforward: independents drilled 85 percent of the exploratory wells in the United States.[11]

This kind of thrust and parry between TIPRO numbers and Treasury tax ambitions was a staple of congressional hearings and after-hours caucuses in Washington. Partly because of the sheer numbers of congressmen involved, sufficient education on the differences between major companies and independents had not been completed by the time the issue came up for its first floor vote in the House. Though the first test vote was by no means lopsided, the result was characterized by George Mitchell as a "clean wipeout" of depletion for independents as well as for major companies. The scene then shifted to the Senate, where the fate of the independent producers was in the hands of Lloyd Bentsen.

It can safely be said that no elected officeholder in Washington had a more thorough grasp of the three core political ingredients that were now at play—the politics of the major companies, the structural needs of independent producers, and the specific climate existing in Washington in 1975 concerning the international oil situation. Bentsen was in total agreement with TIPRO's position that it would be foolhardy to risk losing depletion entirely through a hopeless battle to save it for the majors. Indeed, the Texas senator had told TIPRO leaders the preceding summer that independents could save themselves only by making a strong, clean case in their own behalf, one devoid of any gestures toward industry unity. Such, of course, was a case of carrying coal to Newcastle: experientially, Texas independents understood this strategic reality at least as well as the good senator. But beyond such strategic considerations, Bentsen brought to the struggle a deep personal knowledge of the world of the independent producer. He intended to bring the realities of wildcatting to the attention of the Senate with a degree of factual specificity that the nation's senators had never before heard.

Toward this end, Bentsen's top aide, Gary Bushell, had made himself an expert on energy legislation. He was aided in this endeavor by TIPRO's research director, Julian Martin, who simply packed up his bags and took up residence in Washington for the duration of the long struggle. But it would be a mistake to see the process through which Bentsen armed himself as simply a product of tenacious staff work overseen by the Bushell-Martin team. Bentsen threw himself into every aspect of what became a three-tiered campaign—research in his Senate offices, endless one-on-one discussions with his colleagues, and legislative performance on the Senate floor.

As Martin himself later recalled, "I think there are times in the lives of some specially gifted legislators when they sense that the balance of forces is such that their own individual effort can make a decisive difference on a major issue affecting the whole nation. The pressure is intense at such times because they know there literally is no margin for error. They know they cannot afford to make a mistake." For Lloyd Bentsen, Martin said, "this was such a time." For Martin, the memories are vivid because the stakes were so high. "I remember one night down in the bowels of the old Senate Russell Office Building. We had had a very frustrating day and it looked like we were going to lose something. And there was absolutely no one in there except the two of us, neither knowing the other was there—until I rounded a corner and saw him under a light way down at the end of the hallway, with his arms spread askew, looking up almost as if he were praying. He stayed that way for some time. I could not bring myself to so much as clear my throat because I felt it would have been such an improper intrusion. I just tiptoed back through the rear entrance of the building and went on to my hotel room. But the very next day, Bentsen delivered on the Senate floor the most comprehensive depletion case ever presented before

Congress. It was absolutely magisterial. But it was a very difficult struggle for long weeks after that. In the end we were all elated, but we were
also all exhausted."[12]

There is a sardonic Washington saying, originally attributed to
humorist Will Rogers, that "No one should be forced to watch two
things in life: sausage being made or legislation being enacted." The key
provision of the legislation ending the oil depletion allowance was an
exemption for independents who produced 3,000 barrels a day or less, or
its equivalent in gas, 18 million cubic feet. For the small producers, this
amendment was the heart of the matter. On the Senate's first test vote,
Bentsen's amendment prevailed, 47 to 41, only to be subsequently
reversed, 44 to 50, under great lobbying pressure. After more maneuvering, another amendment, offered by Oklahoma's Dewey Bartlett,
provided a 2,000-barrel daily exemption on a complex "plowback" basis.
Though royalty owners had been excluded from this plowback requirement in Bentsen's version, such, unaccountably, had not been the case
in Bartlett's. TIPRO's Martin noticed this oversight and set in motion
the last-minute move to rectify it. As it happened, the eventual conference committee of the House and Senate knocked out the plowback
requirement while preserving the exemption for independent producers
and for royalty owners.[13]

The New Understanding of Industry Politics

For the first time in the twentieth century, the U.S. Congress, on a
basic structural issue affecting the American petroleum industry, had
made a historically coherent distinction between the integrated companies and independent producers. The 22 percent depletion formula that
dated from the 1969 Tax Reform Act remained intact for the small producer; it was gone for the major companies. The result was an inflow of
literally billions of dollars to the U.S. Treasury and—a rarity in oil and
gas production—a modicum of comparative advantage for independents
over the majors.

But an even more profound achievement, embedded in the language
of the new legislation, was that for the very first time in American history a definition for an "independent producer" was established in the
basic U.S. tax code. This specific goal of independents had historically

been denied them because, in real political terms, the integrated companies did not wish legal distinctions to exist between themselves and independent producers. The achievement of an explicit legal definition of independents became a milestone—one from which independents have reaped tangible benefits in a variety of ways down to the present.

TIPRO's Martin subsequently emphasized this historical perspective: "We have since had a whole series of exemptions that dealt with the independent producer as defined back there in 1975. There were no less than twelve—and some people say more—major pieces of legislation in which that key definition of independent producer has been employed since it was developed. It has saved the independent producer arm of the industry hundreds of millions of dollars over the past 18 years. It is interesting that no one has written about that. As a result, I'm not sure it is fully appreciated."[14]

At the time, George Mitchell, for one, was anxious for independents to focus on the politics that producers needed to employ to achieve a separate identity for themselves in the world of petroleum. "In the depletion fight, we went a long way to communicate the viewpoint that our industry is not one giant monolith intent on gouging the public. For the first time ever, the man on the street seems aware that there are some 10,000 independent producers as well as some 35 big oil corporations."

But TIPRO was just as concerned that appropriate credit be given to the many producer groups who had risked the wrath of the major companies—explicitly the "masterful leadership" of IPAA's John Miller, who was "solidly backed" by all the nation's independent associations represented by the Liaison Committee. It was by no means a one-night stand. "During the past two years, at the call and under the guidance of IPAA's president and staff, independents time and again rallied to lay strategy and then do their best to communicate facts to all in Congress and the Administration who would listen. At times the effort seemed hopeless. But the amazing thing to many was the willingness of congressmen from non-oil states to meet with authentic independents and frankly discuss the issues. Some of us approached this kind of 'lobbying' effort with serious misgivings, fearing our motives would be misunderstood. To the credit of the congressmen, including some of the industry's most severe critics, this did not happen."

TIPRO's Earl Turner stressed the underlying politics: "Certain members of Congress who had long been identified with the challenge to oil depletion flatly switched sides and voted to preserve some portion of it for the independent producer and royalty owner. It was the willingness of the independent to stand up and be counted apart from the major companies which did more than anything else to gain understanding and sympathy for his role."[15]

The majors, of course, had a different view. One spokesman described Bentsen's amendment for independents as a "carveout" that was "discriminatory and unjust." It happened, he said, because "certain large integrated petroleum companies indicated to Congress that depletion is no longer vital to their interests." These comments infuriated independents, who mobilized a blizzard of evidence that major companies, in the words of the *Oil and Gas Journal*, "weren't lifting a finger to save the deduction for independents."[16]

If anything, this put the case too softly. The initial governing position of the majors' lobbyists centered on the argument that "if the majors lose depletion, independents will too, so producers had better get on the team." It was this rather naked form of intimidation that lay behind all the Treasury briefings to the effect that the majors find the oil and, thus, by implication, no special case could be made for independents above and beyond the general case for the industry as a whole.

Nor did the behind-the-scenes maneuvering stop there. TIPRO had carefully preserved evidence of several key junctures where vote switches away from the independent position were made by congressmen who were not consumer champions but rather, as detailed in the *TIPRO Reporter*, were "known to be more favorably disposed to the interests of the major companies than to independents." The intricate tax struggle of 1975 was one congressional maze whose twists and turns independents had followed with carefully assembled knowledge of all the relevant players.[17]

It was, of course, by no means unusual for players, including major company executives, to conduct postmortems according to their own preconceptions. But the simple political reality in Washington in 1975 was that the reach of the independents had been far longer and wider than in the past. It extended to both Democrats and Republicans and deep into the ranks of liberals as well as conservatives. Indeed, a number of the "clean-sweepers" in the freshmen congressional class of 1974 had learned, in informal seminars conducted by Frank and Shelby Pitts, of the critical distinctions between integrated majors on the one hand and independent producers on the other and had, as a result, come down on the side of the independents. The value of not writing off anyone, even so-called implacable opponents, was verified in the depletion fight. But it involved an immense amount of education on the practical differences between independents and majors and the ways in which those distinctions affected American petroleum reserves. Frank and Shelby Pitts were not alone in the task of educating congressmen on the necessary distinctions within the oil industry. Among the many other key players was Max Thomas, a quietly effective independent from Dallas. His work drew special praise from Gary Bushell of Lloyd Bentsen's staff: "Max Thomas had an amazing capacity to get the job done without leaving his office in Dallas—just by utilizing two phone lines. He worked constantly with us on the definition of the independent producer, garnering support both in Texas and in other southwestern producing states. Max Thomas was extremely well informed." To major company executives accustomed to old habits of political thought, the depletion fight of 1975 was a puzzle that was not easily comprehended. What the majors did not know were the details of the enormous effort mounted by TIPRO.[18]

Within the complexities of American politics, the idea of genuine communities of interest between producers and consumers was by no means an organic contradiction. Indeed, if some vertically integrated company stood between the producer and the consumer, the likelihood that both were being routinely victimized was the kind of verifiable fact that was literally strewn through the margins of the nation's history books. On those occasions (not too frequent in American history) when all concerned took it upon themselves to get properly educated on the precise issues at stake, it was not at all remarkable that producers and consumers could frequently find common areas of accord. The 1975 oil fight on depletion for producers proved it. The votes in Congress on behalf of independents came literally from every quadrant of the political spectrum. Indeed, given the oft-demonstrated power of the integrated companies, victory for independents could not have happened otherwise.

But such a broad-based coalition would be a difficult political feat to reproduce because the near-cataclysmic repercussions of the Arab oil embargo changed all the customs surrounding the way energy issues were debated—in the United States and everywhere else. The sharp escalation of crude oil prices affected both the marketability and the availability of all competing fuels, producing a seeming unending array of unexpected consequences. One of the first to emerge in the United States was an instant rise in coal prices and a general inflationary pressure on the costs of every conceivable chemical compound capable of serving as an energy source.

The Natural Gas "Shortage"

Another consequence was the abrupt surfacing of a natural gas "shortage." This discovery was traceable to three suddenly admirable qualities the substance was seen to possess—first, its availability from domestic sources rather than the Persian Gulf; second, its status as an environmentally "clean" fuel; and, finally, its attractive price. These circumstances, of course, created a radically different domestic political climate than the one governing the confused debate over the Harris bills in the 1950s. However, the mere existence of a different climate in no way suggested that any new experiment in national legislation on natural gas would somehow avoid the mind-bending complexity that attended the tortured legislation of the Eisenhower era.

As a degree of normalcy returned, on new terms, to the Middle East, it gradually became clear in America that two profoundly different options had emerged as potential policies governing that newly emergent fossil fuel—natural gas. The nation could either make a conscious decision, through legislation decontrolling gas, to let market forces control entirely, or it could go the opposite route by introducing broad new forms of control over prices. The latter approach, of course, would necessarily have to be augmented by a system that created priorities as to which types of consumers—industrial, agricultural, or residential—would be permitted to gain access to the fuel and at what price levels. But if this range of possible scenarios sounded elaborately complex, it soon became clear in the mid-1970s that other, deeply fundamental questions would also have to be provided with some kind of nationwide answer before anything approaching rationality could be embedded in a national energy policy.

For the average American consumer, the single most powerful

cultural intuition about "energy" was grounded in a daily anxiety that everyone experienced during the Arab oil embargo—namely, the long lines of automobiles at the nation's retail gasoline pumps. This sobering experience translated into a new folk wisdom: the belief that America had run out of oil and gas.

The reality that independents knew—along with certain experienced petroleum geologists, engineers, and geophysicists across the nation—was much different. While domestic reserve production capacity in oil was limited, an outcome confirmed after a century of conscious oil exploration, no such body of experience had been accumulated in natural gas. Rather, the producing gas fields in existence had been essentially uncovered as a tangential byproduct of independents drilling for oil! Indeed, in all the years before World War II, the discovery of gas rather than oil constituted for many wildcatters the functional equivalent of a dry hole.

Within the ranks of TIPRO, a truism had long since prevailed: so scarce were markets for natural gas that the sparse existing networks of field pipelines had created a classic buyer's market; pipeline companies were willing to take a wildcatter's gas only at near-confiscatory prices and then only on long-term life-of-field contracts. If a field had modest reserves or was remote from existing facilities, its gas could not be sold at any price. Thus, when both oil and gas were mixed in a well, the custom developed for independents to produce the oil and "market" the gas by flaring it into the southwestern sky.

This economic fact of life generated among independents a highly differentiated way of talking about gas and oil: "We drilled to 6,000 feet," wildcatters would report to one another, "and it was bone dry. Every stratum. Lots of gas at two or three depths, but not a smell of oil in any of them. Not a whiff." Such areas were, therefore, hopeless. Independents would follow the in-group practice of lessening everyone else's pain by confiding, "No promising shows over there. I'm letting my leases lapse. Nothing but gas."

"There" could mean a field, or a county, or even a whole subsurface stratum running under several counties. For independents schooled in finding oil and further educated by rampant gas pipeline discrimination, natural gas was a negative term of description. Production payments on a gas well could be so small that a decision to undergo the expense of laying pipe to complete a well could tie up capital that might take decades to recover. Experience was the guide: small producers husbanded their capital to finance oil wildcats. In characterizing exploratory acreage that had "turned to dust," oilmen could discredit an area by referring to it as "infested" with gas. In the prewar days, natural gas was like a virus. A prudent independent simply avoided "infestation."[19]

This bizarre state of affairs began to change after the government's wartime Big Inch pipeline was sold to long-line transmission companies that thereupon began to develop markets in the eastern United States in the 1950s and 1960s. While producers hamstrung with life-of-field contracts remained imprisoned at the three- to seven-cent level, pipeline prices for new gas discoveries slowly began to rise to fifteen and then to twenty cents per thousand cubic feet. A modicum of incentive for gas exploration thus began to come to the oil patch—enough to keep some TIPRO meetings in the 1950s intermittently focused on ratable take, price equity, and other matters of contention embroiling independents with the emerging giants of the postwar gas pipeline industry.

Anticipating even richer new retail markets in the future, integrated companies initiated the wild Washington controversies over natural gas decontrol that, as we have seen, brazenly attempted—through cultural campaigns for "industry unity"—to co-opt independent producers into support of the succession of Harris bills that entangled the U.S. Congress in the 1950s. Thus, despite efforts, sometimes energetic efforts, by the IPAA, so relatively inexperienced was the nation's independent sector in that era that producers were fortunate to emerge from those controversies with adequate prerequisites for future struggles.

In any event, the gas industry's basic strategy of "price levels follow markets" inexorably continued to work its will as industrial, agricultural, and retail use of natural gas grew exponentially in the 1960s. As their markets grew, especially retail markets in America's proliferating suburbs, the long-line transmission companies actively began to seek more production contracts. Within the confines of federal price regulations, they also proved willing, in competition with one another, to pay more for them. By the end of the 1960s, the standard wellhead price for new interstate gas connections stood in the vicinity of twenty-five cents per thousand cubic feet.

All of which introduced new complexities into the internal life of organized independents. TIPRO's Gas Issues Committee began to attract more and more engaged participants, producers willing to put long hours into collective self-education and experiments in autonomous planning aimed at shaping an independent policy within the growing field of natural gas development. True, many a devoted TIPRO veteran still regarded gas as an "infestation" and stuck with almost religious zeal to the oil-finding art that had historically paid the family bills. Such producers took their accumulated experience and maturing political style where it was needed—to TIPRO's struggle with the majors over imported crude and its seemingly controlling impact on the cost-price squeeze that was strangling independents. (Despite inexorable inflation across the whole of the U.S. economy, the historic postwar price of crude remained securely within the $2.65 to $3.00 range, verified by the fact that at the outbreak of the 1973 war, Arabian light crude stood at $3.01 per barrel.) The agony over prices was not entirely futile; as we have seen, prolonged Washington contentions taught independents the essential political lessons that were successfully employed in the mid-1970s to prevail in the depletion fight.[20]

But in natural gas, the struggle entered a wholly new stage in the 1970s. The initial sticking point that independents encountered was the nearly universal popular wisdom—fully shared as inside-the-Beltway wisdom in Washington—that new incentives for natural gas exploration were unneeded because the country had "run out of oil and gas." This notion translated into a simple question: why should Congress provide production incentives when the bulk of domestic subsurface mineral deposits had already been found and any price incentive would merely raise consumer costs? For independents, the problem had a stark simplicity because the error was in the premise: it simply wasn't true.

Perhaps the most graphic way to spell out the intervention of Texas independents into the national politics of natural gas in the 1970s lies in tracking the actions of TIPRO's most tenaciously persistent activist on the issue, Frank Pitts. His story is highly germane because his engaged focus on the issue predated that of virtually everyone else, and the knowledge he gained armed him to become a central actor in the formulation of TIPRO's overall natural gas policy.

Long before the issue of a natural gas shortage surfaced in the public mind, Pitts had begun to conduct his own exploration business on precisely the opposite supposition—namely, that natural gas was the household and industrial fuel of the future. It was environmentally clean, a great deal of it was there to be found, and the time of serious efforts in that direction would not appear until incentives were dramatically transformed. Since no one seemed to understand this, Pitts reasoned that demonstrations were in order.

"Around 1969," Pitts later recalled, "I thought I saw a niche where an independent could make some headway. The public had certainly indicated they loved natural gas. But because of the low price at the wellhead, new reserves were not being found commensurate with increased consumption. So I became absolutely convinced that if I went out and caused a lot of wells to be drilled, found a lot of natural gas and then withheld my gas from market until I had a substantial package with a lot of additional acreage that could be drilled, that I could force the price up. How much I didn't have any idea." Natural gas, clean and cheap, had by now become the preferred household fuel in Texas; once the availability of the fuel was assured in the state, the kitchen gas range and gas-powered air conditioning became a fixture in new suburban homes. Pitts's strategy was to use the uncontrolled intrastate market in Texas to demonstrate that the controlled federal price was the one reason why production for the national market was being held back. If he couldn't win the argument on intellectual grounds, he would prove it in actual practice. To get what he called "the wherewithal" for this project, Pitts and his brother Shelby (also a future TIPRO president) sold their geophysical company and set up shop in Denton and Wise counties where they had previously successfully explored for gas in 1966. "I had two wildcats on the line between Denton and Wise but they were about seven or eight miles apart and far enough away from a pipeline and low enough producers that I couldn't get a pipeline connection. So my brother and I went out and bought thousands of acres of leases and started drilling. The first well was in December of 1971. The way we proceeded was drill, drill, drill. We had a number of rigs running and by January of 1973 I started negotiating. The first thing you know I had twelve prospective [intrastate] buyers; yet very few of them had pipelines in North Texas, so the maximum going price in this area was still the controlled interstate gas price of 25 cents. I negotiated until May 4th and then entered a contract with an intrastate pipeline for 82½ cents per thousand cubic feet."[21]

Needless to say, word of this transaction whipped around the Texas oil patch. The Pitts brothers had also taken leases on 15,000 acres in Palo Pinto and Parker counties where other independents had sixteen wells not under contract. "These other operators said to me 'We ought to negotiate a contract down there.' So about four weeks later I negotiated a contract there for 78½ cents per thousand—that gas was not as rich as the gas in Wise and Denton. To preserve capital, I was buying leases for a dollar an acre and another four dollars if I didn't drill a well on it in a year. By now everybody and his brother was coming in to me, ready to buy our leases and saying, 'What about we drill five wells, or we'll drill ten wells if you give us a deal on acreage.'" The Pitts brothers made a wide variety of deals. "We were drilling high, wide and handsome."

By this means, Frank Pitts attempted to prove—on the ground in Texas—that exploration to increase gas reserves would happen the minute drilling made economic sense. In the meantime, no independent was going to risk wildcatting for an interstate market, controlled at twenty-five cents per thousand cubic feet, when the intrastate Texas market commanded eighty-two cents. It was simply a national illusion to believe that incentives to level the playing field were unnecessary because "there was no gas to be found anyway."

But in the aftermath of the oil embargo, it was an illusion that had deep resonance both in the highest levels of the Gerald Ford administration and in the American population generally. The United States was understood to have an energy shortage and, therefore, in need of an allocation system so that everybody got at least something. This understanding governed the writing of the Natural Gas Emergency Act of 1975, which was specifically fashioned to deal with the shortage by creating nationwide price ceilings and instituting elaborate supply allocations both by regions and by types of users.

As chairman of TIPRO's National Energy Policy Committee, Frank Pitts decided to test the waters. He went before the House Interstate and Foreign Commerce Committee with an entirely new view as to how a nation newly rattled on energy could go about the business of maximizing low-cost natural gas in an era of soaring crude prices. The pending legislation, he said, proceeded from an assumption that was precisely backwards: it proposed that the United States attempt to deal with the shortage problem by sharing the shortage. "You will not find a single cubic foot of natural gas unless you drill more wells," he said, but "nowhere in the bill is there any suggestion that new natural gas prices should be deregulated permanently to provide an incentive so that new wells could be drilled to find new sources of supply."[22]

The basic intellectual roadblock that Texas independents encountered in Congress was anchored in the very common misunderstanding that the selling price of a raw material was a centrally decisive factor in its ultimate cost to the consumer. The entire history of agriculture in America flatly contradicted this assumption, as all farmers of the nineteenth and twentieth centuries could document out of their own experiences. Indeed, the cost of a cereal box on a supermarket shelf was more than wheat farmers were paid for the grain in the box. This modern economic reality applied to virtually all producers of basic commodities, be it corn, wheat, cotton, oil, or gas. It was the old truth TIPRO had attempted to popularize in the 1950s through the story of Mrs. Willie Lee Hill of Panola County, who sold her wellhead gas to a pipeline company for 3.6 cents per thousand cubic feet and then paid $1.33 per thousand cubic feet when it was piped back into her home. Despite the fact that the numbers translated as a 3,700 percent increase in price, it was a difficult case to make because it contradicted the most commonly held popular assumptions about how the American economy worked.[23]

Frank Pitts attempted to instruct the Congress in the real cost factors at work under any "share the shortage" plan. "With regulation, the consumer will still pay the full amortization costs of pipelines running at only 55 percent capacity—and we would still have no new reserves to call upon because all incentive to find them would have been stifled. If you buy a five-room house and shut off two rooms, you still pay the mortgage on all five."

It made historic economic sense. But it did not sell. In Washington the political actors changed as Republican Gerald Ford was replaced with Democrat Jimmy Carter, but basic attitudes on natural gas remained the same: Carter's energy proposal in 1977 proceeded from the same assumptions about "exhausted gas reserves" that had controlled the Ford administration. Aggravating the situation was the dramatic growth in noncontrolled intrastate prices that assured that all new nondedicated gas supplies would flow into intrastate markets. The Federal Power Commission did its best with its limited pricing authority, granted under the Natural Gas Emergency Act of 1975, to make interstate gas competitive. Indeed, at one dramatic juncture, FPC chairman Dick Dunham, who was appointed by President Carter in early 1977 to be administrator of the emergency act, even went so far as to unilaterally raise the price for newly discovered gas to $2.25 per thousand cubic feet. Although the increase represented a jump of virtually 50 percent, Dunham did it on his own authority after a weekend of thought. But this breakthrough, while helpful, did not touch upon the long-term problem of overall pricing control. In the aggregate, Washington hands, both in Congress and in the bureaucracy, looked for new controls as a means to secure pricing and supply parity between intrastate and interstate markets.

Frank Pitts decided to try his hand again. He called the governor of Texas, Dolph Briscoe, and through him got an appointment with Jack O'Leary, head of Carter's energy team. Their discussion did not begin on what could be considered common ground. Said Pitts: "I had heard him say that morning—and it just burned me up—that there were very few places to find any new natural gas in this country, so why give the producer any incentive to drill? He said the gas we did have should be held as a premium fuel. That was basically wrong, and he knew it was wrong." Having been head of a geophysical company, Pitts possessed elaborate subsurface maps of the entire United States. "I took data to convince him that there were plenty of places to drill but we had to have a price high enough for a producer to drill the wells. I spent an hour and fifteen minutes with him. But I didn't get to first base. I knew then we were in for a long uphill fight."[24]

Thus began the intricate congressional wrangle that would culminate in one of the most complex pieces of legislation ever to pass the U.S. Congress, the Natural Gas Policy Act of 1978. During the entire struggle, Pitts toured the country in what he called a "two-pronged attack" aimed at both consumers and congressmen. He took with him his detailed maps showing trend lines in each area where he spoke. "I would show them the map of their state, the location of the potential places for wells to be drilled, new reserves to be drilled." He endeavored to show congressmen "they would be voting against their own interests to vote for the continuation of the control of natural gas."

Independents started in a deep hole because they were the most readily visible target for expanded natural gas regulation—and would remain so as long as Congress presumed the wellhead price was the decisive arena of cost for consumers. Meanwhile, the long-line gas transmission companies, with a careful eye on all the players from wellhead producers to retail customers, reserved their most sharply focused gaze

for the fine print in the avalanche of amendments that historically tar-
nished natural gas legislation.

Caught in this vise, independents appeared to have few of the assets
that had served them so well in the long contest over depletion—
except, of course, the separate legal status as independent producers that
had become part of the depletion solution. This separate status would,
of course, stand all independent gas producers in good stead in future tax
legislation but had little direct effect in natural gas pricing other than
stimulating a generalized political sympathy for small producers and
their specific functions within the industry. In short, none of the contentions over natural gas had the clear-cut quality that gave the depletion allowance for small producers the clarity it possessed in 1975.

Yet the issue was the same, as Frank Pitts was laboring to demonstrate: provide wildcatters with a reasonable incentive, and they would
find the reserves. As far as producers were concerned, all of the desperate efforts by FPC and FERC officials since the twenty-year-old Phillips
decision to control independents (and somehow do it in such a way as
to stimulate wildcat drilling for new reserves) had been wholly counterproductive. Indeed, the effort had failed so miserably it had created the
illusion of a gas shortage that now had everyone in Washington rushing
toward a regulatory dead-end. The task at hand for independents, then,
was the same that existed during the depletion fight: educate Congress
on the real economics of exploration. This time it was gas, not oil, and
this time it focused on interstate market prices rather than on the depletion allowance.

Veterans in TIPRO had acquired, and passed on to each other, a
great deal of institutional knowledge in the two depressed decades since
the Phillips decision. One of those who helped this process along was
the Midland independent Malcolm Abel. Abel pushed a number of producer-sponsored initiatives in area pricing as a solution to the routine
forms of discrimination practiced by pipeline purchasers. After Netum
Steed stepped into the TIPRO presidency in 1966, he repeatedly
appeared in Washington to provide a producer perspective on the reasons behind the growing constriction of interstate markets. Both Abel
and Steed made some headway; by 1967 the strangulation of interstate
natural gas markets was increasingly being recognized as a critical
national problem—even by regulatory officials.[25]

What Pitts, Abel, Steed, and other TIPRO leaders were able to establish was this fact: national control of natural gas prices was a transparent failure. If the country did not have a gas shortage, it clearly had a shortage of gas in interstate commerce; increasingly the only consumers in the nation who could count on a steady supply were in Texas and the other producing states where the intrastate market was not controlled. Therefore, since efforts to regulate interstate wellhead prices had proved successful enough to throttle the search for new reserves, the nation needed a new gas decontrol bill that would unshackle wildcatters so they could do what they did best—discover fields.

But twenty years of producer-sponsored reform efforts had essentially revealed that the political playing field was an awesome maze. In the 1950s, Senator Ralph Yarborough of Texas had unsuccessfully sponsored early efforts to create a legal distinction between small producers and integrated companies. A decade later Congressman Bob Krueger had narrowly lost his bid to steer gas decontrol legislation through the House of Representatives. With historical hindsight, it can be said that both men were just a bit ahead of their time. Since the nature of the global energy situation was not yet grasped by political leaders in the nations of the West, the preconditions for a broad new approach to policy in Washington were simply not yet in place in those years.

What the congressional debates essentially revealed was a kind of distant and largely uninformed difference of opinion among those politicians who thought the nation might have a shortage of natural gas and those who detected a shortage of wells. Rank confusion therefore surrounded the basic question of what any new price should be: since natural gas as a commodity was relatively new on the national scene, no historical guideposts existed to which to link any price. Members of Congress were uncertain whether to go with people like Jack O'Leary who said we had to live with a shortage or those like Frank Pitts who said the necessary reserves existed if only the nation gave wildcatters the incentives to find them.

The two analyses were, of course, fundamentally incompatible. To those like Pitts who saw the basic problem as tied to incentives, the market conditions that had worked to encourage intrastate production could be easily reproduced nationally to unlock interstate markets. But to those like Jack O'Leary with a shortage mentality, the basic national problem was perceived to be the existence of "high-priced" intrastate gas that was "drying up" interstate markets. Yet the question could not, and did not, hinge on simple differences in perspective. From a producer standpoint, the issues were weighted against them for the elementary reason that constituencies in consumer states far outnumbered those in producing states. As a matter of simple political reality, Washington policymakers were not going to consider seriously any approach grounded in granting decontrol to the intrastate market; rather, they hoped to find a way to add controls there that were similar to those already in place in interstate commerce. This being the case, producer representatives found themselves, willy-nilly, accepting as a best-case scenario the necessity of working for a bill which might eventually lead to decontrol but which in the short run would result in the creation of controls where they had not previously existed—in the intrastate market. Producer representatives (including TIPRO, the IPAA, and state associations generally) discovered that, to have any voice at all, they would have to participate in a process that would end in something their members did not want—namely, the extension of controls to the intrastate market. This reality sat alongside—but did not by any means overwhelm—the earlier divisions of opinion about whether the country did, in fact, have a natural gas shortage. For the great number of people who shared O'Leary's perspective, the solution was transparent: extend control to the intrastate markets and gas would flow everywhere, though even O'Leary conceded that distribution would have to be carefully "monitored" so everyone got a little something! The byproduct that no one wanted to talk about was, of course, that consumers in producing states would soon be forced to discover they had made a mistake ten or fifteen years earlier when they bought their gas kitchen ranges. Without gas, such regionally fashionable home appliances would be unusable. New regulations might improve the market for electric ovens in Texas and Louisiana, but suburbanites would also have to wonder what to do with their discarded gas ranges once the gas sources supplying producing states had been pirated away. The "regulate the shortage" mentality produced this kind of insanity.

If more than a half-century of lurching, lobby-ridden bureaucratic controls had taught the nation anything about how power really worked in America, it was that such a quasi-administrative approach was a blueprint for a perfect regulatory nightmare. Indeed, even proponents of enhanced bureaucratic tinkering conceded that any effort that was national in scope would be "difficult to administer." To say the least.

But the real problem was much deeper than mere administrative complexities. As historians of twentieth-century America had long since agreed, the effort to cope with enormous integrated companies by regulating in the public interest had been thwarted throughout the so-called Progressive Era, the New Deal, and the postwar years precisely because the agencies charged with regulation had come under the effective influence of the very corporate giants they were supposed to be regulating. Rather than a passing failure, this process had been a century-long failure.

But this insight was not restricted to historical scholars and political scientists. No one in America had more detailed evidence about the political reach of integrated companies than independent oil and gas producers: the decades-long inability of the Federal Power Commission to function independently of integrated gas pipelines and the transparent nonfunctioning of the mandatory oil imports program had taught independents a great deal more than they wanted to know about this ongoing political fact of life in America. Pundits across the entire range of the political spectrum could analyze and complain all they wished about oligopolies and monopolies and, satisfied that they had done their duty, go on the next day to other things in the further practice of political punditry. But independents could not go on to other things because they lived every day of their lives in the very world of the integrated giants. Accordingly, they brought a knowledge of the pitfalls inherent in any national energy legislation that was considerably more subtle and historically grounded than the assumptions most other Americans brought to the same project.[26]

This was the situation when Congress began to formulate what would eventually become the Natural Gas Policy Act of 1978. Needless to say, there were many interested parties, led in influence, of course, by the major integrated companies. Each of these titans was quite capable of acting individually, and they could also mobilize a potent collective input through such entities as the Business Roundtable. Their reach also extended through the American Petroleum Institute and the Mid-Continent Oil and Gas Association to thousands of other participants—not excluding small independent producers who were not well enough informed to work for their own self-interest. But any congressional intent that was truly national also attracted so many other forces that the legislative scene quickly became a maelstrom. In addition to the historic role that the IPAA traditionally played on behalf of independents, a newly formed Natural Gas Supply Committee appeared, primarily as a voice for large but nonintegrated gas-producing companies. In addition, a variety of consumer groups endeavored to get well enough informed to play some sort of role, a process that uncovered differences among them based on regional considerations and underlying attitudes toward the regulatory process itself. And, of course, independents longed to protect themselves, primarily through the IPAA and TIPRO, but also through such smaller entities as the Houston Wildcatter's Group that had first appeared in the 1975 taxation struggle as well as the Louisiana-based producers group that had organized over the same issue.

These dispersed industry segments had wildly differing priorities. Some wanted decontrol of high-cost gas, others wanted newly discovered gas to be exempt, others wanted to protect the freedom of the intrastate market, and still others wanted to phase out control of dedicated interstate supply as soon as possible. With literally billions of dollars at stake, the infighting escalated as the dreary months of congressional battling unfolded. These contentions even invaded the ranks of producer groups. Indeed, not only were all independents not alike, neither were all the majors, some having a far different mix of foreign and domestic production than others and thus a somewhat different set of individual corporate objectives.

It turned out that TIPRO had learned a great deal about coalition-building in Washington during the 1975 depletion struggle. In a congressional environment that in no way could be described as "reservoir sophisticated," producers needed to find some informal vehicle through which they could communicate with each other across as wide a spectrum as circumstances permitted. To this end, an ad hoc group came into being, self-labeled the Boll Weevils. They numbered five participants: Harry Barsh, representing Louisiana gas producers prominent in the interstate market; Wayne Gibbens, representing a wide cross section of large and small producers through the Mid-Continent Oil and Gas Association; Dick Klein of the Houston Wildcatter's group; Texaco's Don Arnett, who had concerns about high-cost gas; and Julian Martin, whose TIPRO members were prominent in the intrastate market in Texas. These men gave themselves two assignments. The first was to communicate with each other constantly on the ebb and flow of amendments dealing with price controls, definitions of markets, and definitions of the proliferating categories of "old" and "new" gas. The second assignment was, quite simply, to stay on the job between committee hearings and mind the store when representatives of other groups went home.[27]

Not all the portents were unfavorable. The Arab oil shock of 1973 had altered the way the lay public thought about energy, and while it by no means produced anything remotely approaching a new consensus, a certain openness now seemed visible. As the *TIPRO Reporter* editorialized in the spring of 1978, "We're well on our road to restoring drilling to the levels of the mid-1950s. Few people realize that drilling was cut in half during our private depression of the 1960s and we still don't have the wellhead incentives to get back to where we were two decades ago when imports were about one tenth of today's levels. There's recognition even among our foremost critics that we must have incentives to drill wells, and that the price of both crude and wellhead gas must and will go up. It's no longer us against the consumer. As never before, the consumer's interest is closely identified with that of the oil and gas producer. The Arabs saw to that."[28]

Throughout oil country, producers endeavored to rethink their relationship to the rest of the industry. Some, not too experienced in the ways of TIPRO, undertook to educate producers on the tactics of integrated companies. For example, Bill Dutcher explained to a TIPRO gathering that the newly formed Independent Gas Producers Committee, of which he was a part, had learned some things in the Washington struggle. "One of the really distressing but perhaps telling arguments against our position," he said, "has come from the staffer of a senator from a producing state who said if we separate independents from the majors, we'll leave the majors out there naked and defenseless against the Senate liberals. We've had representatives of the majors tell us in effect the same thing, that we need the independents out front running interference for us. Now, how long do the independents want to continue playing this role when the result as we have seen over history is 25 years of price controls on natural gas?"[29]

Needless to say, no group of independents had worked through this problem more thoroughly and over a longer period of time than had TIPRO. As a result, no one had a more subtle grasp of how the politics of decontrol had changed as a result of OPEC's alteration of global pricing realities. TIPRO therefore fashioned a broad approach and encouraged other independents to do the same. The Boll Weevils took the pulse of Congress wherever they could and passed their findings back to Texas and Louisiana independents and, through the Liaison Committee, to producers active in other state associations. The phalanx of Texas independents who put in long hours on the natural gas bill was led by Frank and Shelby Pitts, Bob Foree, Chet Upham, Max Thomas, George Mitchell, John Watson, Malcolm Abel, Gene Wright, Jack Warren, Netum Steed, and also Alan King, president of the Wildcatter's Group in Houston. Among independents nationally and also within TIPRO, the cooperation fashioned in the 1975 depletion struggle served as a foundation for 1978.

Given the crazy quilt of pipeline practices and the myriad refinements that had accompanied every piece of natural gas legislation for a generation, the puzzle of how best to structure a measure of decontrol gave rise to an odd (but oddly appropriate) goal: the regulation of decontrol. What emerged as the Natural Gas Policy Act of 1978 fell considerably short of what producers needed, but the alternatives were likewise so bleak that producer associations across the nation found themselves in an extremely awkward position. The measure created a maze of new categories of gas products based on whether they were sold in interstate or intrastate commerce, on whether there were exploratory or development wells involved, on how deep the wells were, and so on—with different prices for each. While the artificial rigidities thus fashioned were riddled with real and potential inequities, the categories treated most favorably were the ones in which independent producers predominated. Through it all, however, and in subtle ways that nonspecialists could not easily identify, the distortion of prices aimed at eventual decontrol had the effect of lowering real competition.

As TIPRO's new president, Chester Upham, put it: "The course which TIPRO chose in working with the gas bill was to keep our hand in the pot as long as possible. We held to the principle of not having the door slammed on our ideas so that we could help fashion the best conceivable bill—just in case we had to swallow some bitter legislation whether we wanted to or not. We never found the bill acceptable after it reached the House-Senate conferees; but neither did we reject it out of hand until we had the opportunity to examine it, and had the opportunity to offer some corrections to the final language in some detail—which we were able to do." TIPRO's Earl Turner explained the political difficulties: "No thinking oilman wants to get labeled 'against' energy legislation at a time when the President of the United States is telling the world that lack of an energy policy underlies the dollar crisis."[30]

But those TIPRO hands most intimately involved in the Washington struggle knew that Congress had brought forth a legislative vehicle of truly awesome complexity. As it happened, the House-Senate conference committee agreement on the Natural Gas Act of 1978 came just thirteen hours before TIPRO's scheduled summer meeting at Lakeway; the bill became the focus on what was perhaps the most intense discussion among TIPRO's members in the entire history of the association. Chester Upham concluded that "the overwhelming numerical opinion among Texas independents was in opposition." In extending price regulation into the intrastate market, the bill lost the support of most independents.

In analyzing the bill at Lakeway, independents heard some truly frightening scenarios, such as the one sketched by Lynn Coleman, general counsel for the Department of Energy: "If we continue to have a more than ample supply of gas in the intrastate market with pipelines incurring take or pay problems, then there is no question in my mind but what the FERC will have to take an expansive view of the Southland Royalty decision. . . . The question could literally be the kind of case where a lease covering acreage—which may have been dedicated to an interstate pipeline some years before—is held to be under such dedication. Maybe there was no way for the producer to find out whether the lease had ever been covered by dedication. He drills a well in good faith, and sells the gas to an intrastate pipeline for maybe $2/Mcf. If it should be held that the gas was still dedicated, two consequences could follow: First of all, the original interstate pipeline might be forced to reclaim the gas. Secondly, that gas wouldn't be $2 gas in intrastate commerce, it would be 29¢ gas, and the producer could be nailed with an obligation to pay back all gas that had been produced for the intrastate market. Nobody can be sure about such consequences, but on the other hand, you can't rule them out either."[31]

As it turned out, none of this happened. But in 1978 this was an outcome that was by no means self-evident and would not become very understandable until the struggle over windfall profits legislation ran its course in the early 1980s and the new regulatory procedures were tested in actual practice. In the meantime, the sheer complexity of the new gas bill kept independents in a constant state of alarm. Nor were they alone. Carter administration officials immediately got into a public intramural argument as to whether the bill, internally contradictory as it appeared, was enforceable. It was a debate within the Carter team that scarcely soothed anxious independents.

In the end the guiding elements of gas legislation turned on the simple fact that no measure designed to create new gas production regulations while also aiming at eventual decontrol could be made workable on a national basis unless the palpable discrepancies between interstate and intrastate prices were removed. There was the added worry that it might not work anyway. What was clear, in any case, was that the 1978 legislation inevitably meant that the intrastate market had to lose its privileged position—a bitter pill for Texas independents to swallow.

Still, some judged the end product to be something producers could live with. "The consequences of not having a bill out of this Congress may be even worse than what this terrible bill could do to us," ventured Bob Foree. And looking back on it fifteen years later, Frank Pitts concluded: "We certainly did not accomplish everything we wanted . . . but we did start the deregulation of natural gas and increased prices so much that within three years of drilling activity—by 1981—we had a surplus of natural gas in this country and we have had a surplus ever since then." On this fundamental point, events proved Frank Pitts to be right.[32]

A Reprise on Unitization

In ways not true of TIPRO's earlier years, the decade of the 1970s concentrated producer energies at the national level. This outcome was, of course, a direct product of the massive impact of Middle Eastern events on the global petroleum market. But there was always one issue close to home in Texas that could be counted upon to exercise independents—the old hobgoblin called unitization. It surfaced again in the 1970s.

The sticking point was—as it had always been—the fact that the

original voluntary statute independents had fashioned in 1949 precluded workable unitization procedures in virtually all fields where there
were more than a handful of producers and royalty owners or more than
a minimum of disputes over the accuracy of ancient land surveys. This
ideal circumstance most often came into being in West Texas, where the
combination of hard-rock formations and deeper depths tended to limit
the number of producer participants, and where large and well-surveyed
ranches similarly limited the number of royalty owners. But these conditions almost never applied in East Texas, where farmsteads under lease
were both small and numerous and the number of producers were routinely large and sometimes downright abundant. Over the years, as
properties (both leaseholds and producing interests) had been subdivid-
ed among offspring and the children of offspring, the number of players
in a given field could literally be counted in the thousands. As fields
depleted and secondary recovery projects became logical, the necessary
arrangements for voluntary unitization became administratively difficult
to complete due to the excessive costs involved in finding all the participants and fashioning their agreement to a unitization plan. Indeed,
by the 1970s the administrative difficulties impeding secondary recovery projects constituted a problem that existed all over the state, even
in parts of West Texas.

Accordingly, the ranks of unitization sympathizers had grown over
the years and, in 1972, TIPRO decided to poll its members. The results
confirmed that the tide had turned: 60.2 percent of the responding independents were for a mandatory unitization statute, 37.9 against, and 1.9
neutral. Yet efforts to craft legislation that would somehow avoid a disastrous rift in producer ranks proved exceedingly difficult. A TIPRO
watchdog committee hammered out some thirty-nine safeguards,
enough to dazzle as well as confuse state legislators. As prominent Texas
independents, including a good number of former presidents of TIPRO,
appeared on both sides and offered complex testimony grounded in very
real case histories, the Texas legislature proved to be as hamstrung by
the issue as had classically been the case with TIPRO itself. Once again,
a mandatory statute died on the drawing boards.

The reasons lay deep in the history of the relationship between
independents and major companies. No one could articulate the matter
more forcefully than TIPRO's old warhorse, Bob Foree. Foree had fought
a rear-guard action for years against compulsory unitization and still

believed no "dire need" existed for such a statute. But rather than cause harm to the organization he had done so much to build, he acquiesced in the 1972–1973 initiative—but only if enough safeguards could be written into the bill itself. Yet no safeguard could deal with his deepest reservation, which concerned the vulnerability of independents should a compulsory statute be formally enacted by the legislature. Even if the initial act were foolproof, Foree said, the very existence of legislation opened it up to future amendments. Foree wanted the major companies and their organizations to agree in writing not to alter the proposed statute for ten years. While this stance exasperated proponents, they had to acknowledge that everyone had vivid memories of price and pipeline discrimination, of nonratable take, and of other distortions of field rules by the most powerful forces in oil country. Perhaps needless to say, no such written guarantees were forthcoming from the major companies. Oddly, the outcome—no new legislation on the subject—demonstrated a bizarre truth about TIPRO's political clout in Texas: the organization could sometimes effectively influence public policy when it was united; it could also influence it when it was divided.[33]

In 1973 and thereafter, Texas remained the only major oil-producing state in the nation with a voluntary unitization statute. The memories of the grim struggle in the 1930s in the East Texas field continued to cast a long shadow in the Texas oil patch. The things Bob Foree said during the 1972–1973 debate had been said before—by Bryan Payne and Guy Warren in the 1940s, by Ollie Hermann and M. D. Bryant in the 1950s, by Robert Payne in the 1960s, and by Malcolm Abel in the 1970s. But more than any one of these partisans, it was tradition itself that defeated compulsory unitization in Texas—the antimonopoly tradition that had guided TIPRO from its inception. Changing circumstances or not, unitization crystallized this tradition in a tactically powerful way. Since some of TIPRO's stoutest independents were on the other side of the unitization debate, the outcome actually verified the strength of that tradition. Proponents, too, respected that tenet of the TIPRO faith. Perhaps nothing illustrated this relationship more clearly than the postmortem on unitization delivered by one of Foree's oldest allies, who also happened to believe the time had come for Texas to move to a workable compulsory unitization statute. He confided to this author, "Old Bob Foree was wrong as he could be in that last fight. But you couldn't oppose him on it; well, you could oppose him, plenty of us did, but you couldn't really do it effectively. Because he was right about where the dangers were. We all understood that. The majors have only themselves to blame for the dead-end we ended up in. The trouble is, the lack of a sound statute now hurts everybody. But that's just the way it had to be. Old Bob was wrong on the issue but he was right about the past."[34]

It was, therefore, not on unitization in the Texas legislature but rather on tax and natural gas legislation in the U.S. Congress that TIPRO made its mark in the 1970s. The long-term result was a verifiable advance in the nation's energy-producing capacity. Indeed, there was no question that the gains were quite tangible—as subsequent U.S. natural gas production would prove. Be that as it may, the Natural Gas Policy Act of 1978 in no way marked the culmination of the tumultuous events of the 1970s. Indeed, that description could only be affixed to the truly apocalyptic happening that soon roared out of the Middle East: the 1979 Arab-Israeli War. Amazingly enough, the scenario of 1973 once again unfolded, literally down to the last detail: first an Arab embargo, following by an instantaneous leap—from one day to the next—in the price of retail gasoline at local service stations across America. Once again the public learned that the immediate price bounce occurred on Persian Gulf crude that had been bought, transported to the United States, and then refined—all under pre-embargo conditions. The drama continued without missing a scene: another round of major company "explanations" and another round of public outrage, one that ensured that Congress would be almost immediately involved in windfall profits tax legislation, which, in due course, became the final extraordinary happening of the decade. Indeed, the windfall profits struggle became so intricate that it occupied Congress through the close of the Carter years, through the entire first term of Ronald Reagan, and then well into his second administration. It would be 1986 before independents had settled knowledge of where they stood. By that time, future prospects for windfall profits had vanished.

As independents looked back over a decade that had been truly transformative, one thing was clear: however complex the pricing and taxation formulas were or might become, the global emergence of OPEC had revolutionized wellhead prices not only for crude oil but for natural gas. Depending on how it was tiered for pricing, old and new crude production in 1982 was bringing independents anywhere from $23.50 to $29.00 per barrel.

These numbers abruptly remodeled the American drilling industry. Old marginal wells that had been abandoned as uneconomic because recovery costs offset revenues were suddenly reexamined and found suitable for redevelopment. The subculture of stripper well production simply exploded. Emerging new technologies employed to increase previous recovery rates through improved reservoir characterization techniques suddenly acquired an attentive audience among independent producers. In a hundred ways—some as old as the art of putting together a sensible deal and some as new as 3-D seismic mapping—new drilling possibilities became the subject of engaged undertakings in oil country. In every corner of the state, independent operators dusted off old maps, geologists restudied old trends, petroleum engineers rethought old formations, and regional banks expanded their exploration loan departments.

The whole climate had changed. America wanted more oil and natural gas. Consumers clamored for it. In ways that had for many years languished in disuse, the nation's politicians cheered the producer onward. The day for which many Texas independents had longed, and most had given up hope ever seeing again, had reappeared. In the oil and gas country of the Southwest, only one word could describe the prevailing mood: exhilarating. Once again, it was the time of the Texas wildcatter.

Chapter Six

AN EXPANDING REALM
OF SURPRISES

The world's fascination with oil has always centered on one intoxicating symbol: the dazzling gusher spewing "black gold" over the countryside. The image has enchanted outsiders every bit as much as it has galvanized oilmen. But as many old wildcatters can attest, this is precisely the reason why heady moments of black gold are always dangerous: intoxication is not conducive to careful economic analysis. Yet euphoria came to Texas at the very end of the decade of the 1970s. When the historic $3 price for a barrel of crude oil doubled after 1973 and then subsequently exploded past $12, then past $20, moved on to $30, and continued rising—all following upon the 1979 embargo— independents found it hard to be objective. In the face of such powerful evidence, all the familiar guideposts crumbled and all the tested rules no longer seemed to apply. The surge of prices developed its own controlling momentum.

So much changed over so brief a period of time that it is no simple task to recreate the ethos of the early 1980s in Texas. It was a moment when the rhythm of history itself seemed to vindicate all the basic principles about exploration that independent producers had always tried to convey to the rest of America. "There are plenty of places to drill," Frank Pitts had told Congress in the mid-1970s, "but we have to have a price high enough for a producer to drill the wells." And, for natural gas, events proved him right.

Now, thanks to Arab embargoes, the incentives were there for oil as well. Inexorably, rig counts began to rise in Texas, from a low of 600 to 1,500, to 3,000, and then to 4,000. The entire economy of fossil fuel production in the United States underwent a revolution. With crude prices ten times their historic levels, everyone's holdings suddenly had a loan value that could underwrite an enormous range of exploratory options. A wide variety of enhanced recovery techniques, previously ruled out as too expensive, now appeared as eminently cost-efficient. All sorts of reservoirs previously considered depleted, marginal, or otherwise beyond practical recovery had abruptly become logical sites for development and further exploration. Across the state of Texas, the fundamental configurations of drilling deals were simply transformed. "It's time," independents told one another, "to drill!"

But there was one other elusive ingredient in the boom of the early 1980s. Simply enough, it had to do with the need of independent producers to verify the endurance of a way of life. As such, a bit of background is needed to explain its impact on the expansion of the early 1980s.

During the long imported crude glut of the 1950s and 1960s—the lean years described in the *TIPRO Reporter* as "the private depression of the oil and gas producer"—independents across Texas had done all the things that hard times force upon self-respecting citizens. They had pulled in their belts and cut expenses. They had fashioned new kinds of drilling deals that spread the risk even wider and softened the cost of dry holes. They had talked over the situation with one another at TIPRO meetings and formulated remedy after remedy to the voluntary imports program and later the grotesquely misnamed mandatory imports program. When politicians in both parties proved more attuned to major companies than to independents, producers had mobilized yet more evidence, devised yet another remedy, and gone back to Washington again. They were unhappy, alarmed, worried, and they complained mightily. But through it all their underlying faith in their own ability as wildcatters was not shaken: the oil and gas was there and they knew better than anyone else how to find it.

But beneath the surface, and to a degree that outsiders never quite suspected, producers in Texas had been privately and fundamentally shaken by the stark evidence that surfaced in the month of April 1972—the proof that the state's historic reserve of crude oil had somehow disappeared. It was one thing to suffer and complain in the face of eight-day allowables at a time when shut-in capacity in Texas exceeded two million barrels daily. A better day inevitably would surely come—sometime. But it was another thing entirely to confront stark proof that 100 percent allowables across the entire state showed conclusively that reserve capacity itself no longer existed. No matter that this raw fact confirmed all the projections that independents for a generation had publicly laid before Washington officialdom—the old adage of the wildcatter that "you can't find new reserves unless you drill, so give us the incentives to drill." It was no consolation to be able to say "I told you so." The raw fact itself simply had too much long-term significance. After 1972, in ways that were quite unspoken and deeply private, a gnawing doubt nibbled away at the confidence of Texas independents.

It did not hinge simply on all the historic imbalances that had always made things precarious for independent producers. Through persistent advocacy, producers had proven they could hack out a place for themselves in a forest of giants. Rather, it was anchored in the elementary fact that without reserves to find, oil-finders had nowhere to go. It was as if nature itself had conspired to put a period to the era of the independent producer in America. This was the unwanted possibility that independents tried to live with throughout the seven long years between April 1972 and the sudden global oil shock of 1979.

The great expansion of the early 1980s cannot really be understood without taking account of the quiet anxieties that immediately preceded it. In the simplest possible terms, Texas independents felt that the amazing turn of events in 1979 had given them a last-minute reprieve. Their fears, it now seemed, had been unjustified; things were going to be alright. The thought, suffused with relief as it was, proved absolutely galvanizing.

"Euphoria," then, was the right word to describe the mood of the early 1980s in the Texas oil patch. The unprecedented escalation of crude prices induced within the entire producing sector the same kind of élan and renewed confidence that Frank Pitts had first felt during his successful foray into concentrated intrastate gas production in 1970. Throughout oil country, independents got busy with a resolve that had no regional counterpart since the heady days of the Canyon Reef and the Spraberry Trend in the late 1940s and early 1950s.

Though the onrush of activity varied with the personality and experience of individual producers, the general upward trajectory had its effect on virtually everyone. It was not merely the fact that crude prices at $30 a barrel made all manner of drilling deals look quite different than in the days of $3 crude, it was the price momentum itself that became a driving engine. The expanding range of possibilities was by no means restricted to producers. Drilling and service company executives of every size whispered to one another about imminent prospects of $100 crude and $5 gas.

Such numbers fundamentally altered the way people thought about drilling proposals in the early 1980s. As one veteran producer confided to this author, "There comes a time when things are really heating up in the middle of a boom, when anything seems possible if not downright probable, and people can more or less lose their moorings a little bit. I remember brooding over a certain deal that a couple of fellows—good men, both of them—brought into my office around 1982. It looked good, real good in fact, but it was very expensive. Enhanced secondary recovery. And I remember thinking to myself, 'I really shouldn't do this, but if oil goes to $60 or $70 a barrel, I am really going to be kicking myself if I don't go into it.' So I did. Well, three or four years later, the mathematics didn't look so hot, to put it mildly. You never get too old to learn something in this business, but that was one I had already learned years ago. But you just get caught up in the general momentum. Truth is, it's happened to most of us, one time or another. It's one of the reasons independents go broke—in good times as well as bad."[1]

In such ways, the rising tide of crude prices carried everything before it, generating an explosion of oil and gas exploration across the state. Every segment and subsegment of the industry gloried in the new activity—pipe supply companies, drilling contractors, landmen of every description, well-testing services, manufacturers of sophisticated new drilling bits and seismic testing tools, and, not least, bank loan departments. As TIPRO's membership rolls expanded, the staid old *TIPRO Reporter* blossomed forth as a dazzling four-color journal that began in 1982 to number over one hundred pages. The journal's readership was deemed large enough, and prominent enough, that ad rates rose in step with everything else, particularly rates for the two sides of the back cover. Predictably, the two biggest names in well servicing and testing, Halliburton and Schlumberger, commanded these favored positions. Everywhere, it seemed, independents could find verification that all was right with the world of the independent producer.

Technological developments wove themselves into the mix, though not quite in the complex ways that would surface a decade later. As early as 1979, the Society of Exploration Geologists reported that seismic activity had reached the highest levels in twenty years. Some 424 crews were at work, up from 365 a year earlier. Meanwhile, Joe B. McShane, a TIPRO member who also served as president of the National Stripper Well Association, said that new price deregulation for stripper wells had begun to cause producers to "think twice before plugging and abandoning even the most marginal of wells." Of the more than 370,000 stripper wells in the nation, only 8,380 had been abandoned in 1978, down from 9,000 in 1977 and almost 10,000 in 1976. These numbers scarcely translated into the raw materials of a boom, since the average stripper well in the nation produced only 2.6 barrels per day. But it did reveal how $6 crude caused producers to rethink enhanced secondary recovery methods in ways that were economically impractical with $3 oil. Another sign of things to come was a 1979 symposium at Southern Methodist University that attracted hundreds of petroleum specialists to hear seventeen presentations on "unconventional exploration techniques." Sponsored by SMU's Institute for the Study of Earth and Man, the symposium explored subjects ranging from temperature analysis of subsurface waters and sediments to electromagnetic sounding and other remote-sensing refinements. These arcane subjects remained, for a time, the special province of technical specialists.[2]

It was, nevertheless, on a rising tide of exploratory promise that Chester Upham turned over the presidency of TIPRO in 1980 to Frank Pitts, ushering in the boom years that would see Pitts succeeded by Gene Wright in 1982, by Bruce Anderson in 1983–1984, and by Shelby Pitts in 1985–1986. The world these TIPRO veterans had to cope with bore little resemblance to the lean decades of oil imports and the desperate wrangles over gas legislation that had dominated the public actions of independent producers since the earliest days of TIPRO's existence. The reason was quite elementary. The transformation of crude prices had led to surging gasoline prices for motorists across the industrialized world. In the natural order of things, this development generated an enormous consumer backlash and an immediate political struggle over windfall profits taxes. The primary targets were the major importing companies, of course, but the task for TIPRO, as always, was to devise whatever protection was possible for small producers. The legal distinctions between independents and majors, first achieved in the tax legislation of 1975, provided producers with a kind of structural protection they had never previously attained. This helped mightily, but it by no means ensured that independents could expect to escape unscathed. And, indeed, they did not. The first result was the Crude Oil Windfall Profits Tax of 1980, which, despite the title, turned out to be a tax on production rather than on profits, windfall or otherwise.

Defining a "Windfall"

For independent producers, an absolutely maddening irony lurked behind this outcome. In each of the four decades since TIPRO had come into existence, the major integrated companies had been able to frame the entire subject of oil and gas taxation as an activity that could only be very narrowly conducted by elected representatives in Washington or Austin. Though the range of commercial operations involved in the exploration, production, refining, and wholesale and retail distribution of petroleum products offered an extremely broad array of sites for taxation, major companies had over the years been able to teach legislators at the state and national levels that the only site that could be depended upon to produce tax revenue was at the wellhead. Any attempt to broaden the tax base through efforts such as the gas gathering and severance beneficiary levies of the 1950s in Texas had been adroitly amended so as to be effectively attacked in the courts as unconstitutional restraints of trade in interstate commerce.

In ways detailed in Chapter 4, the political reach of the major companies had been uniformly effective on central elements of national taxation policy; moreover, the issues being debated were so legalistic and abstruse that the practitioners of daily journalism in the nation's press had never been able to clarify for laymen what issues were actually being contested. So murky was the debate, and the press coverage of the debate, that both the gas gathering tax and the severance beneficiary tax disappeared from public view with little more than a bare ripple of popular response. Beyond the informed veterans of TIPRO, scarcely a corporal's guard of observers in Texas had any real grasp of the intricate politics that surrounded the legislative debates over petroleum taxation. Only highly informed producers understood the subtleties at work: in blocking off all other sites of petroleum taxation, the major purchasers of oil and gas were restricting popularly elected assemblies to choosing between production taxes or no taxes at all.[3]

Close observers of the legislative process mumbled to themselves about this state of affairs and even developed some rueful euphemisms to describe the political clout of the major companies. In such knowledgeable circles, oil and gas taxation was known to be subjected to "lobbying legerdemain" by major companies, producing legislative outcomes that abounded in "legalistic hocus-pocus." However described, publicly orchestrated attempts to achieve social equity in oil and gas taxation routinely ended in the same meek dead-end—another round of production taxes. The realpolitik of the major companies was such that the independent producer was always front and center in the public mind when the issue was tax policy.[4]

For small producers, the escape hatches contrived over the years by long-line gas transmission companies were all quite frustrating. But in no area of national debate did comparative tax advantages work in a more profoundly unfair manner than in the production and marketing of Middle Eastern crude oil. Very early in the postwar years, the major importing companies managed to convince Congress that their lucrative concessions from Middle Eastern countries needed to be understood as liabilities rather than assets. The international companies took the position that their oil concessions were anything but free. They had to be "paid for" through royalties retained by the producing country. The majors argued—convincingly to Congress—that all royalties paid to the Arabs should be considered as taxes paid into the U.S. Treasury. Any additional taxes would, therefore, be "discriminatory."[5]

To independents, of course, this argument was wildly inappropriate. If the identical principle were applied to domestic production, all royalties paid to Texas landowners by independents could be counted as taxes paid by producers and, as such, deducted from the tax payments otherwise due on income from production. Though such a bizarre proposal was never suggested—by independents or by anyone else—it was precisely this principle that governed U.S. tax policy with respect to Middle Eastern crude from 1946 to the present. All efforts to impose import fees were stigmatized by the majors as tariffs that would dislocate international trade. In raw economic terms, of course, this made no sense at all, since in any postwar year from 1945 to 1980 and beyond, the differential in production costs of Middle Eastern and domestic crude were enormous; yet both, after refining, commanded the same price at the corner service station. The real differential, of course, was in the truly impressive profit margin importers enjoyed on every barrel of Persian Gulf crude over and above the margins accruing to domestic producers.

During the forty-year period between 1946 and 1986, TIPRO submitted a variety of proposals to bring production costs of foreign and domestic crude somewhat into line. By no means was this a partisan argument: the position of independent oil and gas producers was bulwarked by pivotal historical dynamics affecting America's relationship to the world economy. In terms of international trade, the United States ceased being a developing nation in the 1890s when for the first time its balance of payments within the world market ceased to show red ink. The happy condition of a favorable trade balance for the United States grew impressively through the twentieth century as America became the world's industrial and agricultural giant and exports far exceeded imports. This historic circumstance came to an end after the 1973 Arab oil embargo radically increased the outflow of payments from oil-consuming nations to the producing countries. In Europe, Asia, and in the Americas, all nations were forced to wrench their national economies in response to these new trading relationships, which created unanticipated deficits, new patterns of deficit financing, and new pressures on every area of national budgets. While some nations, notably Japan and Germany, seemed to do better than others in negotiating this transition, the United States after 1980 began running historically unprecedented deficits that imperiled the entire long-term structure of the economy.[6]

Ironically enough, it was amid these global dynamics that international oil companies obtained for themselves a level of prosperity that was historically unparalleled. Two highly visible national realities underlay the public outrage over windfall profits. The first, of course, was the red-ink hemorrhaging all over the nation's trade balances as well as the national budget. The second was the immediate jump in gasoline prices, including prices on imported crude produced, transported, and refined at pre-embargo prices. The majors had always enjoyed this bonanza in that the two-cent production cost of Arabian crude got the same world price as the much more expensive crude produced by everyone else. Therefore, the public explanations by major companies failed to convince anyone that the importers had not helped themselves to an authentic windfall. No matter. The Crude Oil Windfall Profits Tax of 1980 did not address the differentiated profit levels of foreign and domestic crude that had been, and remained, a historic constant. It therefore did not address the source of windfall profits—namely, the untaxed concessions that were the real source of all windfalls before, during, and after the embargo. Rather, the 1980 levy was once again, simply enough, a domestic production tax.

For the wildcatters, this was the most exasperating aspect of all comparisons between majors and independents. In the copious detail in which independents understood this issue (as well as the structural implications for themselves and American consumers generally that grew out of this detailed knowledge), the historic experience of independents separated them from the assumptions governing American public opinion. To the small producer, the crude price increases of the 1970s constituted a belated compensation for more than two decades of depressed wellhead prices that had persisted at a static $3 level in the face of constant structural inflation in the rest of the U.S. economy in every year since the end of World War II. The American wage earner who made $3,000 in 1949 did not regard his 1979 income of $30,000 as some sort of unearned windfall. Texas producers had the same attitude toward the rise of 1949 crude from $3 to a 1980 price of $30. Not so to the man on the street who saw the sharp crude hike as just as much a windfall for the producer as was the tax-free profits the major companies had always enjoyed on their Middle Eastern production—and were enjoying now more than ever.

In vain did independents once again try to explain the profound structural differences in the taxes paid by majors and independents. In the early 1980s, the announced purpose of windfall legislation was to raise $80 billion over the life of the tax, ostensibly to develop new sources of domestic energy. A second purpose was, simply enough, a recontrol bill—in the aftermath of the Carter and Reagan decontrols. The levy hit "old oil" (pre-1970 production) particularly hard—with contradictory and unforeseen results. In the first instance, the tax was a substantial blow to royalty owners. In response to the fact that 1.9 million of the nation's 2 million royalty owners averaged their royalty on two barrels a day or less, a number of transparent inequities were, fortunately, removed through amendments in 1982. But any tax on old oil also hit the major companies hard because they had over the years acquired title to a great deal of production, either by direct purchase from wildcatters or through developmental wells drilled by majors on offset acreage they had retained (see Chapter 5). So the majors were taxed; the irony here is that the levy was on old domestic oil, not incoming foreign imports. Thus the most lucrative production owned by the majors remained untaxed. But outside the pages of the *TIPRO Reporter*, this fact was largely unexamined in the nation's press.[7]

There were, however, some interesting sidelights that prevailed for a time—traceable in part to the prior victory by independent producers in achieving in 1975 a legal distinction from major companies. Though it was—understandably—scarcely good manners in producer circles to talk about yet another production tax in positive terms, the new legislation did establish differential tax treatment that generally favored independents over major producers in five controlled production categories. Almost uniformly, the categories most favorably treated were the ones in which production by independents predominated. These included exploration, of course, along with waterflooding and stripper well operations.[8]

None of this, of course, touched upon the stunning tax advantages major companies enjoyed through their Persian Gulf concessions. In 1983 and again in 1986, TIPRO raised the issue of equalizing tariffs on imported crude as a means of dealing forthrightly with the realities surrounding the global production and marketing of petroleum products. In 1983 an extended discussion by TIPRO members of tax avoidance by the majors revealed an overwhelming preponderance of sentiment in favor of import fees. Bay City independent Stanley Rosenthal summarized all the arguments against an import tariff as "the same as those devised by major oil companies" and pointedly concluded that "independents should be concerned about protecting themselves." Similarly, a 1986 report in the *TIPRO Target* defined the stakes as starkly as possible: "A Way to Stop the Bleeding." In Texas the issue of import fees became highly politicized in debates between Marvin Zeid, chairman of TIPRO's task force on imports, and George Strake, state GOP party chairman, who defended the administration's opposition to oil fees. The eventual outcome merely verified where the real fulcrums of influence lay in the Reagan administration—as had been the case at the presidential level ever since imports first became a central petroleum issue in the 1950s. When the shouting died down, TIPRO's proposals on import fees had gotten nowhere.[9]

In any event, as it was subsequently amended by Congress in repeated redraftings in the 1980s, the windfall profits tax as a legislative idea gradually strangled to death. After repeal, the end result was a mixed bag for independents—relief from some truly inequitable tax provisions balanced against the loss of some of the comparative advantages temporarily written in for independent producers. The 1986 tax reform bill attacked domestic production in ways that went quite beyond the windfall profits tax while at the same time leaving imports alone—a testament to the profound political reach of major companies even in the midst of a public backlash over the continuing bonanza enjoyed by international companies from Persian Gulf crude. The biggest of the big had found ways to protect the comparative advantages they possessed and even create new ones. Everyone else in the energy economy had to scramble as best they could.

"Scrambling" was the operative word for Texas independents amid the changing field practices of the 1980s. Once again the eternal verities of surprise and change characterized the world of the small producer. This became abundantly clear with the appearance of a dismaying innovation by gas pipeline purchasers known as "special marketing." It turned out that the essential remedy independents had suggested in the 1970s for the domestic gas market had proved workable: higher wellhead prices had at long last unleashed production for the interstate market. Pipelines rushed in to sign dedicated contracts and, with their supply channels in good order, set about expanding industrial and retail sales across the country. However, the expected rise of wellhead gas to $5 per thousand cubic feet—a widespread anticipation throughout 1980–1981—did not materialize. On the contrary, gas prices began to slide in 1982 and continued softening thereafter. Pipeline companies promptly discovered to their horror that they were obligated in "take or pay" contracts to buy gas at levels that now exceeded prevailing market prices.

The solution was special marketing. Pipelines saddled with long-term contracts simply told producers they were suspending purchases because they had no markets. The pipelines then created shadow companies that sent emissaries to the same producers with offers to buy the gas at rates substantially below the previously contracted price. Producers could take the lower price or have no market for their gas at all. Such were the broad configurations of special marketing. Independents howled in protest, and a bevy of lawsuits began wending their way through the courts. Eventual judicial settlements tended to turn on fine points of specific contracts as well as field location and sites within fields. Among producers, there were a variety of outcomes, but the generalized effect was a broad quieting of price levels at the wellhead across the country.[10]

The phenomenon of what TIPRO called "monopolistic abuses at the hands of 'shadow pipelines'" galvanized producers to generate initiatives aimed at market-demand proration for natural gas. During his tenure as TIPRO president in the mid-1980s, Houston's Bruce Anderson consistently pushed for a system that would moderate the behavior of shadow pipelines and protect correlative rights of producers while at the same time permitting new marketing techniques to develop. These efforts were partially successful. Failure of the Railroad Commission to react favorably to the TIPRO initiatives, combined with the onslaught of special marketing, left independents with little recourse in the marketing of their natural gas.[11]

No longer did producers, suppliers, and bankers whisper to one another about the imminence of $5 gas in the U.S. market. In natural gas, the high tide of prices had come and gone—even before the same phenomenon came to crude oil.

The Crash of 1986

But it came to both. Indeed, the collapse of the crude market hit Texas independents with the destructive power of a Gulf hurricane. In a ninety-day period early in 1986, world crude prices plummeted from $30 to under $10. The precipitating cause was a decision by the Saudi Arabian government that was made essentially in exasperation at other OPEC nations. Ever since the end of U.S. reserve capacity in 1972 and the 1973 embargo that followed, the Saudis had attempted to function as a kind of Texas Railroad Commission of the Middle East. Unfortunately for the Saudis, their attempt to create a system of market-demand proration hinged on a degree of restraint by other producing nations that was—to put it mildly—not forthcoming. The only way the Saudis could hold Persian Gulf production at levels anywhere near world market demand was through cutbacks in their own production. But the more the Saudis did so, the more other Persian Gulf producers proved gleefully ready to take up the slack—in the face of reiterated warnings from Saudi officials. Finally, late in 1985, the Saudis turned on the spigot, and in January 1986 the world price of crude collapsed.[12]

It is not an easy task to describe the psychological as well as the economic consequences of this shock, other than to suggest that fallout from the crude price crash of 1986 has influenced in large or small ways every subsequent development affecting independent producers down to the present. The immediate effect, of course, was excruciating economic pressure that, for a good many Texas producers, proved too much to bear. Bankruptcies coursed through every sector of the drilling industry, including, of course, wildcatters. Several regional banks, heavily invested in exploration loans, went under, leaving a trail of independents in their wake. A number of other small producers, including several prominent in TIPRO, received bone-jarring jolts that necessitated wholesale reorganization of the family economy.[13]

One way to avoid such a fate was to follow a variation of the "Bill Rutter Rule," which, as the Midland independent explained, was this: "Never take on an exploration debt in excess of what ninety days of in-hand production could pay off." Rutter, who cut his teeth in the Spraberry in the early 1950s, watched a close friend as well as his hometown bank disappear in the 1986 cataclysm. The friend, in common with many drilling contractors, had taken on large debt obligations to finance expensive new rigs. Given the abrupt decline in drilling that followed hard upon the price collapse, the contractor was undone. Rutter's summary of the costs of the 1986 contraction echoed the sentiments of many Texas independents. Noting the $4 billion loss Exxon experienced in a misplaced secondary recovery venture, Rutter observed, "If the majors can make a mistake that big, then how can we fault a little country bank or a small independent? During the boom, banks were very aggressive in encouraging independents ever onward. I, for one, certainly did not anticipate any such price collapse and I don't know anyone who did. We rode it out because we stayed within our long-term means. Most old-timers did, you know." True enough, but whether individual operators found themselves in the red or black in 1986, the era of expansion for independent producers had clearly come to an end.[14]

A massive downsizing engulfed the entire producing industry, touching every individual and company involved in any aspect of petroleum exploration—drilling, testing, lease acquisition, and all aspects of development, including finance. Everyone hoped these slashes were merely temporary expedients, pending more information as to when and at what level prices would actually acquire some measure of permanence. Amid the immediate shock of the 1986 whirlwind, independents were too busy trying to create a survival economy for themselves to have much time for long-range planning. Accordingly, rig counts plummeted as exploration budgets for producers of all sizes shrank precipitously.[15]

But as the months passed into years, a fairly clear outline of the shape of the future began slowly to emerge. After the early free fall in 1986, the price of crude vacillated in the $13 to $15 range for the better part of four years before achieving a rough stabilization in the vicinity of $18 per barrel, where it remained through the first half of the 1990s. A similar stabilization for natural gas also developed, roughly between $1.60 and $1.80 per thousand cubic feet in most regions of the country. To the extent that anything at all was predictable in the global petroleum market, a general trajectory seemed evident: world energy prices had achieved a settled level that could probably be expected to increase in the future only in step with global inflation rates.

The Independent and the Environment

While this organic shakeout was wreaking havoc throughout the nation's producing industry, one other issue increasingly came to occupy independents—the mounting national concern about the environment. From the very outset of heightened scientific anxiety about the earth's ecology, beginning with the first speculations about global warming, TIPRO adopted a stance of engaged interest. After specially appointed task forces surveyed emerging data on oil exploration, storage, and transportation, TIPRO moved in the early eighties to augment its primary forum for Texas matters, the State Petroleum Issues Committee, with a new subcommittee devoted exclusively to environmental issues. Al Dillard of Midland moved in as vice-chairman of the State Petroleum Issues Subcommittee for Environmental Affairs, which developed a number of ideas about oil and gas exploration in wetlands that were soon adopted by the U.S. Corps of Engineers. In this early phase of TIPRO's exploration of the issue, the association assigned itself two tasks—to inform producers about pollution remedies and to work with regulatory agencies and environmental groups on technical aspects of proposed compliance procedures. Producers themselves moved in the same direction, particularly in Central Texas, where a Giddings Producers Association was established as a nonprofit group to assist local independents in meeting federal and state environmental requirements. The group purchased spill containment equipment for producers to use.[16]

Independents gradually informed themselves in the 1980s on two broad environmental subjects—the variety of ways exploration and development practices could affect the ecology of Texas and the equally wide impact of regulatory procedures on the economics of petroleum production. TIPRO participated in an employee right-to-know program that involved workshops on the handling of hazardous chemicals as well as with the Superfund Amendment and Reauthorization Act (SARA) on a broader community program. This initiative took the form of six Oil Patch Right-to-Know Seminars, conducted by TIPRO across the state, detailing how producers could comply with OSHA and SARA regulations. The information workshops were held in Midland, Abilene, Wichita Falls, Houston, Kilgore, and Amarillo.[17]

As ecological knowledge became more widespread among independents, a rather broadly differentiated range of opinion developed in producer ranks. As on most issues that seized producer attention throughout the life of TIPRO, this range of opinion was too diffuse to be easily characterized. Speaking broadly, however, it could be said that independents were of two minds on the subject—those who shared in popular concerns about the environment and wanted TIPRO to develop a cooperative posture and those who tended to grow exasperated at environmental "extremists" who were seen as favoring regulatory procedures that were so sweeping as to put workable solutions beyond the capabilities of small producers. In 1989, TIPRO president Jim Russell created a new and permanent TIPRO Committee on the Environment and named a prominent "cooperationist," Albany's Jon Rex Jones, as its chairman. Jones said independents were "going to have to exercise discipline, because if we don't the American public is going to discipline us. We won't have to be on the defensive if we show our concern for the ecology." He added that his primary goal was to establish TIPRO as "a credible source for politicians and the public when they seek solutions to environmental problems." For his part, Russell said he welcomed the "challenges and opportunities for the association" on the ecology front and added that TIPRO "can't find a better man" than Jones, who had served as a member of Task Force 2000 and also as president of both the IPAA and the West Central Texas Oil and Gas Association. Jones was also a current member of the National Petroleum Council. The new environmental chairman promptly announced his intention to "maintain the high road," and Russell added in support: "Reasonable preservation of the environment is necessary to maintain quality of life and this preservation will demand an increasing amount of our attention and economic resources as time passes."[18]

Soon thereafter, TIPRO became involved in the migratory bird issue. Responding to warnings by the U.S. Fish and Wildlife Service, TIPRO and other members of the Liaison Committee of Cooperating Oil and Gas Associations undertook to address the problem of "migratory birds dying in open pits, tanks and ponds containing oil accumulations." At an environmental committee meeting in Austin in October 1989, producers learned from government and university specialists that flags, noisemakers, and other decoy devices did not offer dependable long-term protection for wildlife. Rather, access to possible contaminated areas could be more effectively reduced through the use of one-inch netting. For example, a sixteen-foot tank could be covered for about $50, exclusive of labor costs.[19]

But a more structurally relevant approach to the problem lay in preventing contaminated pits and ponds in the first place by properly plugging abandoned wells and by cleaning up old well sites. Responding to both public and government pressure, TIPRO played a major role in helping to draft and subsequently in supporting legislation to provide the Railroad Commission with an annual $10 million cleanup fund. The money for such an undertaking would come from the petroleum industry through revenues from fees, fines, drilling permits, and other regulatory taxes. Indeed, the method of financing led to a muscular struggle between independents and major companies on whether a substantial portion of the $10 million should be raised through fee increases on drilling permits (borne, of course, chiefly by independents) or though a fee increase on production, which would involve major companies to a more comprehensive degree. After the extent of legislative lobbying pressure exerted by major companies became apparent, the entire initiative appeared to some observers to be fundamentally threat-ened. When TIPRO's Julian Martin had earlier predicted that the cleanup bill would become law "within six months," his forecast was greeted with considerable skepticism, reaching as high as Commissioner Jim Nugent. But the environmental needs were quite clear, and the plan of dividing funding between drilling permits and production taxes made too much sense; TIPRO won the intraindustry scuffle and the bill passed in 1991. It has been working ever since.[20]

Among its features was an incentive clause making compliance less burdensome for producers with good environmental track records. In due course, the commission established a pollution prevention program to assist producers in minimizing and managing oil field wastes. The effort focused on source reduction and recycling opportunities in the field, offering training and technical assistance for producers attempting to establish waste minimization plans for their operations. A TIPRO-sponsored oil pollution seminar in Corpus Christi in February 1994 proved even "more timely than expected" as attending speakers from the Environmental Protection Agency took the opportunity to announce inspections along the coast beginning in sixty days.[21]

In a further effort to help independents establish themselves as good environmental citizens, TIPRO began to compile a 675-page *Environmental Reference Manual*, published in 1992 as the first of many comprehensive editions. By 1995, the manual had grown to 900 pages and was, reported the *TIPRO Target*, "selling fast" at $75 a copy.[22]

Among the more complex aspects of environmental practices in which TIPRO actively came to involve itself was the Coastal Management Plan, first initiated by the state of Texas in the 1980s. George Mitchell and John Watson of Mitchell Energy were among those concerned about pollution problems in Galveston Bay, and Watson, as TIPRO president, worked closely with state land commissioner Gary Mauro on developing the Coastal Management Plan. "It was one of the world's broadest-based coalitions," Watson said with a smile, explaining that interested participants ranged from oil producers to the League of Women Voters, the Sierra Club, and the AFL-CIO, among other parties. The general approach of these groups remained broadly harmonious as long as details remained vague; the task became far more difficult when implementation plans reached the fine-print stage. By 1993, Tom Coffman and Scott L. Anderson were complaining to Mauro about increasing difficulties that operators were experiencing in getting drilling permits, and both men testified publicly against some of the proposed components of the plan. A negotiated settlement was finally worked out in 1995, to the satisfaction of independents as well as state and federal environmental officials.[23]

TIPRO's struggling search for a middle ground continued to give it a somewhat distinctive cast among commercial groups. George Mitchell's concern about pollution in Galveston Bay was one aspect of TIPRO's approach while strains over multiple requirements for drilling permits was another reality. Among business groups, TIPRO's quest for the high road placed it in a distinctive position: in place of a routinely negative response to ecological concerns, the association mirrored the competing interests of the nation at large on all matters touching upon the environment. In short, among committed environmentalists, TIPRO could not be viewed as a routinely dependable ally on all matters touching upon oil waste, though it was clearly more responsive than many others.[24]

But while the internal pulling and hauling over the fine points of environmental procedures was both instructive and revealing, the issue was vastly overshadowed within TIPRO by the general crisis in the global crude market. The price collapse had abruptly shoved producers back to the depression-level status of the 1950s and 1960s. As had been the case in the Eisenhower-Kennedy-Johnson years, their very survival seemed fundamentally questioned.

What now for independents? Nature itself seemed to suggest one inarguable route: they could just die off. At the very end of the first year of the crash, TIPRO's founding president, Jack Porter, died in Houston at the age of ninety. Two years later, Bob Foree, the man who had led independents on a course different from Porter's, died in Dallas. In an organization too diverse to be dominated by anyone, Foree had been the single most influential figure in TIPRO for forty years. And when TIPRO decided on a route different from his own—as it once appeared ready to do on unitization—he acquiesced rather than tear up the organization he loved and had done so much to build. Similarly, Guy Warren, Bryan Payne, M. D. Bryant, and Ollie Herrmann, the early pioneers who along with Foree had led TIPRO through the crunching constraints of the 1950s, were all gone.[25]

Was their passing symbolic of the way of life they had labored through TIPRO to preserve? A good many producers began to act as if they thought so. They cut exploration to the vanishing point and seemed to be content to play out the string, some electing to put a period to their wildcatting days by selling all their production to the majors and closing shop. However, others, including independents heading small producing companies, probed the possibility of merging with other independents, in some cases with specialists in selective kinds of recovery operations and in other cases with larger independent companies. In this way, the ranks of independents became at one and the same time leaner but also stronger and more flexible.

A Technological Option Emerges

But there was another conceivable route—one that might prove workable whether independents merged or not. In the spring of 1988, possibilities of new exploration and recovery techniques began to surface in TIPRO. At a Dallas regional meeting of producers in April, Dr. William Fisher of the University of Texas at Austin laid before independents both a new strategic analysis of exploration and an array of new tactical approaches to drilling, all flowing from new ways to conceptualize subsurface reservoirs. Fisher's emergence in TIPRO deliberations was not accidental. A distinguished geologist, he had developed a close relationship with TIPRO's Julian Martin when both served on the advisory council of the Gas Research Institute. Martin encouraged Fisher to share his technical ideas with producers and to become an active participant in the association's internal deliberations. Fisher's address in Dallas was one of the early tangible results.[26]

As director of the university's Bureau of Economic Geology, Fisher brought a rare combination of talents to the world of independents. He had the scholar's focus on pure research, but also a unique ability to recruit teams of specialists to work together on reservoir analysis and recovery techniques as well as a driving interest in seeing how technological innovations could effectively be applied on a day-to-day basis in oil country. A number of new technical institutions had formed in the 1970s and 1980s—including the Gas Research Institute. Along with the Bureau of Economic Geology, they brought together geologists, geophysicists, engineers, and testing specialists, who (among many other areas of specialization) had begun to develop increasingly sophisticated methods of 3-D geophysics in testing reservoirs—or, in producer parlance, "3-D seismic." Collectively, the multiple technological developments already in place, and the exploration techniques they made possible, convinced Fisher that the collapse of global crude prices need not be fatal to the oil-finding sector of the industry. But for this result to be realized, some fundamental shifts needed to be achieved in the way everyone thought about exploration.

In actuality, Fisher's message for independents did not date from his 1988 appearance in Dallas—he had placed before independents his basic strategic analysis of oil production years earlier. Indeed, in a comprehensive article in the *TIPRO Reporter* in 1981 entitled "Oil in Texas: Yesterday, Today, Tomorrow," Fisher had outlined his vision of a future in which radically enhanced recovery techniques were the essential component in unlocking previously unrecoverable oil. In a subdued scholarly manner, he endeavored to shock people into a new awareness through a quiet recitation of some truly startling numbers. As of 1981, some 153 billion barrels of oil had been discovered in Texas, of which roughly 51 billion barrels could be expected to be marketed through conventional techniques of primary and secondary recovery. What Fisher was endeavoring to induce producers to focus upon was what he called "unconventional oil"—the phrase he helped popularize as a means of characterizing the 100 billion or so barrels of crude that was "conventionally unrecoverable" through traditional techniques. In this way, Fisher endeavored in 1981 to introduce independents to unconventional techniques ranging from tertiary recovery to strategic infill drilling. His conclusion was either sobering or tantalizing, depending upon how one elected to read the options: the future of producers depended "more and more on our technical know-how in enhancing recovery from oil already known in place, and less and less on the wildcatter of yesterday."[27]

Surfacing in the heady early days of the 1980 boom, Fisher's central emphasis on technology more or less blew away on the wind. But then came the crash of 1986 and the massive downsizing in the producing industry that followed. When Martin arranged for Fisher to speak to surviving TIPRO members in 1988, the prestigious geologist had their rapt attention. By this time, Fisher himself had benefited from seven years of increasing technological breakthroughs in well testing and drilling. He had also taken due note of the wholesale changes in the domestic ener-gy picture brought on by the near collapse of the producing industry. In the new climate, Fisher set for himself two initial tasks. The first was to sound a warning about the structure of the industry. If the nation's pri-mary oil finders, independent producers, passed from the scene, the inexorable result would be immediate stasis in drilling followed by long-term exhaustion of the nation's developed reserves. The second item on Fisher's agenda concerned the independents themselves: they needed to rethink the time-honored approach to wildcatting in order to take advantage of the technological breakthroughs both in advanced seismic testing and horizontal drilling and in the data-gathering process neces-sary to make the new procedures work as a practical tool of reservoir characterization and development.

Independents could attest to the fact that the first assignment con-stituted a knotty task they themselves had been engaged in for many decades: convince the country that the health of the producing sector was essential to the maintenance of domestic petroleum reserves. No easy task, this.

But the second item on Fisher's agenda was also difficult. As a topic, technology was scarcely a new subject among Texas independent pro-ducers. Ever since Spindletop, where the Hamill brothers had pioneered drilling mud and Anthony Lucas had fashioned the first back valve, technical advancements had been part of the way of life in oil country. Indeed, the idea of electrical measurements of the subsurface had occu-pied Conrad and Marcel Schlumberger as early as 1911, leading to their eventual perfection of the electric log in 1927—that is, at a time even before the East Texas field had made independent producers a real fix-ture in Texas.[28]

So it was not technology itself that was distinctive about William Fisher's conceptual initiatives. Rather, what he and the other scientists at the Gas Research Institute and the Bureau of Economic Geology were pioneering was an entirely new way to think about exploring and developing oil and gas reservoirs. One of the central features turned on new methods of creating and then reading testing data so as to uncover segmented reservoirs, which, in earlier days, would have been passed over as unpromising after random drilling based on inadequate testing and analysis. Here is where strategic infill drilling became relevant. Research by the Bureau of Economic Geology had developed evidence that fundamentally challenged long-standing assumptions about homogeneous reservoirs. What actually existed beneath the surface of the earth in a vast number of cases were sealed-off or segmented reservoirs, some containing oil or gas while others did not. So the new 3-D seismic testing approaches went beyond reservoirs to the acquisition of elaborate subsurface data suitable for testing entire plays—data that might run through a half-dozen or more counties! Specialists began talking about reservoirs in terms of "clusters."[29]

For the average independent, the outlines sketched by Fisher and his colleagues at the University of Texas looked like a whole new universe, one by no means easily grasped. Even the precise point of entry into this realm was unclear, as it applied to the decisions independent producers would be called upon to make. For TIPRO members, the one ingredient that seemed unmistakable was that everyone had to learn more. A number of technologically inclined producers, including Frank Pitts, Jim Russell, and Tom Coffman, pushed for a systematic internal educational program on the new exploratory options. It was an influential trio, since by the late 1980s Pitts had already served as a highly active TIPRO president while Russell and Coffman followed each other in that role from 1989 through 1994. It was, in any case, a TIPRO tradition to pioneer for the producing sector, so the association moved on a fairly steady pace toward a systematic inquiry into the dimensions of the new technology.

Early in 1990, Russell created an Applied Research and Technology Committee, with William Fisher as chairman. Veteran wildcatters like Dallas's Patrick Gratton, who had trained in geology before becoming experienced in the other arts of the independent producer, also worked to propel the effort by taking an active role in the Fisher-led committee. A comprehensive internal survey by TIPRO had yielded an interesting point of loyalty: independents trusted their own association more than they did any other governmental or scientific institution. Fisher included this bit of information in a magisterial report to the U.S. Department of Energy outlining new areas of potentially fruitful cooperation between producers and the federal government.[30]

What ensued over the next five years was the product of the coordinated initiatives of Fisher, Martin, Russell, Coffman, and Gratton. Through technical channels, independents made contact with specialists in the Department of Energy in Washington, particularly with James

Randolph, director of the Fossil Fuels Division. Martin and Russell labored to get TIPRO's administrative ducks in a row, notably the creation of the Applied Research and Technology Committee and the scientific contacts that flowed from the work of that new forum. For his part, Coffman effectively shepherded an intensive internal education program aimed at reaching every member of TIPRO. The central idea behind all of these efforts was to establish in TIPRO a comprehensive program that could become a national prototype for petroleum development in a technological era.

In September 1990, the Department of Energy sponsored a day-long seminar on technology transfer in Austin. Agency officials were astonished, as well as impressed, by the unanticipated turnout of over 400 independent producers rallied by TIPRO. The agency announced the creation of a Petroleum Technology Transfer Council (PTTC) to coordinate what quickly began to take on the appearance of a massive educational campaign on the specifics of the new exploration technology.[31]

In measured steps, an elaborate informational program was persistently pushed by Tom Coffman and Jim Russell. TIPRO's internal survey had determined what producers thought they needed in terms of the new technology. Armed with these replies, TIPRO and the Bureau of Economic Geology orchestrated a series of workshops, conducted around the state in the fall of 1991. Workshops were held in Corpus Christi, Abilene, Midland, San Antonio, Amarillo, Wichita Falls, Dallas, and Houston. Governor Ann Richards was responsive to the TIPRO initiatives, and the state's energy office, headed by Bob Armstrong, provided some financial help to assist in funding the workshops and the specialists who provided the professional staff for them. These sessions were by no means one-way streets where information flowed from technical experts to producers on such topics as 3-D seismic applications, recovery from tight gas sandstones, or improved conventional oil recovery strategies. They were, rather, two-way dialogues with the reservoir and recovery specialists—from a half-dozen Texas universities as well as DOE officials—seeking to learn more about the technological needs and capacities of local producers so they could better shape their presentations at future sessions. By 1993, these information exchanges had reached more than one thousand Texas producers, a testament to Coffman's driving energy and the organizing intensity of Martin and the TIPRO staff.[32]

The Department of Energy was also sufficiently impressed with the TIPRO program to provide some technical and financial help, and the Gas Research Institute developed a technology transfer program to provide research results to producer members. As a conscious model of technology exchange, Terry Ramsey was installed on the TIPRO staff as the program's first transfer agent to conduct seminars on such topics as "Management Decisions in the Application of Hydraulic Fracturing Technologies." Meanwhile, Jim Russell, having turned over the TIPRO presidency to Austin's Tom Coffman, moved on to head IPAA's newly created Advanced Recovery Task Force, which encouraged other producer associations to monitor the TIPRO program as a prototype that could be exported to other state and regional associations through the PTTC.[33]

Coffman proved to be an articulate advocate within TIPRO ranks, and Russell, citing TIPRO examples, broadened the message to the nation's producers through the IPAA and, later, as board chairman for the DOE's new PTTC, which did, in fact, become a functioning and ongoing national institution. It was thoroughly grounded in the TIPRO prototype of two-way workshops, followed by intensive seminars, capped off by the creation of informational centers to disseminate PTTC programs as they materialized. The entire informational sequence had been designed by TIPRO and tested throughout Texas. Among the many specialists who contributed besides Fisher, perhaps none proved more helpful than Dr. Myron Gottlieb, who pioneered, through the Gas Research Institute, the transfer agent program and who also shepherded into being a technology alliance of TIPRO, the Oklahoma Independent Producers Association, and the Independent Petroleum Association of the Mountain States. In these multiple efforts, TIPRO was the beneficiary of contracts from the Department of Energy, the Gas Research Institute, and from the State of Texas. DOE's James Randolph, GRI's Myron Gottlieb, and Governor Ann Richards were instrumental in facilitating these cooperative breakthroughs. Gottlieb continued his contributions through 1995 as an influential member of the national board of the PTTC.[34]

The challenge, it turned out, was more than technical. Large-scale seismic testing procedures were not cheap, particularly when covering many miles of Texas landscape. To function as a practical cost-effective stratagem for independents, producers not only had to think in terms of plays rather than individual leases or even fields, but they also needed to find a method to share both information and costs. Where subsurface strata across a number of counties might have similar characteristics, independents needed to think in terms of practical working cooperation with one another. In essence, DOE terminology—"technology transfer"—described a process that went quite beyond merely transferring technical information from specialists to independent producers; it involved wildcatters in freely transferring information among themselves and even larger producing companies. In the natural order of things, this might conceivably stretch to include major companies!

The entire history of wildcatting in America pointed in precisely the opposite direction. To find oil, independents made a habit of venturing into uncharted terrain. Conventional wildcatting technique called for speculative ability, data acquired as a result of speculation, lease acquisition based on the data, and—only then—the drilling of a wildcat well. One did not broadcast to the world one's intentions at any one of these stages. Indeed, as a great many TIPRO veterans knew—and practiced—there were "wildcats" and there were "rank wildcats." While enormous variations in risks attended diverse exploratory efforts, common to them all was silence—as much silence as one could manage. As an occupational inheritance, mystery surrounded the wildcatter's planning strategies. And nowhere was the silence greater or the mystery more enveloping than when independents were contemplating drilling "rank wildcats." In short, what the university specialists and the DOE intellectuals were asking independents to consider was nothing short of a complete reversal of the habit patterns of a lifetime.

In Pat Gratton's phrase, the new technology handed independents "a cultural problem." Though independent producers like Gratton, Russell, and Coffman were very much in favor of innovative approaches to exploration and field development, they also freely acknowledged that TIPRO's new Applied Research and Technology Committee was, as Gratton put it, "controversial." Nevertheless, the logic driving the new technology—as well as some demonstrated examples of the implicit rewards—generated a compelling momentum. Led by Myron Gottlieb, the Gas Research Institute established four Natural Gas Supply Information Centers across the country to provide producers with access to GRI's most recent research results. At the same time, a routine perusal of the institute's own descriptions indicated rather starkly that producers had to rise to a new technical level to be able to participate in the emerging world of exploration—as when it described its new FRACPRO system as "the industry's only real-time three-dimension hydraulic fracture modeling system." It was all very esoteric—but in the tight sands of the Travis Peak or Cotton Valley formations, the new exploratory techniques seemed quite relevant. And throughout the fractured sands of South Texas, there was scarcely any innovation more relevant than the new horizontal drilling techniques. Or, as specialists would add, "especially when integrated into a three-dimension fracture modeling system."[35]

How to fit it all together—literally, how to *think it all through*—remained the problem. It was as if modern science were telling independents that, to survive, they had to forgo all the customs they had learned that made them independent. Pat Gratton was right: it was a cultural problem.

For most independents, the immediate uses of technology turned on the possibility of lowering production costs. Over the longer term, producers tended to think the wholesale use of sophisticated new drilling and testing techniques could come into widespread use only after prices staged a significant recovery. Even some of the advocates of technology among independents emphasized a direct connection between prices and enhanced recovery approaches and tended to place their advocacy of technology in a contingent context of higher prices. As Abilene's Russell Taylor put it, "When other independents complain that the crude price is too low to apply new technology, I tell them to never mind that: 'Read up on new technology, go to seminars and get yourself ready so that when prices do go up, you'll be ready to apply it and not lose precious lead time. If you lose that, you may well lose your opportunity. And I am convinced the price will go up in the foreseeable future."[36]

This put technology in a different context than the one William Fisher had originally framed. To the director of the Bureau of Economic Geology, technology was not conditioned on higher prices; rather, it needed to be understood as a *substitute* for price. All the seminars and workshops on technology transfer were geared to the here and now, in the belief that they made immediate economic sense even without higher price levels. Toward this end, TIPRO's new computer bulletin board for independents was instituted to provide producers with ready access to specialists in a wide variety of exploration activities and field development enterprises. Interestingly, independents such as Abilene's Taylor stepped forward in 1995 to provide corroborating evidence that technology could be combined with the bulletin board service to produce payoffs for independents. "I had an engineer in here this morning with a computer program to keep track of some wells in a field," said Taylor. "I hadn't heard of the program, but it had an e-mail address on it, and we contacted them through the bulletin board. I had a hole in the casing of a well in Menard County. Normally I'd go in with a packer and pump truck and find the hole that way; but we found out about a new kind of log and ran it yesterday. This log finds the hole and tells me the condition of the casing. In this situation, we not only found the hole we were looking for, the program told us about two places in the casing where there were weak spots that presented problems. We were able to repair all three problem spots. That saved us time and money. That's the kind of information that people on the bulletin board would like to know. We can share information with other producers."[37]

As Fisher's successor as chairman of the Applied Research and Technology Committee, Taylor became a leading advocate of advanced technology, a role he shared with Frank Pitts, Jim Russell, and Tom Coffman. Pitts himself embodied the change in TIPRO thinking on the subject when he said in 1993, "A year and a half ago, I knew nothing about 3-D seismic. Major oil companies have been using it offshore and in foreign lands for many years and to a limited extent on land in the south Forty-Eight. I didn't know it. I don't think the average independent knew it. But I have become really sold on the use of that technology today. I will drill at least seven wildcats this year and four of the seven will be drilled on 3-D. I predict personally today that within two years the average independent will not drill any wells, either exploratory or development wells, unless he has 3-D–type technology."[38]

This prediction proved to be premature, at least within such a short time span. Not only are large-scale seismic mapping and intricate enhanced recovery strategies very expensive; they are products of a level of producer cooperation that is unprecedented. Beyond cooperative production efforts, independents began exploring various approaches to marketing co-ops only to discover such efforts were impeded by, of all things, legislative and judicial outcomes traceable to antitrust statutes. Indeed, the need for reform legislation on the subject became a focus of producer efforts in the mid-1990s. At the exploration and development end, but also in marketing, the evidence seems conclusive that cooperative modes of producer operation are coming, but by 1995, the jury was still out on whether such fundamental shifts could materialize fast enough to save independents.[39]

What, then, are the long-term prospects and what is the ultimate verdict on all the initiatives that TIPRO generated through the five decades that have elapsed since the furor over the Anglo-American Treaty precipitated the formation of a statewide association in Texas? Applying a historical perspective to the full half-century of TIPRO's efforts, it is evident that the association found a way to shape the diversity of its membership into a source of long-term strength when it just as easily could have turned into sustained internal rancor and eventual disintegration. From the earliest days, when some of the more outspoken of the founders molded the swashbuckler image, TIPRO's executive committee generated a less flamboyant approach that proved both more enduring and more tenacious as a style of independent advocacy within a centralizing national economy. Over these five decades, three ingredients seem to have contributed to TIPRO's historic achievement in carving out a niche for Texas independents in the global realm of petroleum. Each one requires a fair measure of explanation.

The first had to do with a component of southwestern life itself—namely, a deep regional appreciation of the merits of candor. The sharp disagreements within TIPRO ranks did not prove to be permanently crippling for the simple reason that their full expression fascinated the membership. While Bob Foree could become exasperated with, say, Jack Woodward, their clashes seized the imagination of everyone in attendance. The founders might, in the earthy phrase of Frank Pitts, "argue with a signpost," but the arguments themselves were, to someone like Bill Rutter, "exciting." TIPRO meetings were neither predictable nor dull. People became active in the organization not only because their future might well depend upon it, but, more prosaically, because TIPRO's people seemed to them to be real. The organization could survive an argument, but given the power of the opposition, it conceivably would have withered and died without this authenticating vitality. The attempt to create TIPRO in the first place probably could not have proven enduringly successful in the absence of the kind of high indignation, alarm, and resolve that so easily translated into "swashbuckling." What seems remarkable is the fact that TIPRO began through the activities of swashbucklers, found itself ineffective for that very reason, and then moved on within the first decade to a fundamentally different stance. By the mid-1950s, TIPRO had unshackled itself from the chains of industry unity and, prodded by Foree's driving initiatives, had begun to carve out a truly independent position for independents.

But it would be a mistake of the highest order to see this shift as one that easily uncovered a pristine route to success. On the contrary, the decades of the 1950s and 1960s added up to a generation of defeat and retrenchment for Texas independents. While the rest of the national economy was expanding and the real per-capita incomes of Americans across the board were rising, wildcatters across the state experienced what the *TIPRO Reporter* accurately described as "the long private depression of the independent producing industry."

Indeed, it was this unwanted circumstance that led directly to the second component of TIPRO's increasingly effective role as the pace-setter for America's independent producers. Interestingly enough, TIPRO had available a measure of historical guidance in how to deal with depressions. After the great crash of 1929, President Herbert Hoover had essentially sat on the sidelines and wrung his hands as the economy worsened. In contrast, Franklin Roosevelt decided to do something, "even if it doesn't work," as one of his advisors once put it. TIPRO, too, decided to do something and to keep trying, even when it did not immediately produce workable outcomes.

The practical result, increasingly accumulated throughout the 1950s and 1960s, was a wide variety of experiences that taught TIPRO's most active participants how political decision-making actually functioned in Austin and Washington. These were the years when major companies created a "Texas umbrella" to keep themselves dry and prosperous within a glutted world crude oil market. Month after month, year after year, major purchasers incrementally reduced their nominations at monthly proration hearings of the Texas Railroad Commission, citing as justification an "overage of stocks on hand." The saturation of stocks-on-hand was attributable, of course, to the relentlessly rising tide of imported Middle Eastern crude that the very same majors were able to channel through the sieve of the "mandatory" imports program. The majors' corresponding reduction in purchasing nominations throughout the 1950s forced the commission to reduce allowables from thirty days a month to twenty-five, to twenty, to fifteen, and ultimately to seven days. The "private depression" of Texas independents was very real.

If these developments in oil were not enough, producers were also subjected to multiple varieties of pipeline and price discrimination in natural gas. The elaborate skewering of petroleum taxes was such that the long-line gas transmission companies as well as the oil-importing companies collectively became one of the world's great sanctuaries for tax avoidance. Indeed, it was by observing the lobbying practices that destroyed all the gas gathering and severance beneficiary bills in the Texas legislature that producer advocates first became exposed to the real world of the major companies' political tactics. The occasional but critical Washington victories achieved by independents in the 1970s were grounded in the lessons learned in these earlier—and losing— struggles in Austin.

Though it was scarcely visible to outsiders, what this whole process created was a new kind of institutional memory inside TIPRO that gradually became the property not only of the association's presidents, executive committeemen, and task force committee members, but also of its regional vice-presidents and representatives across the entire state. In no formal sense could this institutional knowledge be genuinely understood as ideological. Rather, it was experiential—the kind of broadly gauged and experimental understanding that men like John Hurd, George Mitchell, Frank Pitts, and Malcolm Abel acquired in the trenches of national and international politics and economics.

The finite components of this kind of political maturity are not easily explained. Early on, TIPRO's most active participants learned in matters of politics that things were not as they seemed. While true, this kind of folk wisdom was not precise enough to be useful: the challenge was to learn how things actually were. The answers that came to the surface through hard experience were very sobering: policies favoring the major companies prevailed as effortlessly in the years of Eisenhower and Nixon as in the time of Kennedy and Johnson. The giants of petroleum sometimes talked as if they were worried about antitrust laws, but much more often they were able to exploit existing antitrust statutes to their own ends. Similarly, they might talk about free trade as a necessary component of a worldwide "level playing field," but much more frequently they employed the rhetoric of global free trade to advance their own insular corporate objectives. Computing Persian Gulf oil concessions as taxes paid into the U.S. Treasury was merely one of the more distorted examples of this kind of political artifice. The practical result was even easier to see: if members of the Texas legislature or the U.S. Congress wanted to tax the petroleum industry, they could do so only by levying a tax at the wellhead rather than at the more visible sites of transportation, refining, or distribution. Similarly, a high-risk activity like wildcatting could appropriately have a depletion allowance, but only if it were extended across the board to major companies that drilled few, fewer, or no wildcats at all. In such a world, TIPRO's people learned that abstract terms of description like "liberal" and "conservative" lost a considerable measure of practical meaning. A liberal like Wright Patman understood the world of monopoly, but a liberal like Harold Ickes only thought he did. A conservative like Price Daniel could sometimes stare a gas pipeline lobbyist in the face without blinking, but a conservative like Waggoner Carr demonstrated he could not. Over time, TIPRO learned the necessity of conferring with all these types of politicians, but it also learned to judge them by actual results rather than by what they said publicly.

It thus can be said that the second component of TIPRO's enduring relevance was not merely that the association decided to be assertively independent, but rather that in so doing it acquired a body of experience that less active producer associations did not acquire. No knowledgeable student of the American petroleum industry would deny that TIPRO veterans not only led in the creation of the Liaison Committee of Cooperating Oil and Gas Associations, but also subsequently provided most of the driving initiatives that eventually became settled policy within the nation's independent producing industry. This capacity to generate national initiatives was centrally grounded in the prior experience acquired by TIPRO members on their home turf. Over time, the multiple experiences that comprised TIPRO's institutional memory became the association's practical guide to policymaking. TIPRO's members learned more because they gave themselves permission to experiment more. Inevitably, they became less concerned about being in the forefront than in whether the particular style they developed in that role proved workable. Win or lose, they knew they would learn something from the effort.

The final distinguishing feature of TIPRO's first half-century was structurally grounded in the first two. TIPRO attracted men of resolve, and their subsequent experiences helped to create a tradition of sustained advocacy for independent producers. But how best to harness this tradition and how best to deploy it became the final challenge. On the eve of the great struggle over national energy policy in the 1970s, Houston's George Mitchell managed to summarize this task in a single sentence: "I don't believe in being more militant than necessary to get this job done." In these fourteen words, Mitchell managed to capsule a generation of experience Texas producers had gained within the maw of American politics. It may be swiftly summarized in three axioms: (1) if producers were passive, they would lose; (2) the alternative to passivity was not unbridled swashbuckling; (3) rather, the appropriate style of advocacy would grow out of the demands of the immediate task at hand—whatever proved necessary to "get this job done."

In practical terms, this translated into calm reflection upon a large number of potential fronts: what was appropriate to say to Republicans, to Democrats, to the executive branch, to regulatory officials, to representatives of consumer states, to people worried about the environmental impact of different kinds of energy policies, and even to officials who were so remote from the world of petroleum they thought it was irrelevant to the nation's economic and political future or to their own. No single one of these varied constituencies was decisive in itself; rather, the key words in this long litany lurked in the phrase "calm reflection."

How capable TIPRO proved to be in strategic reflection was absolutely a function of the range of its prior experiences. At any one moment of TIPRO's history, the keepers of this experience were the organization's most active and dedicated participants, including a number of former and future presidents, its executive committeemen, and, additionally, its permanent staff. The role of the association's most visible leaders has surfaced again and again in this half-century chronicle: the labors of McCarthy, Porter, Foree, Warren, Payne, and Kadane in the founding decade; the work of Foree, Hurd, and Abel in creating an effective consensus during TIPRO's change of front in the 1950s and 1960s; the leadership of Bill Murray in testing allowables in the 1969–1972 period; George Mitchell and Frank Pitts in the period of political breakthrough from 1975 to 1980; the proposals to modernize gas prorationing advanced by Bruce Anderson in the 1980s; and the technological initiatives of Jim Russell and Tom Coffman in the

1990s—to name only a few of the more energetic participants and the issues they stressed.

But the role of TIPRO's two long-term executive vice-presidents has not yet been adequately addressed. If the "private depression" of the independent producing industry proved educational as well as agonizing for Texas wildcatters, for no one was this instruction sustained over a longer period of time than it was for Earl Turner and Julian Martin. Events forced them to pay close attention not only to the complex ways in which major companies dominated decision-making in Washington, but also the equally subtle explanations the majors' spokesmen offered everyone else within the industry. Both Turner and Martin observed the precise ways in which major gas purchasers lobbied the gas gathering and severance beneficiary tax bills into judicial unconstitutionality; they dutifully tracked the escape hatches built into the mandatory imports program; they watched the independence of the Railroad Commission be mocked by crude purchasers through elaborate posturing about "stock overages"; and, perhaps most instructive of all, they analyzed the truly intricate process through which independents were placed under utility-type regulation by FPC commissioners as a precursor to an industrywide attempt to "deregulate" such transparent inequities through lobbying tactics that left producers breathless, powerless, and—in the end—subtly instructed. For almost a half-century, they experienced it all.

Earl Turner came on board within a year of TIPRO's founding and soon shepherded into being the association's first publication, the *Independent News*. As he surveyed the industry's own publications, elaborate and multiple as they were, he soon came to realize that something more substantial than a newspaper format was necessary if anything approaching in-depth analysis for producers was to be attempted. The *TIPRO Reporter* was the result. The journal emerged in full flower during the time Robert Foree assumed TIPRO's presidency and independents across the state first began feeling the cold winds of Middle Eastern imports. For Turner, the most dismaying component of intraindustry politics was the way ostensible facts and statistics could be mobilized in industry publications to fashion a Washington context in support of the major importing companies. The seemingly random way the voluntary imports program came upon the scene, soon followed by an equally ephemeral mandatory program, convinced him that producers suffered less from an inadequacy of facts than from an almost total absence—in Washington, where policy was made—of a statistical context that reflected the real world in which independent producers lived.

It was not so much that the TIPRO staff needed a research director; the operative problem was too large to be so easily defined. Rather, the association required a research director with the political sophistication to place raw numbers into an authentic producer context that influential laymen in Washington might have a chance of understanding. After Turner became executive vice-president in the mid-1950s and after a protracted search through the labyrinth of Austin's political and intellectual circles, he found what he wanted. Turner hired Julian Martin away from the Texas Research League and put him to work deciphering both oil numbers and the public politics of oil, ostensibly based on the numbers. Martin surveyed the mandatory imports program and in due course characterized it as a permanent sieve.

What both Turner and Martin found—right on their doorstep in Austin in 1959—was also instructive: the triumph of gas pipelines over the severance beneficiary tax, the continuing practice of nonratable take in gas fields, and, as the sole alternative for embattled gas producers, the ongoing persistence of life-of-field contracts at near-confiscatory prices. Both Turner and Martin also noted that while some conservative legislators in Texas supported independents over the pipeline companies in 1959, a great many did not—when the chips were down. And both further noted that most state senators and representatives, whether liberal or conservative, did not really know much more about the day-to-day realities of the state's oil and gas fields than Harold Ickes had known in the 1930s with respect to the operative dynamics actually at work amid the tumult of the East Texas field.

In short, what both learned was that they faced more of a challenge than readily met the eyes of laymen scattered throughout the rest of the society. This specifically included self-described "informed" laymen who prided themselves on how consistently liberal or consistently conservative they were. To be a consistent advocate of independents was an art that required a good chunk of staying power. It was a lesson every TIPRO president and every task force chairman learned in his own good time, but it was one that Turner and Martin had beaten into their heads every day on the job, decade after decade. And staying power they had:

Turner served from 1947 to 1980, and Martin from 1959 to 1994. Their combined tenure in the position of executive vice-president of TIPRO was just short of forty years.

It was just as well—indeed, it turned out to be a blessing—that TIPRO's ranks included a good number of producers who could move with ease through Democratic administrations as well as others who felt at home with Republican presidents. Independents were routinely out-gunned by major companies no matter who occupied the White House, and TIPRO needed help wherever it could find it. The enduring reality was this: the lessons derived from each of TIPRO's struggles in Austin and Washington became part of the association's experience and also part of the personal memory of its presiding staff officers. From the aura of international politics that surrounded TIPRO's founding in the wake of the Anglo-American Treaty controversy in 1944–1945 down to the present when technological breakthroughs have created the context in which the future of independent producers will be shaped, TIPRO's spokesmen—presidents and staff officers alike—learned that indepen-dents could not afford to be provincial if they wanted to survive. To Turner fell the task of creating, out of the fractious discord stirred up by the more outspoken founders, both a sophisticated staff and the task force forums that by the 1960s had made Texas independents the most informed producers in the nation. And to Martin fell the intricacies of coalition building that produced the victories of the 1970s and 1980s in Washington as well as TIPRO's technological initiatives in the 1990s. Whatever else Turner and Martin were (and both bore the scars of inevitable intraproducer controversies), they were instrumental in ensuring that TIPRO remained a broad-gauged and resilient voice of America's wildcatting fraternity. The fact that both men enjoyed the continuing support of such a politically diverse membership attests to that central feature of resilience within TIPRO. A verifying character-istic of this producer ethos was that Turner and Martin had on occasion tactical disagreements with one another, as did producers generally. They, like TIPRO's membership at large, took it all in stride.

Martin's successor as executive vice-president, A. Scott Anderson, came on board in 1980, became general counsel in 1984, and took the staff helm at the same time in 1994 that Austin's Rex White succeeded Tom Coffman as TIPRO president. While Coffman was a dedicated and consistent technology advocate throughout his three-year term, White thought the whole matter should be subjected to a comprehensive review by TIPRO's broad-based executive committee. Sustained over many months in 1994–1995, the reappraisal yielded a consensus that TIPRO should continue leading the nation's independents on the issue. So guided, Anderson extended TIPRO's information network, which, along with all the other technological initiatives pioneered by TIPRO, became a model for the IPAA and the nation's other independent producer associations. By 1995 Anderson could report—in an article entitled "What's New on the TIPRO BBS/Website?"—that "over 10,000 e-mail messages have passed through the system, and the 3,000th call was received on July 27, 1995." The number of registered users had passed the 100 mark, and the Web page has experienced approximately 2,000 "hits" per month.[40]

From TIPRO's home page on the Internet, one could learn that the Bureau of Economic Geology had opened a PTTC resource center in Austin. The Department of Energy, together with the IPAA, TIPRO, and other associations, cooperated under the umbrella of the national PTTC while, in Texas, a thirty-member Producer Advisory Group (PAG) was created as an integral part of the information network that Fisher, Russell, Coffman, Martin, Gratton, Taylor, and others had envisioned since the early 1990s. Coffman was named to chair the new PAG group, and Gratton moved in as chairman of a smaller operational task force. The PAG voted unanimously to ask the TIPRO Foundation, chaired by John Hurd of San Antonio, to be the regional lead organization. This function was soon moved to the Bureau of Economic Geology, which proved better placed to handle the private and public grants that were an integral part of the evolving program. Noel Tyler, successor to William Fisher as the bureau's director, and his associate, Ray Levey, both played an instrumental role in further developing the technology informational network for Texas producers.

In these sundry ways, the future of America's oil and gas finders gradually took shape along a trajectory that was substantially different from anything that independents had previously experienced. White, Anderson, and the rest of TIPRO's leadership faced the task of carving out new ways to advance the cause of producers in a structurally revamped industry floating within a transformed world economy. Anderson, an ardent believer in the potential of Internet technology, saw TIPRO's on-line service as a way to broaden the association's traditional constituency and to reach out to new subcommunities. Beyond the utility of computers in storing and retrieving information, noted Anderson, "the thing that is truly revolutionary about the Internet is that it turns computers into a communications medium." Anderson added that on-line communication "works best when the people involved feel like they are part of a community. Even though the day-to-day concerns of building an on-line service focus more on adding content and helping newcomers get familiar with the technology, our fundamental task is one of community-building. I am optimistic that we can succeed. If there is one thing TIPRO has absolutely achieved over the years, it is the creation of a genuine community of independents. We have stood many a test. Granted, this one is huge, but we have a strong track record. Independents have survived individually because they have learned to hang together."[41]

It has now been almost a full century since Anthony Lucas first brought in the great discovery well at Spindletop and ushered in the era when the Texas wildcatter became a resonant example of the entrepreneurial spirit in America. TIPRO's pacesetting on the technology front has gotten the attention of the IPAA and the nation's smaller oil and gas associations, all of which are continuing to experience the same precipitous downsizing that has radically reduced the aggregate number of surviving independents throughout the nation. For America's producers, technological planning has as its objective the fundamental reduction of costs of exploration and development and, therefore, long-term production costs. This conceivably could maximize the differential between costs and prices sufficiently to provide a margin of survival for independents.

In the 1990s independents found themselves surrounded by an industry in organic structural transformation. There were several ways of reading future prospects. To Tom Coffman, big producing units were trying to act like smaller units at the same time that mergers were reducing the overall number of players: "There are examples of larger producing companies like AMOCO seeking to emulate the decision-making capability of small independents by creating 'business units' composed of a geologist, a petroleum engineer, a geophysicist, and a landman, the whole group capable of screening a proposal from an independent and reacting within one day. That is one new trend. Another is companies like UNOCAL selling off production and even a company like Texaco selling off its production in what it considers its noncore areas to independent companies like Apache—and Apache selling off its noncore production in the Rockies. There is tremendous upheaval. There is Wall Street money for acquisition but not for exploration. Yet some of the larger companies like AMOCO actively want partnership arrangements with producers on drilling deals. None of the old patterns are holding.

"The good news," summarizes Coffman, "is that the technology continues to get better, continues to lower costs and creates dramatic opportunities for new exploration alliances. The bad news is that a great many independents, especially among the older veterans of TIPRO, are experiencing a kind of information overload, one that produces inertia. The simple fact is that you can't any longer 'do it the way Dad did it.' It's not just a matter of learning to live with 3-D seismic, for example. Advanced seismic is just another tool: all the high-tech tools must be mobilized. Yes, it is costly. However, it can be incorporated, but to do it we have to learn to make deals in a new way—in order to pay for the advanced reservoir analysis that determines where and how to drill. The oil-finding potential is absolutely astronomical, but to achieve it, independents are going to have to rethink what they are doing. It's proving very hard for a lot of people."[42]

Despite these wrenching changes, one constant has always remained. In the energy mosaic of the world, the responsibility of oil and gas continues to be enormous and, within that reality, the United States still remains the most prominent producer and consumer of energy in the world. Oil and gas production inexorably will continue far into the next century or even longer. As presently constituted, the structure of the modern world depends on it.

How America's wildcatters will fit into this spectrum remains an open question.

Chapter Seven

THE WAY OF LIFE

I s there an aura of romanticism about the oil business? "Why should-
n't there be?" says Houston's Scott L. Anderson. "We're living every
kid's dream: I'm looking for buried treasure. I'm the luckiest guy on
earth."

Finding the treasure is, of course, another story. Scott Anderson is
the son of Bruce Anderson and the brother of Neal, Craig, and Kevin—
oilmen all. With a geologist, a petroleum engineer, a landman, and a
lawyer, the Anderson family is a small conglomerate of petroleum
crafts—with the sole exception of daughter Karen, who did not go into
the business. Scott Anderson on the family approach: "We like to think
we're professional enough that we get the odds starting to work more in
our favor, but that is the best you can do. I mean, I can sit down and list
fifty different things that can go wrong with a well other than just being
dry. You can lose some drill pipe down the hole and have to redrill it.
You can have sloughing shales that come in down-hole and increase
your costs horribly. You can have human error—somebody doesn't
watch their mud weights. It's a fine line: you have to have enough
weight on that mud to make sure what's down-hole doesn't spit out on
you, but it's got to be not too much weight so that the hydrostatic column of that mud doesn't break down the formation underneath you and
get put away."[1]

Scott Anderson talks like a petroleum engineer because he is one.

His brother Craig is the geologist, Neal is the lawyer, Kevin (knowledgeable in both geology and engineering) is the landman, and the father, Bruce, a one-time TIPRO president, is the lead horse of the family enterprise. Despite Scott Anderson's knowledge of the importance of the technical side, he does not feel it is the central part of the oil business. "Land is the most important thing. It doesn't matter how good a geologist, how good an engineer you are. If you can't get the land that the oil's under, it doesn't matter what you do: you have got to have the acreage. Granted that the geologist tells you what acreage to get, and the engineer tells you how to drill the hole and get it done, and the accountants tell you if you made any money. The bottom line [is] you've got to have an appreciation for that lease, not for the play. But every independent company is absolutely different and has its own niche that it tries to fill. And it makes it really hard for the independent industry to get together because we're always at cross purposes with ourselves: you go to a TIPRO meeting and we have incredibly heated meetings sometimes—people who feel very strong about some point and somebody just as strong feels the opposite. It may be the simple fact that one of them is working South Texas and the other West Texas; or one is basically gas prone and the other oil prone. Everybody's got a different way of doing it, and there is no formula for success."

Indeed, given the diversity of specialties, there is no single style in the way oilmen talk to each other. As Dallas's Pat Gratton puts it, "Just from the kinds of things they talk about and their attitude in general, I can tell when I am in a social gathering with geologists, exploration geologists in particular, as distinct from being in a social gathering with landmen. I don't mean to run landmen down. They are effective and necessary, take care of a lot of details. But they don't really know the value of anything, they just know the price of it. Their great strength is in dealing with people, and you have to do that because this is a people-oriented business. You can't get lease one unless you are good with people. But landmen don't have much scientific capability."[2]

The polar opposites of landmen are, for Gratton, the geophysicists. They are "so technically oriented that that is about all they are interested in. Hardly any of them become successful independents on their own. They can't quite embrace the whole bundle, which is what you have to do to be a true independent. Petroleum engineers have a lot more job opportunity because there is much more work to be done that way." But Gratton points out that engineers cannot be easily character-ized because there are so many subdisciplines in the field: "A lot of them are good in drilling wells and doing it mechanically correctly. Reservoir engineers are good at evaluating what you find. Others are good on com-pletion work—how to get what you think is there out of the ground."

"You Have To Be an Artist"

Gratton's appraisal of oilmen, like everybody else's, reflects the per-spective of his specialty—in his case, geology. "To be a really effective geologist, you have to be an artist and a scientist. The requirements are conflicting. Geologists are the romantics of this business, but the people who go into geology have to be strong in physics and math and chem-istry and at least acquainted with biology, and these things take an awful lot out of people who are artistically inclined. Geology is the least pre-cise of the scientific disciplines—maybe anthropology would fight it out for that honor. People who are effective geologists need a lot of imagi-nation, which of course is something an artist considers almost to be his monopoly. We are talking about having the imaginative capacity to visualize. I'm not talking about visualizing something that is not there—which the artist does when it is a new concept—but to do the next step down from that: and that is to visualize what might be there and hope-fully is there that Mother Nature left you [as] just a few clues. It is like painting with water colors—representational. We are trying to do an accurate job, but we are going to let our imagination run a little bit. Mother Nature. She knows she has to have a tree in there and a hill in there and a stream. But we do not know where the stream is for sure except that the tree cannot grow unless it is near water—that kind of thing. She does it all and it is for us to try to recreate it, to imagine from a few clues."

Another practicing geologist, Robert Foree Jr. starts not with disci-plines but with rocks. As he put it in the office of Foree and Company in Dallas, "Misconceptions about oil fields essentially stem from the fact that people don't understand rocks, sedimentary rocks. We are con-strained by the rocks, which are hidden, put there in ways that confuse man. When you're drilling with an eight-inch bore hole, you're just taking a minute pinprick deep into the subsurface. Even in the event you get a show of oil, how limited is the reservoir? Is it actually commercial? There is the matter of structural visualization. If you cannot see the thing in three dimensions, you can't do geology because it is all in three dimensions." But even if all signs are positive, nothing in petroleum production is permanent. "Remember," says Foree, "all wells are declining from the day they come in and if you want to stay in the oil business, you somehow have to find a way to keep drilling. Technology is not only necessary, it's downright exciting now, but oil-finding still involves something beyond science and technology: intuition and imagination." These are qualities that have carried Foree into a sustained investigation of the potential for oil in, among other improbable places, Portugal.[3]

Thus, in the 1990s, something old and something new is embedded in the way producers talk about exploration. Technology is increasingly a centerpiece, but different specialists continue to think about it differently. Just listening to three oilmen talk about a new technology such as horizontal drilling reveals the different emphases they put on the same subject. A dialogue recorded in 1992 runs this way:

OILMAN 1: The last five years have been exceptional, particularly the last two.

OILMAN 2: The breakthrough has been the computerized end of it.

OILMAN 3: The whole thing is a matter of quantum leaps. Five years ago it cost $5 million to drill out 200 feet. And then a year after that, costs down, drill out further. I was talking to a field superintendent, and he says that they can't believe the things they were doing six months ago, because they seem so backward now. The learning curve on horizontal drilling is moving so fast that they can't keep up with it.

OILMAN 2: Clayton Williams just set a record for an onshore horizontal well. He went horizontal 8,000 feet for a mile and a half.

OILMAN 1: Controlled all the way.

OILMAN 2: Computer-driven.

OILMAN 3: Actually, it's mechanically driven. The computer keeps you on target.

OILMAN 2: But you control it just [by] physically turning the pipes certain fractions.

OILMAN 3: You still have to imagine your way through it.[4]

"I Think I've Been Had, But It Was Fun"

Despite these acknowledgments of both technology and intuition, the older romance of getting the lease still shines through the narratives of Texas oilmen. There is, for example, the 1930 tale that Jon Rex Jones's father told about an incident near Avoka, Texas. Jones's father had a well he wanted to drill but could not get offset acreage because the adjacent landowner—a fellow named Bland—would not trade with him.

As Jon Rex Jones tells it, "The challenge was, 'We have to figure out a way to get next to Bland.' So my father hired a surveyor to go out and stake a drilling location offsetting Bland. 'Stake that location exactly 330 feet from Bland's line and you put down the tallest stick you can find and put ribbons all over it so that when Bland steps out of his house he can't miss it.' So the surveyor says, 'Okay, I will do that,' and my father repeated, 'I want a big stick out there.'

"'So then after the location was staked, Daddy went out there and stopped at Bland's and the conversation goes like this:

"'How are you doing today, Bland?'

"'Fine. Noticed you boys staked that location.'

"'Yeah, staked that location 660 feet off your lease line.'

"'That's closer than 660 to me.'

"'No, it's 660.'

"'Well, it's not important; you're going to drill it wherever you are going to drill it, but, Jonesie, I know how far apart those rows are on the offset track, and that location is not over 400 feet away.'

"'Well, Bland, it's not important, but it's 660 because I told the guy to stake it.'

"'You got an argument on your hands.'

"'Well, I'll tell you what I'll do. I've got a hundred-foot tape in my car and if it's important to you, Bland, we'll go out there and measure the bloomin' thing.'

"'You're on.'

"'I'll tell you what, Bland. Just to make it interesting, why don't we bet a cold case of beer?'

"'I'll do it—there ain't no way I can lose.'

"'Well, you're just wrong.'

"So they shook hands on a cold case of beer and go out and measure it. Dad gum. It wasn't 660. It was 330 right on the button. So Daddy says, 'Well, gosh, Bland, I guess we're going to have to load up in the car and go to Breckenridge and get that beer—I don't have any beer with me.' So old Bland gets into the car and they drive to Breckenridge, which is wet, and Daddy buys a cold case of beer. And he and Dad drink that beer on the way back to Avoka. When they get back, Daddy has his lease and Bland says, 'I think I've been had, but it was fun.'"[5]

Bland became an oilman, too; one of the artifacts in the Jones family is a photograph of a well blowing out in what came to be known as the Avoka field.

"Bruce, Will You Sell That Lease?"

But the land story to top them all may be the one that Houston's Bruce Anderson tells about his very first gas well—in Kansas in 1953. "The niche I had worked out for myself at that time was to lease federally owned land. I had someone in every land office—Billings, Montana, which also handled North and South Dakota, Cheyenne, which handled Kansas and Nebraska in addition to Wyoming, and additional offices in Denver and Santa Fe. I also had someone in Silver Springs, Maryland, at the federal land office for the eastern states, where there was very little federal land. I hired people to work exclusively for me. There was no sense hiring someone who had buddies that he might call instead of you. This is where I learned my lesson: don't work with men; work with women. I hired women. You can trust them. Remember, in the late 1980s in the state of Texas, every single major city had a female mayor. This is the only state I've ever heard of like that. Every single town! Down to Corpus Christi. A gal over in San Antonio, a gal in Austin, Dallas, Fort Worth, El Paso, Houston. Because people just feel in their heart that women are more trustworthy. When my gals found a federal lease, they phoned me. They're trustworthy. I didn't have to worry about them tipping off one of their friends instead. In my own mind, I had two categories of leases—ones I had for sale that I had bought in speculation and then there were those I called my Red Star Leases that were not for sale. They were for production. I knew this Kansas lease was a sleeper because it was a unique situation—a federal lease in a state that had almost no federal lands. It was a stray little piece in Morton County, Kansas—Section 8 of 34-42. The government had taken it in somewhere in a bankruptcy and most people didn't realize that the government owned the minerals. My gal in Maryland found it and when she told me, I just automatically leased it. I couldn't lose because almost every county in Kansas produces. You know the adage: 'Stand in the shadow of a derrick and you're in good country.' Though it was really a small piece, 360 acres, I took it. I didn't do any geology; I just leased it and forgot it. It cost fifty cents an acre for a three-year paid-up lease. It was stealing, but that's the law! That's the way the government was run! I look back on it and I say, 'Why didn't I lease America?'"

Less than a year later, Anderson went to lunch in Casper, Wyoming, with Walter Whitlinger, the head landman for Cities Service Oil Company. Anderson mentioned in passing that he had noticed in *Petroleum Information* that Cities Service had drilled a well directly off-setting his Kansas lease. "I said to him, 'Nobody ever called me, but I think that's very sporting of you guys.' So Walter kind of laughed and said, 'Well, Bruce, I don't think Cities Service—you must have something wrong. We don't do that.' I said, 'Well, it's all the same to me. I hope you get a well.' After lunch, he went to his office and right away he's on the phone to me: 'God Almighty! First, tell me, Bruce, will you sell that lease?' And I said, 'Obviously not.' And he said, 'You ought to be over here—the phone is ringing off the hook. We drilled down there. We had the north half of Section 9.'

"The thing was," said Anderson, filling in the rest of the background on this unusual case, "you have to have 640 acres to drill in Kansas. Most states it has to be square. But Kansas is funny: you can have it any shape you want as long as it is a contiguous 640. So Cities Service had pooled their Section 9 with the north half of 8. They had gone to the landowner and gotten a lease, not realizing he had bought it from some bankruptcy thing of the government and the government had held back the minerals. Walter said nobody ever thought to check for federal minerals and the landowner thought he had them.

"So Walter said on the phone, 'Frankly, I'm authorized to tell you— I told them the best approach with you was just to tell it straight out the way it is—we drilled the well to 3,400 feet. We've already run pipe on it; we've already logged it; we've already tested it. It tested 17 million cubic feet a day. You've got us. What do you want to do?'"

Bruce Anderson called his partner in the lease, Maury Machris of Los Angeles, who said, "Theoretically, we don't have to do anything. We can just take half the gas. However, it's only 3,400 feet, and the joint bill can't be much over $15,000–$20,000. Let's just call them up and say we appreciate them drilling a well, we appreciate them telling us about it. Now just bill us for half and there won't be any problems."

"So we did that," recounted Anderson. "The drilling and completion costs were about $18,000. And it is producing today. It has produced over 10 billion cubic feet. Unfortunately, gas was only six or seven cents per thousand in those days. We had a twenty-year contract. We got a much better price in 1973.

"My partner, Maury, had a lot of little sayings," continued Anderson. "One of them was: 'You don't take advantage of another man's mistakes.' You might take advantage of his stupidity, but not his mistakes. This was my second big well. The first one was an oil well in Glenrock, Wyoming, after the war. I knew a lot of people in Casper; we were all friendly, and we drank coffee together. And right after the war, we didn't any of us have any real money at all. Five of us would flip for coffee and whoever lost, it was a financial disaster. But I noticed that some of them really didn't want to be around me anymore after we made the big find in Glenrock. So I turned to Maury for advice and he said, 'Well, Bruce, there are a couple of rules you'd better learn early in life. Your friends want you to do good. They really do. They think the best of everything for you. But they can't stand it if you do too good. The other thing to remember is, you never desert your friends; they desert you. If you remember that, you'll never get upset.'"[6]

The Andersons and Joneses of TIPRO tell land stories that emphasize people while the Forees and Grattons of the new generation talk about imagination coupled with the new technology. Says Gratton: "There are fifteen ways to make money in the oil business—from taking leases, peddling leases, trading them to somebody else, and all of that. But the people who really have the most fun fall into two categories. First of all, the people who drill wells or get wells drilled. But the cream of the crop are the people who are drilling where nobody else will drill, or have never drilled, where you are not near any production. This is rank wildcatting—new-field wildcatting. I can't very easily sell that to my associates who have risk money. But every so often we roll one of those cards into the hand we are dealing—to see if they want to play, you know. And if we can make it enticing enough—big enough—and not do it too often, they will do it."[7]

But still another route oilmen followed in becoming independent producers was through engineering. One of TIPRO's old hands is Abilene's Jim Russell. His introduction to oil country properly begins with his father, an old-time cable tool contractor. "I was born on the derrick floor of a cable tool rig," said Jim. "I made up my mind I was going to be a petroleum engineer because of growing up in the oil patch during the Depression—there weren't too many opportunities." After getting an engineering degree in 1941, and spending three years in the air force, most of it in Europe, he went to work in Conroe for Texaco in 1945 and later signed up with a Tulsa-based independent who focused on waterflood engineering, reservoir studies, and core analysis work.

The desire to go independent is an idea; actually doing it is another matter entirely. It is a juncture that all wildcatters remember in great detail. Though Russell and his wife liked Tulsa and had bought a home there on the GI Bill, by 1949 he felt "it was time to stretch out. I'd always had visions of being on my own even though I was satisfied with my work that I was doing and was learning a lot." So Russell set up shop on his own in Abilene.[8]

The big news in West Central Texas was the newly discovered Kelly-Snyder field. Secondary recovery was then in its infancy, particularly for new fields, but, in Russell's words, "the technology was coming onstream whereby, okay, why wait until you've depleted a field before you start putting water in? But the early days of waterflooding were very helter-skelter. People thought that all you had to do was put water in the ground and the oil would come out. Then they discovered bad water and everything else—you were plugging up your own wells. It took more technology really to be successful because in the early days probably seven out of ten waterfloods were failures because of mismanagement or bad operation. There was very little engineering attached to it. So I was at the right place at the right time. My business grew by leaps and bounds. I began to hire people. We started doing a lot of reservoir studies, and we'd do it for major companies and independents. Then they'd form an operators' committee of all the people involved, and we'd make these studies for the group and make estimates of the reserves and procedures that could be utilized for that particular type of reservoir."[9]

In light of this history of early involvement in secondary recovery, it is no surprise that Jim Russell later on became an articulate voice among the "pros" rather than the "antis" within TIPRO's long-running internal argument over statutory unitization: "Of course, in those early days we had to do it voluntarily, but it was fairly well accepted in the bigger fields—in the Permian Basin, for example. I had a broad base to work with and because of that we were in a position to work with both the independent segment and the major companies. We put in our own laboratory and did a lot of core analysis work for people in competition with the old Core Lab Company. We went into the operating business, too, and started operating wells for people on a contract basis."

How does a small but technologically sophisticated service company get into the exploration end of petroleum production? Much of it had to do with one of the basic iron laws of the oil industry—the presence or absence of adequate capital. Jim Russell is unusually well placed to summarize these dynamics: "We'd done a lot of experimental work with fire floods and CO_2, but we kind of zeroed back into waterflooding because it was the most economical way for small operators to increase recovery rather than going into more exotic types of things like steam injection—thermal methods. We tended to end up doing what most of our customers, independents, needed done."

But then came polymer-augmented waterfloods. By the 1960s, Russell's small band of engineers had established themselves as an experienced and dependable group of independent service specialists. They were approached by Dow Chemical engineers who were pioneering enhanced recovery through chemicals. Says Russell: "They had their minds set that they were going to put in some field demonstration for polymer flooding, so we worked with them on one of the first polymer-augmented waterfloods in the world. With our background in secondary recovery and theirs in chemicals, it was a very good relationship. It was a joint venture—very exciting times—and the experimental project was very successful in developing the equipment and the procedures and how much polymer to put in—a lot of experimental laboratory work to see what the viscosities are and the technicalities that go with it. We were one of the few independents that were really getting involved in it." So this became the route Russell followed to acquire the capital to drill wells on his own. "We expanded in the 1970s and started doing a lot of drilling and exploration on our own."

The paths to exploration, then, were quite varied and often turned on expertise in different specialties. The arguments between geologists and engineers were both structural and never-ending. An independent like Houston's George Mitchell, with a background in both, acknowledges the gap—in fact, he emphasizes it. "Engineers are too conservative. They have to have everything spreadsheet out for them. A geologist may be too optimistic, but you have to be optimistic. I've had Ph.D.'s working for me in geology that couldn't find—they were pessimists—couldn't find oil in a 55,000-barrel tank. You have to have optimism; you just can't let it run away with you. Most engineers really don't think that way. I really think you have to do both; one of the big failures of our universities is they don't train people to do both. I think I was fortunate that I was good at both, able to bridge the gap."[10]

Jim Russell proved the engineering route to becoming an independent was workable, without ground-floor help from geologists in the industry. In the course of time, Russell developed production in Texas, Oklahoma, and Kansas, and it was in Kansas that he got his first introduction into the grimmer side of intraindustry relationships. "One day in western Kansas, we learned we had gotten a ten-cent increase in the price of oil and, boy, we were ecstatic—ten cents was a big raise on three-dollar oil, you know. So we decided we'd stop in Wichita and buy a bottle of whiskey and celebrate. So we did. When we got back to the office the next morning, we were devastated because that morning the pipeline company we were selling our oil to raised the pipeline fee ten cents and wiped us out. So one day you think you've got something, the next day you don't. The market price is not at the calling of producers." Like all independents, Russell is capable of waxing at length on the subject of the obstacles, inside the industry and outside, that confront independents. And, like them, he is also capable of a swift summary: "The public doesn't know these things; even the government doesn't. So we have all of these forces working against us. That sounds like sour grapes, but that's a fact."[11]

"Once They Got Hooked on It, It Was Like Heroin"

Any details that Jim Russell doesn't supply on this front can be rounded out by Neal Anderson. As spelled out in Chapter 6, special marketing by gas pipelines became in the 1980s another cross for independents to bear. At the beginning of the decade when the retail price of gas began to rise, pipelines were desperate to get more production under contract and they began offering producers "take or pay" clauses, which meant, as summarized by Neal Anderson, "'Every month I'll either buy your gas or I'll pay you for your gas that I didn't buy, and then later on I get the right to take it and make it up. But this way, you'll have a certainty of income each month.' It was really wonderful for producers, but then 1986 rolled around and the price of gas went through the floor. At $4 per thousand cubic feet, take-or-pay would have broken every pipeline company in the industry because the retail price was going down. So the pipelines told producers they weren't going to take any more of their $4 gas, 'We can't market it'; and independents said, 'But we have a contract,' and they said, 'To hell with you, sue us.'"

Continuing his summary, Neal Anderson said, "In the meantime, though, because gas was still needed and they still wanted to stay in business, pipelines formed subsidiary companies that created what they called 'special marketing' programs in which they said, 'We have a market and we'll take your gas for $2.75 or $1.50 per mcf,' or whatever. Every single pipeline did this. They all said the same thing: 'You either take this price under this contract with this special marketing program or we're going to cut you off. And if you want to sue us, fine, but we'll tie you up in court for five years and cut off your cash flow.' And they did it. The average small independent, particularly if he owed money to the bank or had overhead he had to meet, had to knuckle under; he had no choice. And so they took it.

"But once you got into the special marketing program, you were almost on a month-to-month contract. This gave rise to what they call the 'spot market,' which is basically where we are now: they'll give us a jingle before the beginning of each month and say, 'Your price this month is $1.25' and you either shut in or sell it at that price. TIPRO got into the deal—there was a hue and cry, the Railroad Commission, and the legislature, too, people wanting to outlaw them, because these special marketing contracts were nothing but a ruse to screw everybody out of their contracts. And it's true, that's what they were. Once the pipelines got hooked on it, it was like heroin—they started having fun. I know companies that created paper subsidiaries with their special marketing contracts and then went on to create yet another company, a third company, another layer so that they could just keep ratcheting down prices paid to producers. Producers who could afford it hung in there and sued the pipelines' brains out, sued them back to the Stone Age."

It was by no means a futile gesture—for the independents who could afford it. Says Neal: "I don't know of a single case where the producer didn't ultimately win his lawsuit. So, basically, it was the little guys who got wiped out. My dad and my brothers and I talked about it, and we were like most other independents who said, 'Hell, we're still making money at $2.75. Let's go along with it.' We were as dumb as everybody else. We didn't think gas would ever go down to $1—but once you gave away your rights, it was too late."

Special marketing was a nightmare for TIPRO because the only independents moving their gas to market were the little producers who had been forced to take the new contracts. In the beginning, stronger independents were screaming for TIPRO to fight to outlaw special marketing, which would have been fatal to smaller producers who—deprived of their cash flow while the test case wound through the courts—would have gone broke. Neal Anderson again: "It was basically a divisive fight between the haves and the have-nots in TIPRO." Predictably, it ended in a compromise because a number of big producers who could legally protect themselves threw in with the small independents. "Guys like Frank Pitts, people like that, said, 'We understand where you're coming from and we'll back you on this deal.' It finally ended up where the majority of the producers, both large and small, kind of settled down and said, 'We've got to do this to try to save the little guy.' But this was after six months of fighting. There was a consensus that was arrived at in TIPRO. I think it was one of their finer hours because people kind of put aside their personal deals and their hatred for the pipelines." Special marketing left an indelible mark, and Neal Anderson spoke for most independents when he said, "To this day, everybody is bitter at the pipelines for what happened."[12]

Stripped of public relations verbiage, the "way of life" in oil country has never possessed the monochromatic quality outsiders have always supposed. Yet amid all the personal surprises and collective disasters that have intermittently afflicted the independent industry, an abiding humor has always been a saving feature. Jim Russell's story of how his father, the cable tool contractor, entered into the world of petroleum illustrates this reality in one of its most oft-repeated forms—namely, tales of how people got into the oil business in the first place: "My dad was plowing corn on his dad's farm, and they were building this wooden derrick over on the next lease across the road. The contractor came over one day and stopped my dad and said, 'Look, one of my tool dressers didn't show up today and I need some help. So the boy (my dad) says, 'Well, we'll have to go up to the barn and talk to my dad.' So they walk up to the barn and my grandfather tells him, 'Well, son, I guess it will be alright if you want to go over and help him out. Go up to the house and have your mom fix you lunch.' Years later, my dad said to me, 'Well, I went over there and I went to work. As far as I know, that team of horses is still in the corn field 'cause I never went back.' Grins Jim Russell, "My dad had some tales, I'll tell you for sure."[13]

Family tradition was also the entering wedge into the oil business for Chester Upham of Mineral Wells. The first member of the Upham oil clan was his grandfather—at the age of fifteen in 1887 in Pennsylvania: "He had a falling out with his brother and felt he was being pushed around, so he just left home." The boy soon found himself cutting lumber in the Pennsylvania forests. "He saw so many of his friends who were drowned in the wintertime riding logs down the rivers that he decided he would go for a safer thing, and he heard about this oil that was being discovered and produced. And I heard from my father many times that when there were three drilling rigs in the world, his father worked on one of them—a cable tool rig. They were always getting stuck and getting tools lost in the hole. Every blacksmith in the area was always coming up with a new fishing tool. By the time a well was finished, there would be a whole pile of these fishing tools.

"My father was born in 1894, and he later would tell me how amazed he was that my grandfather was the person they used to call and say, 'Davie, come on out and check these tools over.' He was the one who recognized the different tools that had been borrowed from different people, and he would sort them out and send them back to where they belonged so the next driller could use them." Chester's grandfather later worked on gas pipelines and on rigs drilling gas wells in West Virginia. He continued moving west and began leasing acreage and drilling wildcats while his son—Chester's father—ended up running the family farm in Vincennes, Indiana. The elder Upham found his way to Ranger during the boom of 1916. "By the time he got here, the Ranger field was bought up and there was no opportunity, but he liked the area between Ranger and Mineral Wells and settled in. He sent word to my father, who was not enjoying farming that much, to come on down and help him."[14]

"They Worked on Halves No Matter How Much the Leakage"

The Upham family's knowledge of gas pipelines and distribution systems proved to be their ticket into Texas petroleum. "They saw that there had been three attempts—fragments of a gas system—in Mineral Wells, which was a resort built on the mineral waters there. And they said, 'Well, they've done it all wrong, and so let's just buy those three companies and build a good system here.' So they built a gas distribution system in Mineral Wells by putting those three together and then drilling shallow wells in different places and serving the city."

Then came the first big wells in the Panhandle gas field. "As is quite often the case when people rush in, people without the ability or knowledge of what might happen were drilling wells, and they would strike gas in much bigger volumes than they thought and have the tools blown out of the hole. Not only fishing problems, but all kinds of problems." Chester's father became very expert at solving those kinds of problems: "Granddad would wheel and deal and buy wells and then tell his son to go fix that well. Some were wells blowing wild. One was eight miles outside Shamrock, Texas, and it was on fire; and another well blowing wild was gauged at 146 million cubic feet of gas per day, one of the largest in the world at that time. It just boggles my mind that with the equipment they had then, they could bring [in] those wells—shut them and cap them—and then make them produceable."

In the 1920s, the Uphams built pipelines to Vernon, later to Wichita Falls, Stamford, Haskell, Iowa City, Olney, Archer City, and eventually to Weatherford and Jacksboro. As an exercise in marketing, it was a seat-of-the-pants operation: "Gas was so cheap they really did not meter it in the wholesale. The deal he would make with these various people who would take gas off of the line was that 'you pipe it and sell it and then whatever you get for it, I get half and you get half.'"

Leakage was so widespread it was just ignored. "They worked on the halves no matter what the value, how much they used, how much the leakage. If a pipeline leaked, well, that was not income, so the person operating the distribution system in the cities did not worry about leakage because all they were worried about was having enough to sell at the end." This may sound strange in the 1990s, but the simple reality was that natural gas was being flared all over Texas and would continue to be flared for years to come. The early days of gas pipelining were, in their own way, as primitive as the early days of oil drilling around Titusville, Pennsylvania, in the mid-nineteenth century.

In his own time, Chester Upham graduated from high school in 1943 and then got a wartime degree in engineering at the University of Texas through a navy program and, following the war, took up station in the Upham Gas Company. The Uphams had their share of difficulties with larger gas pipeline companies and eventually sold out in 1956 shortly before the senior Upham died. (The grandfather had died in 1935.) Since then, Chester Upham has focused on exploration.

The routes into the world of wildcatting, though varied, suggested one undisputed commonality: it appeared to be a male community. But this, too, was considerably less than the whole story—and had been ever since Anthony Lucas and his Georgia bride lived out of a shack the entire time Spindletop was being drilled back in 1901. In comparative terms, a shack can be understood as a step up from the tent that Bruce Anderson's grandmother called home in the early days of wildcatting in California. "My grandfather was, at times, a strange man," recalls Bruce. "When he'd hear about a possible oil boom somewhere, he'd go off maybe four or five months. He had a very spartan way of living, and he thought any woman who had a twenty-dollar gold piece and a good tent never had it so good. He'd leave my grandmother in 110-degree heat in the desert, no water within miles, and a scarlet fever plague running through camp, and leave her with a couple of twenty-dollar gold pieces and a good tent. Grandmother thought it was fine, too; it was just a way of life."[15]

The wives of western oilmen, like those of early ranchers in West Texas, remember the wind, remember it as an enemy, an ever-present, soul-attacking enemy. Jacqueline Anderson reconstructs her early days with Bruce in Casper, Wyoming, in a language that brings to life the experience of thousands, perhaps millions, of western women over the past three generations. "We had regular forty-mile-per-hour winds. This was typical. And they would go up—I mean, we'd call them hurricanes here in Houston if something like that came up, except, of course, they weren't circular. They were just steady, solid winds. In the winter, a blizzard, and after the blizzard you'd have the ground blizzard, which was the wind picking up the snow and whipping it around and piling it up. It wouldn't melt, you see; it was so cold that it would just stay fine snow. It would blow tremendously all the time—cold. Cold! You'd see people walking down the street, you know, at an angle, leaning. Hard winters. Hard winters."[16]

In the male world of wildcatting, something odd—something really out of phase—had to happen to create an opening for a woman to step into an active role in an independent oil company. Catherine Terrell Smith's father was a medical scientist specializing in contagious diseases. He was, it turned out, exceptionally good, and the Terrell Laboratory in North Texas eventually became one of the largest private labs in the world. It became so elaborate, in fact, that it required a business manager; it was the manager who got Catherine's father into the oil business, setting in place the dynamics that got her involved, too.

In the fullness of time, there came—for Catherine Terrell, as for every other independent—a particular deal. The man involved was, she says, "a very nice person, but he was the type of person who—if he said something cost one hundred dollars, multiply it by ten; and if he said you were going to have a hundred-barrel well, divide it by ten. He was enthusiastic, you might say. A salesman type. Well, one day a fight developed in the office, one man threw a typewriter at the other, and suddenly here was this white coat in my office—my father always wore a white coat—with an armful of books of a new corporation they were supposed to be creating, and my father said to me, 'You run this.' I said I didn't know anything about it and he said, 'It is high time you learn.' And I said, 'It will cost you,' and he said, 'I'm willing to pay,' meaning, I think, it would cost him through my mistakes. Anyway, that's how I got into the oil business. Generally, we drill shallow wells and usually go it alone. If we make a mistake, we don't have to answer to anybody. When I started out in West Texas, we had sour crude, which meant a lot of corrosion. In Crockett County, I think we had all the problems in the whole wide world—my early indoctrination covered a multitude of problems."[17]

Catherine Terrell's company was a two-person operation—a geologist and herself. "The geologist was a man about my father's age—a very qualified geologist. I was in the field for years, wanted to see everything that happened. Shooting the early wells with nitroglycerin, I got very near the rig floor and so forth; after seeing how it was done, there's no sense in being closer, just getting in someone's way. I moved back after that."

She joined TIPRO in 1959. "It's very well named—independent oil people are very independent, all different." Echoing a central theme of TIPRO veterans, she said, "It's hard to get a consensus."

"Did We Buy This Coat for You, Irene?"

The saga of Irene Wischer's Panhandle Producing Company is one that encompasses a story of independent versus independent, as well as female entrepreneurs versus their male counterparts. The company itself had its roots in the old Hugoton field of the 1930s in the Texas Panhandle—a time, says Irene, when "you couldn't sell gas." The company came to be based in San Antonio, where Irene worked initially as an executive secretary. She founded the San Antonio Desk and Derrick Club, becoming its first president and, eventually, president of the International Desk and Derrick Club. She was smart and she came to know the oil business. The partners in Panhandle Producing gradually died off and, in the 1960s, Irene Wischer stepped in as CEO. Soon thereafter, she generated the story that since has become part of the folklore of the Texas independent community.

It seems that the sons of one of TIPRO's early presidents, Amarillo's Ollie Herrmann, still had a number of marginal wells in the Panhandle in the early 1970s. In reconstructing the details, Irene Wischer said: "In addition to Panhandle Producing, I had a small workover company named Pinto Well Servicing. Well, Pinto really needed some business. Also at the time, there was a sudden shortage of pipe; a number of independents needed to drill to hold their leases, but couldn't get pipe. So we looked over the Herrmann properties—they had a large number of declining wells. We thought we could go in there, clean up a number of them, fracture a few, various things, generally improve production. My thought was, any well that didn't respond, we'd just shut it in, pull the pipe, and sell it. We paid the Herrmann brothers $650,000 for about 300 wells and went to work. That pipe shortage got very severe. We pulled pipe and sold it for a pretty good price. Real good—enough to pay out the whole investment and then some. Also, we increased production on the remaining wells. The price of crude went up, you know—the Arab oil embargo." All things considered, it was, as they say in the oil business, "a ten-strike of a deal" for Wischer's company. The punch line of her story is this: "I thought a little celebrating was called for. I bought a fur coat, a mink stole, to wear to a meeting of the Panhandle Producers Association because I thought the Herrmann boys would be there. I was right. Dick Herrmann ran his fingers over my new fur coat: 'Did we buy this coat for you, Irene?' I just laughed. I don't remember acknowledging to him that he had. He laughed, too. He wasn't bitter."[18]

The slices of life in the oil patch made visible by men like Bruce Anderson, Jim Russell, Chester Upham, and Jon Rex Jones—and by women like Catherine Terrell Smith and Irene Wischer—all have a successful ring about them. But so is the litany of failure—such as the nineteen consecutive dry holes that Bob Foree of Dallas once drilled. Or the dramatic ups and downs of one of TIPRO's most celebrated wildcatters, Netum Steed of Wichita Falls, who had some substantial strikes and agonizing failures before hitting it big on the famous 6666 Ranch in the 1960s. Or, more poignantly, the one "dry hole" that Lester Clark drilled in the 1940s in Stonewall County that was to haunt him the rest of his life. "It was a deep well that I had sold interest in to a lot of people," recalls Clark. "Big core structure. We drilled right through the pay and lost circulation—but in those days you didn't have the mud you do now. We put cottonseed oil in it, plugged it as a dry hole. It was in the middle of what later became a big oil field—maybe a hundred wells in it— but I missed it. When I really needed it, I missed it. That's right. But there were other geologists from other companies that had an interest in acreage around the well and all of them missed it. We brought in the Schlumberger Company to run a log—that was the first log I had ever seen—and everybody on that machine spoke French. We ran the log and still weren't able to see it. I think it was 1941. The logs weren't sophisticated like they are now. I never did go back into it. Somebody else got the whole field, and it is still producing. The Flowers field in Stonewall County."[19]

There were no missed plays in Bob Foree's nineteen straight dry holes: they were all routinely and prosaically dry. Foree's entrance into the oil fields came as a teenager when he got a job as a pumper on a producing lease—keeping the pumps running and gauging the oil produced.

He was nineteen. He saved his money and got a toehold in the oil rental tool business. He worked himself up to the point where he traveled around buying used oil field equipment and transporting it to new plays where demand might be high. Gradually, Foree became a modest entrepreneur, a drilling contractor owning three tiny oil supply stores in remote towns.

"Old Moncrief Wouldn't Let Anybody See That Core"

And then—as for so many Texans—came the East Texas field. Of the three big strikes that defined the field—Dad Joiner in the south, the Bateman well in the middle, and the huge Moncrief strike in the north—Bob Foree was the drilling contractor on the Moncrief well. In the Foree family lore, passed on by his son, Bob Foree Jr., "everybody was spreading the risk, of course, and Dad struck a deal to drill the well for Moncrief—some cash and also a good deal of offset acreage. When they cored the pay sand, old Moncrief didn't want to let anybody, including my father, see the core. Eventually, of course, they completed the well and it came in at 10,000 barrels a day. But Moncrief wouldn't give my dad the assignment for the offset acreage! While that well was producing, Dad camped in Moncrief's office day after day until he got it. Dad's wells were also 10,000-barrel producers, though no one wanted to take that much oil. But of course that's all part of the East Texas story—for Dad, Moncrief, Bateman, Joiner, and everybody else. It was a great struggle." The Foree family contribution to the folklore of the famous field comes from Della Foree, Bob's wife, who remembers that one of the Joiner women missed the big day because drilling the plug took second place in her priorities to going to church. As Della Foree puts it, most everybody in Rusk County was present, but the Joiner woman didn't come to the well on the big day. At the time, it was the most important oil discovery in history—"but she missed it."[20]

The East Texas field, with its massive and organized campaign of waterflooding, brought technology deep into the consciousness of Texas independents—whether or not they uniformly possessed the scientific skills to apply it. As in the case of Russell, Anderson, Foree, and many others, the sons of oilmen were encouraged to go into petroleum engineering and geology as the soundest way to buttress the family enterprise. These developments changed the way the next generation talked about prospecting for oil and gas. This is not to say that this sea change altered the disagreements among independents about what the essence of wildcatting entailed. Rather, the diversity of perspectives simply became more elaborate.

As Pat Gratton puts it, the sons of wildcatters "took degrees in geology or petroleum engineering or petroleum land management or geophysics or business degrees with a focus on natural resource development. So it has become a lot more technical. That is just the name of the game. It is appropriate that it is that way."[21]

There is a connecting link, then, between Patillo Higgins and Dad Joiner on the one hand and the wildcatters of today—intuition in the discovery years and intuition plus technology in the modern era. But as a mode of entry into being an independent operator, a majority of Texas independents more or less followed the basic trajectory that George Mitchell did. "We didn't have our own capital at first. We stayed afloat by consulting. We would put together a small deal and sell it in the Esperson Drug Store—the drug store in the Esperson Building in downtown Houston. We'd try to clear out a one-sixteenth for ourselves. Then later an eighth and then a fourth—working toward the day when we could have some good acreage and prove part of it up with a small override for ourselves and then, when proven, drill on our remaining acreage straight up."[22]

With small variations, this is the way oil people—whether landmen, engineers, geologists, or service specialists—worked their way into being producers. But it would be a mistake to portray the road to wildcatting solely in terms of romance when so much that is ordinary is also a factor. There are some very sober, mundane, and bureaucratic aspects to modern petroleum—and one of them certain to crop up in conversations with independents deals with the legal side of petroleum.

Jerry O'Brien's education on the subject came at an early age when he was working for a small independent company in California, the Sunset Oil Company. "We were operating a joint well with George Getty, J. Paul's dad, the old man." One of Sunset's young engineers fresh out of college noticed that a joint well the company had with Getty had been operating for seven or eight years without a written agreement. "'Oh, can't do that,' he said." Jerry O'Brien continued: "So a thirty-two-page operating agreement was drafted for Mr. Getty to sign. My job was to take it uptown to him, which I did. I got into his office and explained I was from Sunset and we felt we should have an operating agreement. 'I have brought it up here for you to look at and, if you approve, well, to sign.' I handed it to him and he glanced at its thickness, sort of mentally counting the pages, and said, 'Where do I sign?' And, I, of course, said, 'Mr. Getty, aren't you going to read it?' And he took his glasses off and looked at me kindly and said, 'Son, let me tell you something. Anything this thick has contradicted itself half a dozen times and I can break it half a dozen times. Where the hell do I sign it?'"[23]

George Getty may have had the legal battalions necessary to support such a cavalier approach, but few independents do. Tediously long lease contracts can become a nightmare for small producers, as Neal Anderson can attest. "It's not unusual to see a thirty-five-page lease and you need a lawyer to read the damn thing because, unfortunately, lawyers wrote them. Little clauses can just kill you. We took a lease on a big ranch—one of the legendary families here in Texas. And we took their thirty-five-page lease which they had some high-powered law firm write. I read through it as carefully as I could and decided, with a few minor changes, that we could live with it. We drilled. Well, one clause that seemed innocuous at the time said 'You'll caliche and maintain any roads that you use.' Sounded reasonable. All of a sudden, they came back and said, 'By the way, that road you drove in on—that three-mile road—we need you to caliche it, since you're using it, and fix it up because there are some low spots.' We ended up spending $40,000 just on road work. In their defense—they're wonderful people—that ranch we were drilling on is their little showpiece. They want it kept beautiful and if an oil company is going to come in there, then they're going to maintain the thing and keep it nice. But those little bitty clauses in leases can really jump up and bite you."[24]

Such stories serve to illustrate the diverse ways in which independents understand their calling and the nature of the specialties that are concealed within the phrase "independent producer." The fact helps explain why TIPRO has always contained such an enormous range of individual strategies for survival and why, too, prominent Texas independents played very different roles when they rose to TIPRO's presidency.

But to explore these roles first requires a measure of background. The half-century story of Texas producers traced in these pages necessarily has centered on political contentions at the very top of national decision-making—at the presidential and congressional level. But any such focus on high politics is seriously incomplete because it passes over the multiple occasions when the people of TIPRO jostled with one another in trying to fashion a workable approach for themselves as independents out to survive in a world of global marketing.

There is a temptation to use the phrase "behind the scenes" to describe this other realm where, for fifty years now, the independents of TIPRO have met, compared notes, and planned their strategies, all in the name of deciding what to do next. The phrase "behind the scenes" has the merit of opening up to view the enormous variety of people who embodied inside TIPRO the mind-bending diversity that has historically always been the essence of the independent producing sector of the American petroleum industry. Nevertheless, the phrase is misleading because it does not do justice to the genuine risks independents took in first creating and then standing by policies that irritated and even infuriated a number of very large players in international energy. Whether in Austin or in Washington, there was nothing "behind the scenes" when TIPRO went public: TIPRO's producer-oriented stands were all very much out in the open and visible for all to see.

Thus, to make the decision to be a TIPRO spokesman, an independent operator had to weigh the responsibilities and risks of not only a public profile that was starkly visible but also a stance that was to some extent personally vulnerable within the petroleum industry. For this reason, to pass over high politics, and its emphasis on results, long enough to see the creative process at work inside TIPRO's own councils is to enter a very personal and emotional realm that lay at the very heart of the independents' struggle for autonomy. In entering this intimate space the first thing that needs to be acknowledged, therefore, is that "TIPRO activism" was not in any way a given. No one was born to it; it was territory that was occupied only through personal struggle of a kind outsiders could not see.

The point merits a measure of detailed emphasis. As has been the case in many other areas of American life, the producing sector of the petroleum industry has always housed within its ranks a certain number of prominent representatives who simply could not find a way to take a public position in opposition to powerful and highly sanctioned forces within their own occupational milieu. When serious conflicts arose between independents and majors, there were always a number of compelling reasons some small producers could mobilize to convince themselves of the merit of remaining silent. The recurring problem was how to take a national issue framed essentially by the major companies and refocus people's attention on the underlying issues that were critical to the survival of independents. Over the past half-century, there have been many occasions when TIPRO was forced to try to address this problem directly—through educating both the general public and the political community of Austin and Washington by spelling out the specific inequities within oil and gas production.

But whether the subject was ratable take, special marketing, other forms of price and pipeline discrimination in the field, or larger political questions that pertained to international trade or to the U.S. tax code, the task TIPRO faced proved to be inherently daunting in two fundamental areas bearing on the nation's political discourse: first, the issues themselves turned on intricate power relations between sectors of petroleum production and marketing that were not popularly understood and, second, the task was made even more arduous because TIPRO's proposed remedies often seemed at first glance to contradict popular assumptions about how the domestic and global economies were believed to function. TIPRO's task was to penetrate the maze of political and economic sloganeering and the sheer popular mythology that surrounded such issues and make the real nature of the political dispute simple enough for the general public to understand.

Compounding this problem is the basic contradiction embedded in the two words "organized independents." In TIPRO, the operative question always was whether diverse and self-consciously independent people could find a way to put aside their personal and political idiosyncrasies long enough to work in prolonged and intimate association with one another. Outside visitors—particularly those from Washington—who attended TIPRO conventions were invariably struck by the immense diversity of views they encountered among rank-and-file TIPRO members.

"Anarchists Unite!"

By way of illustration, there is the tale of bafflement told by a visiting Washington bureaucrat who was a minor functionary in a division of a federal regulatory agency that focused on coal. He was fairly well informed about certain aspects of national energy policy, but was relatively unfamiliar with the oil industry and particularly the independent segment. It seems that within a single hour of conversation at a TIPRO convention, the visitor was treated to three separate critiques of the incumbent Washington administration of which he was a part. While all three critiques were vigorously articulated, they were also organically contradictory: the first flowed from the belief that the administration was too hidebound and conservative, the second that it was too activist and socialist-leaning, and the third that the administration was essentially irrelevant because it was mired in a proven inability to act at all. Somewhat dazed, the visitor felt it appropriate to mention an old Washington joke and suggested it could be applied to Texas independents. What TIPRO needed to do, he said, was get itself a campaign button directed at its own membership. The button should read, he said with a wan smile, "Anarchists Unite!" He quickly added, "I have no idea how TIPRO can mobilize its membership behind the kind of clear-cut stands it so often takes in Washington. I really have no idea how they manage to do that."[25]

Through a half-century of advocacy, the answer is, of course, "not easily." But the fog can be lifted somewhat if TIPRO's presidents are broken down into categories defined by the different skills they brought to the job—as public spokesmen and tacticians, as recruiters, as mobilizers, and as coordinators on certain key issues that over time came to the forefront of the industry.

The association generated a number of widely admired public spokesmen—Robert Foree, John Hurd, Frank Pitts, George Mitchell, and Bruce Anderson, among others. In the immediate postwar period and for three decades thereafter, Foree played a seminal role in TIPRO. He had two qualities—a talent for calm, clear advocacy and great patience. In both Austin and Washington, Foree took the political scene as it was, rather than as he wanted it to be, and endeavored to deal with the reality that independents were routinely outgunned when it came to global oil policies. His aim was to formulate a strategic approach that might offer independents a chance to be relevant players no matter which party was in office.[26]

To Foree's admirers, he was a man of enormous persistence. His detractors regarded the same trait as a matter of stubbornness. Both agreed he took on TIPRO's early swashbucklers and that he played a major role in altering TIPRO's political posture as an association of independents. Pitts, who watched this struggle firsthand, singled out TIPRO's founding executive vice-president, Tommy Thompson, as the style-setter among the founders. "There was only one way to do it and that was the way Tommy wanted to do it. He was the toughest-talking one: 'It's got to be this way.' But Bob Foree could handle him, and some of the others could. It might take them much longer than it should. It was kind of an art for them to do it. Foree carried the day because he was a very smart fellow."[27]

John Hurd had a similar memory of the founders—as men "not noted for their ability to compromise." Most of the founders came and went with comparative speed: in length of sophisticated service in behalf of independents, few in Texas besides Foree could match the record of John Hurd. A tall, handsome westerner, Hurd became active in TIPRO in the 1950s, assumed the presidency in 1960 at the very beginning of the oil import crisis, and continued playing a crucial role over the ensuing thirty-five years down to the present. In his own personal economy, he has lived through the rise to prominence of natural gas production. As late as the 1970s, some 70 percent of his production was in oil. "It's about 90 percent gas now."[28]

Hurd's special gift to TIPRO was his ability to shepherd politically diverse—and politically argumentative—executive board members into a workable team on complicated issues. It was an art that seemed all the more remarkable considering the fact that, in the larger Texas society, Hurd was an early mover and shaker in the fledgling Texas Republican Party during the days when the GOP was languishing in the Texas wilderness. Though it was a stance that might easily have caused problems with some of the old-line Rayburn-style Democrats in TIPRO ranks, it never did—largely because Hurd carefully orchestrated TIPRO's positions in terms of the needs of independents, keeping his TIPRO work separate from his political work. As Earl Turner once privately confided, "TIPRO is blessed by the fact that John Hurd is not the kind of person who feels an irresistible need to make long speeches to impart moral instruction to his fellow man. He has great patience and an understated sense of humor that helps get all of us through some tight spots."[29] Over the years Hurd acquired admirers from all parts of the TIPRO political spectrum, and his style gradually became a model for a number of subsequent TIPRO presidents. Though now in his eighties, his contributions and his prestige among independents continue at a high level.

Frank Pitts, who once characterized Bob Foree as a "stalwart," came to have precisely the same standing himself within the producer community. In the early days of Foree's influence, TIPRO was, said Pitts, "very aggressive in the national picture. I thought it was the one organization I could go to where I could listen to the discussions and become much better acquainted with the problems and what the solutions were."

Indeed, so impressed were executive board members with the intellectual powers of Pitts that Bill Rutter, for one, found it hard to believe that Pitts claimed to have learned about intraindustry politics in the Foree school. "I don't think Frank Pitts takes a back seat to anyone when it comes to brains," says Rutter.[30] But what especially marked Frank Pitts—in the years before he assumed TIPRO's helm as well as during his tenure as president—was not only his creativity in articulating the cause of independent producers, but also his unrivaled energy. His leadership on natural gas, spelled out in some detail in Chapter 5, set a national standard for independents.

As chronicled in Chapter 5, George Mitchell played a leading role in crafting a tactical course of action for independents in their defense of depletion in the 1970s. Together with Pitts and Anderson, Mitchell provided TIPRO with some hands-on advocacy throughout that complex and ultimately successful struggle. And, of course, his career in building Mitchell Energy into one of the premier independent enterprises in oil country has a legendary quality about it.

Bruce Anderson's path to leadership in TIPRO is somewhat distinctive in that he cut his teeth as a producer advocate not in Texas but in the Rocky Mountain Oil and Gas Association. After he moved his base from Casper, Wyoming, to Denver in the mid-1950s, Anderson became state treasurer of the Colorado Democratic Party. "Some of my oil friends looked upon me as virtually a bomb-carrying Communist, because being a member of the Democratic Party was, to them, unthinkable. On the other hand, when Jack Kennedy was elected president, they didn't hesitate to say, 'Bruce, you go back and talk to Jack.' And I could, too, because a good friend of mind from Green River, Wyoming, was the liaison man in the White House. But after the assassination, I did not have the same intimacy with the Johnson administration."

A TIPRO member since moving to Houston in the 1960s, Bruce Anderson became especially active in the natural gas controversies of the 1980s, during which time he moved into the association's top position. In the divisive fight over special marketing, he was one of those who, like Frank Pitts, tried to keep the membership's policies in harmony with the most pressing needs of its least affluent members. As Anderson puts it, "One of the enduring philosophies of our company has always been to remember who you are. We're little bitty guys. We don't try to play with the big boys. The oil business is very similar to playing poker. I don't care if you've got four kings in your hand, you don't take everything you've got and shove it out in the middle of the table. The guys who go under are the guys who do that. Our unwritten rule—and we live by it religiously—is, don't do any single deal that will put you out of business if it goes bad. TIPRO occupies a very special place in Texas because it is the last holdout, in my estimation, of the independent."[31]

Gradually over time, TIPRO developed an attitude toward its own internal diversity—namely, that it wasn't a bad thing. No one has summarized the matter more succinctly than Midland's Malcolm Abel. "Disagreement is what makes the oil industry go round. If all geologists agreed upon the geology, you would never find anything. It takes a difference of opinion to find oil and gas."[32] With this outlook, Abel, along with independents such as Johnny Mitchell of Houston, Shelby Pitts of Dallas, and John Watson of Houston, brought to the TIPRO presidency a capacity to recruit membership. Abel became president in the early 1960s, after the plays along the Canyon Reef and the Spraberry Trend had brought the Permian Basin to prominence. Area pricing controversies helped energize new Permian Basin producers, and Abel tried to ensure that many of them followed his path into TIPRO's ranks. As a result, the association became measurably more technology-friendly.

Houston's colorful Johnny Mitchell brought an earthy vibrancy to the TIPRO helm in 1962, one that generated substantial new membership. An engaging extrovert, Mitchell beat the bushes throughout the state in quest of new members. It was a focus that Shelby Pitts raised to a new level of visibility in the 1970s by transforming the structure of membership dues and, eventually, creating the Explorer's Club.

Actually, when Shelby Pitts first became membership chairman in 1976, it is not accurate to say he "transformed" the structure—because there was none. "There was no set schedule of dues," Shelby recalled.

"We had one member who was getting four copies of the *TIPRO Reporter* for four people in his organization, and he was paying $30 a year. I didn't think we could get any work done going that route. So I got TIPRO's approval of a minimum membership of $50. Well, it was a case of one step forward, two steps back. People who had been giving more than $50 cut back to $50. I knew that unless something was done, my tenure as membership chairman was flopping. So that's where the Explorer's concept started."[33]

"When We Get to Ninety-Nine, I Won't Need You"

The concept was to create a group of deadly serious independents, producers willing to give TIPRO some genuine heft. The admission ticket was $1,500 per year for one hundred members. "I started by signing up ex-presidents. It wasn't all that easy. One told me, 'Shelby, when you get ninety-nine, I'll be the hundredth member.' I told him, 'When I get ninety-nine, I won't need you.' So I kept him informed of how I was doing. Every time I saw him I would tell him: 'I'm at thirty-seven . . . I'm at seventy-one.' When I got to ninety-nine, I called him and told him to get his checkbook out. 'We have arrived.'"

But this puts the story, and Shelby Pitts's contribution, much too swiftly. Actually, the road to one hundred members was a long climb. "I had gotten forty-two and from then on it seemed like I'd gotten a chicken bone in my throat. I just couldn't move it. My brother [Frank Pitts] suggested we cut it off at fifty. But I said no. We wanted to add staff and do things that TIPRO should be doing and make it a real viable, energetic, aggressive organization even beyond where we were, and that meant we needed money. We scraped the bottom of the barrel. It was a lonely journey trying to get someone to commit to $1,500 a year—and not only $1,500 that year but every year." The advent of the TIPRO Explorers altered the long-term structure of advocacy for Texas independents by underwriting improved research and informational services for producers and for the general public, including legislative bodies. Shelby Pitts played a central role in this development.

Houston's John Watson brought to the TIPRO presidency two ambitious tasks, both grounded in what might be called a populist vision of internal democracy. While he found TIPRO to be just as freewheeling as he and everyone else believed it to be, Watson did not feel it was necessarily as internally democratic as it needed to be. Watson's vision was an association whose policymaking at all times needed to be driven by the membership. Toward this end, he set for himself two ambitious tasks: to educate the membership on what they had to do in order to effectively guide association policy, and to add new members oriented to the same goal. "I just thought that, on occasions, too many policy decisions were being made by staffers instead of members." Watson formed a blue-ribbon task force, the TIPRO 2000 Committee, and appointed D. F. Jack McKeithan of Milwaukee to be chairman. Additionally, he induced Tom Coffman, John Hurd, Rusty Howell, and John Bennett to help "get more TIPRO members involved in the leadership role."[34]

Watson thus endeavored to address an almost intractable problem that has baffled democratic theorists and organizational theorists for ages—how to make an organization, any organization, functionally democratic on a day-to-day basis. Democracy is much easier to talk about at the level of high abstraction than it is to implement on a long-term basis. Watson's efforts had the effect of guarding against complacency within TIPRO's ranks, but he would be among the first to say that the problem is not solved.

John Watson was another TIPRO veteran who regarded Bob Foree as his mentor. And it showed in the way Watson proceeded to get TIPRO involved in the Clean Air Texas campaign launched by the commissioner of the General Land Office, Garry Mauro. The campaign was an effort to rally a coalition to support legislation mandating the use of cleaner alternative fuels in transportation. The group focused initially on converting buses and vehicles in state, county, and city fleets, including school districts that had fifty or more buses, to fuels other than gasoline or diesel. "A lot of them converted to compressed natural gas. The City of Houston converted to liquefied natural gas. There is no question in my mind that the compressed natural gas market is going to grow significantly in this country. However, the big—the really big—potential for natural gas is still electric generation."[35]

Closely akin to the recruiters were a group of TIPRO spokesmen who could more accurately be described as coordinators and mobilizers. Among the earliest members of this breed was Lester Clark who, as recounted elsewhere in these pages, pioneered the creation of the Liaison Committee of Cooperating Oil and Gas Associations in the

1950s. Dallas's Tom Medders followed up on Clark's initiatives and helped fashion the Liaison Committee into a more cohesive force. Gene Wright of Tyler was another TIPRO activist who spent a great deal of time and energy coordinating joint TIPRO-IPAA and Liaison Committee efforts on the gas decontrol issue during his tenure as TIPRO president in the early 1980s. Wright pushed this initiative with zeal because, as he put it, "I really had a lot of trouble with IPAA because their tax committee was against an import fee." Even before becoming TIPRO president in 1982, Wright had served effectively as chairman of TIPRO's task force on oil field theft, shepherding into being a cooperative effort with the Texas Rangers and the FBI that brought serious field problems under control through successful sting operations. "It was very effective," says Wright, adding with justifiable pride, "and they still are effective."[36]

Searching for the High Road

Jim Russell played a pivotal early role in shepherding TIPRO into two new areas—first in environmental cleanup, naming and then aggressively supporting the energetic Jon Rex Jones as TIPRO's first chairman of the Environmental Committee, and also mobilizing independents on the broader issues of technology. Following Russell's tenure (detailed in the preceding chapter), Austin's Tom Coffman became without question TIPRO's most dedicated spokesmen for technological initiatives, winning the admiration of Hurd, Russell, Pitts, Upham, Anderson, and many others of the older generation for his efforts in the early 1990s to set independents on a new course: thinking and—the more difficult task—acting in terms of heterogeneous reservoirs rather than homogeneous reservoirs.[37]

Jon Rex Jones also became an early advocate on both the technology and environmental fronts. He sees TIPRO in the 1990s as "more proactive than in the past, looking for the next problem before it gets on top of us." As an oilman, Jon Rex takes on the environmental challenge frontally: "The issue is, how are we going to operate as producers with the environmental movement and do it and stay alive and allow them to do what needs to be done to this whole earth—and that is protect it? I have been so proud of TIPRO because they have not come out and said, 'Okay, you environmentalists are a bunch of crazies.' They have not always been crazy and, in fact, they have been right. All you have to do when you are driving around old Breckenridge outside of town is see all the salt-water-damaged areas done by the deposition of salt water on the surface as opposed to disposing of it properly. I am not pointing fingers because our company was a part of the old way of doing things. But TIPRO encourages its members to be a part of this cleanup effort. I have received strong support as environmental chairman and I really was pleased about that. I don't think that the old guard would have put up with that much of a progressive attitude, but we have to do it right. This earth cannot afford to haul off our trash any longer. And the quicker we business people realize that, the better off we are going to be as an industry and as a nation."[38]

Issues aside, Jones also tells an oil-finding story that fits snugly into the industry's folklore. For Jon Rex, the drill-stem test on the South Green Ranch back around 1959 began the best day he ever had in the oil business. "It was at night on Easter Eve and my brother didn't want to open a test at night—too dangerous. He said, 'Let's just go out there on Easter morning and have sunrise service right there on the grounds.' We called the landowner and he joined us the next morning about 6 A.M. It was already light, but the sun was not up. And then it peeked over the horizon, right up over the rig. Now, we're sort of religious folks, so this meant something to us. When that sun first peeked on Easter morning, my brother makes a big gesture, making a production of giving the signal to open the test. Well, that well gassed to the surface in three minutes and flowed in seven—oil to the surface. There we were on an Easter morning with that sun not up—it wasn't all the way off the horizon—with that oil flowing right there. It was something alright. That well just recently quit producing—over thirty years and something like 400,000 barrels. For us it was a big-time well. It was a gift of God."[39]

After all the stories,—whether nostalgic, realistic, or whimsical—the saga of the independent producer properly ends where it began: with the art of the deal. Bruce Anderson's description captures much of the essence of the process as it surfaced in dozens of the interviews comprising the TIPRO Archives. "When it comes to exploration, you deal with people you know well. I'll call somebody I know well and say, 'I'm going to drill a well. If you want a quarter of it, you can have it.' He asks, 'Highly promoted?' And I say, 'No, it's ground floor—you know about it, that's it.' And he says, 'Fine.' And that's the end of the deal. He doesn't even ask me what county. Now, by the same token, if he calls me up and says, 'There's one I think is going to be pretty good and I'd like to have you in it, Bruce. I'm going to drill down in the Rio Grande Valley and it's going to be a 6,000-foot well.' I'll say, 'Fine. If you want me to take a quarter, I'll take a quarter.' We just know each other well, and I know he wouldn't lead me wrong. There's a lot of business being done that way now because you need to have partners. You need to spread yourself out."[40]

Though Bruce Anderson was talking specifically about the art of the deal in drilling, his final sentence also serves as a summation of TIPRO's first half-century as the unrivaled voice of Texas independents. Simply stated, TIPRO provided the organizational means for individuals to "spread out" in an effort to survive in a global market.

As such, the independent's association provides an intricate and revealing insight into the long-term dynamics of a modern industrial economy, one that is highly stratified and increasingly centralized. Indeed, the TIPRO story is an institutional one that has few counterparts in American history. For fifty years, everything TIPRO has done or tried to do has revolved around the same central message: the only way small-scale enterprise can hope to survive in a global market is through constant innovation and adaptation. Admittedly, these bedrock requirements are demanding. But they are precisely the dynamics that have always governed the world of the wildcatter.

EPILOGUE

TIPRO's journey has been a half-century voyage of discovery, a quest for democratic space that has necessarily proceeded in an American political system that sits atop a complex economy. In the nature of voyages, the pattern that materialized was sequential: an almost imperceptible launching, from Spindletop to Daisy Bradford, of a subculture of exploration that over time became a way of life. The world of the wildcatter was fashioned through experimentation and polished through a regional oil-finding experience unmatched elsewhere on the continent. Through a series of events that were constantly edged with surprise and change, producers gradually learned that the independent craft they had created were destined, like well-built but tiny canoes, to bob in a perilous sea prowled by ocean liners. Wherever oceans of oil existed, there were independents and there were major companies.

The maritime metaphor is appropriate. For the people who built the little one-man craft, life was dangerous out there on the high seas. It was not only that a lonely sailor could easily be run over and sunk without a trace, even a passing ship could create waves big enough to capsize the unwary. Moreover, protection could not be achieved simply by sailing out of harm's way—for the big ships had many scouts trained for long-distance reconnaissance to help them clog all the well-traveled routes. But, as it happened, the great liners were also very clumsy and they tended to be captained by overconfident skippers. Though all the people in all the boats thought of themselves as dedicated explorers, most of the significant discoveries were made by the adventurous rowers in small canoes. They were really very good at what they did and their numbers grew. In Texas, independent producers became an enduring species.

They experienced a kind of life that was not easy to explain to the vast majority of Americans who made their living in other ways. The men in canoes came to know more about the great ships and how they operated than anyone else, but this knowledge did not help them explain themselves to the rest of the country. For one thing, viewed casually and from a distance, all the seagoing craft seemed to look alike: people were constantly mistaking the hardy rowers for the great ships. This did not help matters at all, for the realm of global petroleum did not have a level playing surface. So the adventurous little craftsmen got together and decided to create their own port in the storm: they named it TIPRO. From the day producers created their own voluntary group, their association embodied a most complicated idea: independents would get together so they could continue to sail alone.

With TIPRO's founding in 1946, the maritime metaphor can be dispensed with. This is so because the collective space independent oilmen created turned out not to be a "port," but rather a schoolroom of self-education. When independents shared with each other their experiences and their insights, they were helping over time to fashion something more than producer policy; they were creating, inside TIPRO itself, an institutional tradition of assertion. In the introduction of this book, an early TIPRO president is quoted recalling his early days as a fledgling member when he "learned how things really worked in Washington, and in Austin, too." Though "sobering," it was also, he said, "real. Very real."

Indeed it was. Inside TIPRO, the world of politics and commerce opened up exponentially, and new and instructive lessons came with great speed. In becoming the most assertive voice of the independent producing industry in America, TIPRO accepted a new kind of exploratory challenge—to craft an approach aimed at maintaining for its participants something very organic to the American idea: a measure of individual autonomy in a centralizing world. In pursuing this end, TIPRO became something more than a schoolroom; it became a high-

powered seminar on the economy, on politics, and on the specific contours of American democratic procedures. Two questions immediately
became clear: how could producers deal effectively with power and how
could they deal with each other?

In the Eisenhower years of TIPRO's first decade, independents were
forced into the tangled Washington world of natural gas legislation and
the Middle Eastern import question. In these early days, it seemed to
independents that they faced two obstacles—big oil and big government. Given the fact that most independents were equally worried
about monopoly on the one hand and socialism on the other, their two
adversaries pulled producers in precisely opposite directions. The one
person in Washington TIPRO's founders felt most at home with was
Congressman Wright Patman of Texas, chairman of the Small Business
Committee and one of the nation's most highly visible antimonopolists.
But while Patman talked TIPRO's language, he was also a liberal
Democrat. This fact reminded independents that the one man in
Washington in the 1930s who thought he could run the world of oil—
even better than major oil companies thought they could run it—was
one of Patman's fellow liberals, none other than Franklin Roosevelt's
interior secretary, Harold Ickes. To the struggling independents trying to
keep a toehold in the vast woodbine sands of the East Texas field, no
one in America personified the perils of Big Brother more dramatically
than Harold Ickes. For producers, it was transparently self-evident that
the good secretary did not at any time in the 1930s have a clear grasp of
what forces were actually at work in the giant field of East Texas. The
clearest outcome was that major oil companies loved what Harold Ickes
was doing in East Texas. But if liberals like Ickes seemed a problem, a
good number of conservatives who made stump speeches against "socialism" were also seen to march in faithful legislative lockstep with the
major oil companies. The long, doomed struggles of independents in the
1950s over the Harris bills and import quotas taught independents this
second unwanted truth. There were so many contradictions suffusing
the world of American independent producers that there was no sanctioned political ideology that could see them through the diverse kinds
of crises that their embattled position in the global market imposed
upon them.

In response to this hard lesson, TIPRO forged in the 1950s, slowly
and with increasing subtlety, an entirely new approach for the nation's

independent producing industry. The slogans of the early founders, and the swashbuckling style they exhibited, were laid aside and replaced with an extremely broad-gauged approach to politics. Though Dallas's Bob Foree was the most visible symbol of this maturing style, TIPRO's executive committee—with its impressive range of committed Republicans and committed Democrats—gave enduring life to the "producer first" policy that replaced the "industry unity" trajectory of the early years.

The farther down this road independents traveled, the more apparent to everyone that TIPRO was "out front." The tensions that developed with the Independent Petroleum Association of America were mediated through a new national institutional structure pioneered by TIPRO, the Liaison Committee of Cooperating Oil and Gas Associations. But of even greater long-term significance was the increasing crisis of the nation's entire producing sector. What TIPRO called "the private depression of the American independent producing industry" cast a pall over the 1950s and 1960s that few outsiders understood or, indeed, tried to understand. Through it all, TIPRO's long-maturing institutional momentum carried producers nearer and nearer to the seats of power where politics happened—and nearer to technological sophistication where the future lurked. The latest chapters of the producer story concern both of these destinations.

Over this half-century of effort, TIPRO discovered, and taught the rest of the nation's producers to discover, how the very existence of independents was used by the major companies not only as a shield on taxes, but as a mechanism through which they could pursue their own ends. The FPC's use of the Phillips decision to place independents under utility regulation became the buffer behind which the industry's giants plied their own politics of decontrol; and the elaborate masquerade of the voluntary and mandatory imports programs taught independents the ways of big oil under Republicans Eisenhower, Nixon, Reagan, and Bush and under Democrats Kennedy, Johnson, Carter, and Clinton. Similarly, in Texas, the ability of the integrated long-line gas transmission companies to keep independents as the focus of all tax legislation took the form of elaborate and successful maneuvering to render gas pipeline taxes unconstitutional. The culmination of this general political trajectory was the generations-long use of independents as justification for retention of the oil depletion allowance for segments of the industry whose basic profit margins did not turn on finding new oil reserves.

The fruit of all the lessons, and of fifty years of TIPRO efforts that were grounded in these lessons, was the successful struggle of independents to retain the depletion allowance in the 1970s at the very moment it was passing into history as a balm for the major companies. The remarkably broad-based coalition of Democrats and Republicans who were persuaded to stand with independent producers on this issue became the ultimate historical justification of TIPRO's well-honed—and often lonely—brand of autonomous assertion for independents.

Indeed, even in the protracted intramural debate among independents over statutory unitization, the enduring reason for the continuing depth of opposition among producers had to do with their interpretation of the power of major companies in unitized fields. As one old hand once put it to this author, "Independents historically have not trusted the very concept of units because they're usually run by major companies and they have big overheads and they'll charge you too much in administrative costs for the privilege of participating in the unit. And they'll manipulate the formula to their own advantage because they've got in-house engineers and geologists fully capable of doing that. Though independents really need mandatory unitization of natural gas, the majors have never wanted to market the gas of independents in a common reservoir and they do not want anyone else marketing their gas. The majors would routinely bring up antitrust reasons why they could not enter into a common marketing agreement." But aside from these differing power relationships that separated independents and majors, producers disagreed with each other on the advisability of a statutory solution to unitization. More than once, TIPRO was rocked by internal controversy on the issue. The partisans on both sides were highly informed, forceful, and confidently articulate. Somehow they learned to live with the tension.

Through all the hazards and all the changes that have transformed the world of petroleum, the independents of TIPRO have survived, though in what is now severely diminished numbers. During the nation's last exploration expansion in the 1980s, the comparative drilling statistics of independents and majors verified one final time the enduring historical reality about petroleum production on the North

American continent. In 1982 independents drilled precisely 88.4 percent of all wells in the United States. That year, twenty major companies spudded in 10,119 wells while independents drilled 76,814. The comparable figures for Texas were 3,550 by the majors and 23,669 by independents.

Independents, more keenly than other Americans, know that such days will never come again. TIPRO's membership losses since 1986 now approach 40 percent. The crisis now surpasses anything independents had to face during the darkest days of the 1950s and 1960s. The survivors, to continue surviving, will have to do what independents have historically always had to do: respond to change—specifically the striking technological changes now coursing through the world of exploration. But the cold reality is that large-scale seismic mapping and enhanced recovery are very expensive. The degree of cooperation among independents necessary to cope with this organic capital problem is absolutely unprecedented. As the new century looms, independents know they will have to find a way to adapt—or fade away. Increasingly, the focus of attention is on cooperative efforts, not only through joint ventures in exploration and advanced secondary recovery, but also through new approaches to cooperative marketing.

In pondering their options, independents at least have the security of knowing that their attempts to adapt place them squarely in the mainstream of a half-century of TIPRO tradition. But whatever independents do, their future is exceedingly perilous. In historical terms, this is not new: wildcatting has always been organically hazardous. But as the producers who have appeared in these pages know in their bones, the hour now is very late. In all societies linked into the global market, concentrations of capital have reached a plateau where they dominate the three fundamental components of worldwide commodity exchange—costs of production, price levels, and access to consumers. For producers of basic commodities around the globe, the storm warnings are up for all the small craft.

To recognize this reality is not to indulge in hand-wringing; rather, it calls for independents to be what Jon Rex Jones calls "more proactive than in the past—looking for the next problem before it gets on top of us." The wildcatters of Texas are alive, but a number of them are not well, and the independent industry as a whole is in a convalescent state.

Yet they are a grizzled bunch of sailors, mature in the arts of small craft and free of innocence about the power of the great liners. Over fifty years of collective assertion, their horizons have been shaped both by provincial needs and by the dynamics of international affairs. TIPRO remains their self-constructed schoolroom where independents continue to teach each other the navigational subtleties of long-distance voyages. They will not go away quietly.

The optimists among them are determined that they will not go away at all.

H. J. Porter, Houston,
1946–1948

Guy Warren, Corpus Christi,
1948–1950

R. L. Foree, Dallas,
1950–1951

Bryan W. Payne, Tyler,
1951–1953

M. D. Bryant, San Angelo,
1953–1954

Jack Woodward, Dallas,
1954–1955

A. P. King, Houston,
1955–1956

A. E. Herrmann, Amarillo,
1956–1957

Jerome J. O'Brien, San Antonio,
1957–1958

Eugene Locke, Dallas,
1958–1959

Harry Jones, Tyler,
1959–1960

John Hurd, Laredo,
1960–1961

J. F. West, Stamford,
1961–1962

Johnny Mitchell, Houston
1962–1963

E. Bruce Street, Graham,
1963–1964

M. D. Abel, Midland,
1964–1966

Walter Koch, Austin,
1966–1967

Netum A. Steed, Wichita Falls,
1967–1968

W. J. Murray, Austin,
1969–1972

George Mitchell, Houston,
1972–1975

John J. Christmann, Lubbock,
1976–1977

Chester Upham, Mineral Wells,
1978–1979

Frank Pitts, Dallas, 1980–1981

Gene Wright, Tyler, 1982–1983

Bruce Anderson, Houston,
1983–1985

Shelby Pitts, Dallas,
1985–1986

John Watson, Houston,
1987–1988

Jim Russell, Abilene,
1989–1991

Tom Coffman, Austin,
1991–1994

Rex White, Austin,
1995–1996

TIPRO Executive Vice-Presidents, 1946–1996

E. I.
Thompson
1946–1955

W. Earl
Turner
1955–1980

Julian
Martin
1980–1994

A. Scott
Anderson
1994–

NOTES

1. Democracy Comes to the World of Oil

1. R. J. Forbes, "Oil in Eastern Europe, 1840–1859," 1–6; Kendall Beaton, "Founders' Incentives: The Pre-Drake Refining Industry," 7–20; Henrietta M. Larson, "The Rise of Big Business in the Oil Industry," 27–42; Arthur M. Johnson, "Public Policy and Concentration in the Petroleum Industry, 1870–1911"; in *Oil's First Century*, comp. and ed. Harvard Business History Review (Cambridge, 1960).

2. The treatment of Spindletop that follows is drawn from Marilyn D. Trevey, "The Social and Economic Impact of the Spindletop Oil Boom on Beaumont in 1901" (master's thesis, Lamar University, 1974); Richard O'Connor, *Oil Barons* (Boston, 1971), 66–90; Daniel Yergin, *The Prize: The Epic Quest for Oil, Money, and Power* (New York, 1991), 82–94; and, especially, Ruth Sheldon Knowles, *The Greatest Gamblers* (1958; rpt., Norman, 1978), 23–43.

3. Knowles, *Greatest Gamblers*, 28.

4. The following account of exploration in West Texas is based on Lawrence Goodwyn, "Lessons of the Permian Basin," *TIPRO Reporter*, April 1961, 9–12; Roger M. Olien and Diana Davids Olien, *Wildcatters: Texas Independent Oilmen* (Austin, 1984); Samuel D. Myres, *The Permian Basin: Era of Advancement* (El Paso, 1977); Richard R. Moore, *West Texas after the Discovery of Oil* (Austin, 1971). Both my original article and this updated account are also indebted to Knowles, *Greatest Gamblers*, 219–231.

5. Goodwyn, "Lessons of the Permian Basin," 11.

6. Samuel Myres's comprehensive work on the Permian Basin and the informed study of wildcatting by Roger and Diana Olien stand apart from most of the literature of oil in Texas in that they steadfastly avoid the two principal weaknesses of the genre—sensationalism and, conversely, excessive technical jargon. I am particularly indebted to the Oliens for their deft analysis of the promise and disappointments of the Spraberry Trend, discussed in Chapter 3.

7. The story of the discovery and development of the East Texas field is drawn from Lawrence Goodwyn, "East Texas: Thirty Years Later," *TIPRO Reporter*, March–April 1960, 11–15; and the works cited in notes 2 and 4 above.

8. Knowles, *Greatest Gamblers*, 260. Knowles was among those who reacted viscerally to what she considered the inappropriate ridicule of Joiner by oil scouts and major company executives: "There was no difference between Dad Joiner and Mike Benedum or Harry Sinclair or any other oilman except that after you hit oil, you were called an oilman instead of a promoter" (251). One might also observe that the impulse of petroleum professionals to denigrate Joiner arose partly from a common human malady—namely, envy of his achievement. Dad Joiner died in 1947 at the age of eighty-seven in Dallas, having made a local reputation among bibliophiles as the heaviest book-borrower at the Dallas Public Library (O'Connor, *Oil Barons*, 304). He made a million dollars out of the East Texas field, continued wildcatting, and died well read and broke.

9. Goodwyn, "East Texas: Thirty Years Later," 12.

10. Ibid., 13.

11. Knowles, *Greatest Gamblers*, 260.

2. "Anarchy" vs "Order": Independents and the Majors

1. Yergin, *The Prize*, 249. Independents, of course, would not have characterized production in East Texas as fragmented since a variety of other terms (such as "fair" and "equitable") would have appeared more aptly descriptive of what they viewed as a level playing field.

2. See J. Stanley Clark, *The Oil Century* (Norman, Okla., 1958), 235–236, for the opinion of the circuit court. For the debate in the Texas Senate, see Robert E. Hardwicke, "Legal History of Conservation in Texas," in American Bar Association, *Legal History of Conservation of Oil and Gas: A Symposium* (Chicago, 1939), 229–237, cited in Clark, *The Oil Century*, 237. Walter Rundell Jr., *Early Texas Oil* (College Station, 1977), 226, also cites a 1931 anti-proration ruling at the district court level in Texas.

3. The conceptualization as well as a good deal of the specific evidence marshaled in this chapter draws on the author's earlier article, "East Texas: Thirty Years Later," *TIPRO Reporter*, March–April 1960, 11–15, which was based on Knowles, *Greatest Gamblers*, 249–269, on the oral tradition of Texas independents, and on Olien and Olien, *Wildcatters*; Gerald D. Nash, *United States Oil Policy, 1890–1964* (Pittsburgh, 1964); David Prindle, *Petroleum Politics and the Texas Railroad Commission* (Austin, 1981); John G. McLean and Robert W. Haigh, *The Growth of Integrated Oil Companies* (Boston, 1954); Clark, *The Oil Century*; and Svante Karlsson, *Oil and the World Order* (Gothenburg, 1984).

4. Knowles, *Greatest Gamblers*, 39.

5. The legal literature is, of course, enormous, with relevant cases ranging far beyond the concerns of the oil industry. See American Bar Association, *Legal History of Conservation of Oil and Gas*; Blakely M. Murphy, ed., *Conservation of Oil and Gas: A Legal History* (Chicago, 1949); Ernest R. Bartley, *The Tidelands Oil Controversy: A Legal and Historical Analysis* (Austin, 1953); Robert E. Hardwicke, *Antitrust Laws et al. v. Unit Operations of Oil and Gas Pools* (New York, 1948); Leo J. Hoffman, *Voluntary Pooling and Unitization: Oil and Gas* (Dallas, 1954); *MacMillan et al. v. Railroad Commission of Texas et al.*, 51 F2d 400–405 (July 1931).

6. Yergin, *The Prize*, 254.

7. James Presley, *A Saga of Wealth: The Rise of the Texas Oilmen* (New York, 1978), 146–180.

8. Ibid., 147, 151, 172.

9. The influence of the major oil companies is a central theme of Chapters 3, 4, and 5.

3. Closing Ranks

1. Yergin, *The Prize*, 281; Aaron David Miller, *Search for Security: Saudi Arabian Oil and American Foreign Policy, 1939–1949* (Chapel Hill, N.C., 1980), 30–38, 131.

2. David Painter, *Oil and the American Century: The Political Economy of U.S. Foreign Oil Policy, 1941–1954* (Baltimore, 1986), 37–55; Karlsson, *Oil and the World Order*, 35–53; Irving H. Anderson, *Aramco, the United States, and Saudi-Arabia: A Study of the Dynamics of Foreign Oil Policy* (Princeton, 1981), 111; Michael B. Stoff, *Oil, War, and American Security: The Search for a National Policy on Foreign Oil* (New Haven, 1980), 52–54; Shoshana Klebanoff, *Middle East Oil and U.S. Foreign Policy: With Special Reference to the U.S. Energy Crisis* (New York, 1974), 25.

3. *Independent News*, June 21, 1948; R. L. Foree, "The President Says," *TIPRO Reporter*, February 1951, 15 (hereafter cited as *TR*). An early biography of Foree appears in *Independent News*, April 29, 1948.

4. Karlsson, *Oil and the World Order*, 48.

5. Yergin, *The Prize*, 396–399.

6. Karlsson, *Oil and the World Order*, 58; Yergin, *The Prize*, 406.

7. Walter Henshaw, "FTC 'Oil Cartel' Report Is Embroiled in Politics," *TR*, October 1952, 19–21. Henshaw, one of TIPRO's more prominent founders, was commenting in 1952 on a contemporary report by the Federal Trade Commission for the Senate Small Business Committee, *The International Petroleum Cartel*, 82d Cong., 2d sess., 1952. In reviewing this document, Henshaw recounted the earliest days of the independents' struggle against the Anglo-American

Treaty and went on to say: "How many of us can deny in good conscience the existence of agree-ments among the five big major [American] companies which can be reasonably characterized as cartel links?" Including the British and Dutch giants, the Seven Sisters owned in 1949, Henshaw said, citing the FTC report, "about 82 percent of all foreign crude reserves and about 34 percent of all US reserves—or 65 percent of the world's estimated crude reserves. Outside of US, Russia and Mexico, the companies controlled about 92 percent" (19–20). For another exploration of the problem, see Elmer Patman, "International Oil Cartel Threatens Independents," *TR*, January 1952, 10.

8. *TR*, Summer 1978, 16. In a retrospective on the founding of TIPRO, Porter put the num-ber in attendance at 39, though contemporary accounts generated by the new association speci-fied "60-odd" (*TR*, March 1949, 5). In the formal filing of TIPRO's state charter, some six weeks after the founding meeting, the names of 86 independents appear (Charter No. 86807, filed in the office of the Secretary of State, May 2, 1946). See also Texas Independent Producers and Royalty Owners Association, brochure, 1946; "Bulletin No. 1," Founding Documents, TIPRO Archives, Oral History Program, Center for American History, University of Texas at Austin (hereafter cited as TIPRO Archives).

9. "Executive V.P. Effective as Organization Ramrod," *Independent News*, October 15, 1947, 4.

10. *TR*, September 1949, 7; *TR*, February 1951, 11.

11. TIPRO charter, May 2, 1946, TIPRO Archives. A complete list of TIPRO presidents from 1946 to 1996 is contained in the Appendix.

12. For TIPRO's relationship to the Patman committee, see *TR*, June 1949, 1; *TR*, January 1950, 9; *TR*, April 1950, 7. For a time, the association's general preoccupation with issues of monopoly gradually became specifically focused on ratable take and field pricing in natural gas. See, for example, "Gas Monopoly Immobilizes Supply and Demand Forces," *TR*, May 1951, 18. In its February 16, 1948, issue of *Independent News*, TIPRO quoted liberally from an antimonop-oly speech by railroad commissioner Olin Culberson: "Monopoly . . . is the most vicious and vir-ulent malady that could ever plague the business fabric of this nation" (4).

13. Porter's polemical style was visible in early TIPRO publications: he described wartime price controls as "stupid and vindictive" and characterized Everette DeGolyer as "thoughtless, ill-advised and contrary to the American principles of private enterprise" when the noted geologist defended continued oil development in the Middle East ("Porter Tells Independent Position in Letter to New York Newspaper," *Independent News*, January 15, 1948; "Porter Refutes DeGolyer's Statements," *Independent News*, March 13, 1948). For examples of the Thompsonian approach to legislative matters, see "The Wonder Is They Are So Good," *TR*, July 1949, 10, and to regulato-ry agencies, "Ratable Take Is Available Practically for the Asking," *TR*, January 1949, 2. Porter's description of DeGolyer, a respected figure in the industry, hurt TIPRO with oil journalists while Thompson's tendency to exaggerate TIPRO's influence and overstate its fears filled them with disbelief (see Chapter 4, note 6).

14. While the grievances of independents with vertically integrated sectors of the industry increasingly seized the attention of TIPRO's executive committee, Fort Worth's Arch Rowan was among the more prominent independents who shared with Porter and Thompson a preoccupa-tion with socialism as the chief threat to producers (see *Independent News*, March 13, 1948, 1). In the early years, both themes surfaced intermittently in the *TIPRO Reporter*, but the antimo-nopoly trajectory gradually became more prominent, attained dominance in the mid-1950s, and remained so thereafter. The specific manner in which these differences were resolved at the pol-icy level within TIPRO is a central theme of Chapter 4.

15. *TR*, March 5, 1949, 9. By the summer of 1949, TIPRO had 4,053 members (*TR*, September 1949, 7).

16. *TR*, August 1950, 13. The first issue of the *Independent News* appeared on October 15, 1947.

The *TIPRO Reporter* made its debut in December 1948. Vandygrift was TIPRO's second general counsel, having been briefly preceded by Weaver Moore, an Austin attorney (*Independent News*, June 21, 1948). The association's need for legal representatives experienced in the subtleties of constitutional law became apparent in TIPRO's struggle with long-line gas transmission companies over the gas gathering tax, a subject tracked in the next chapter.

17. *Independent News*, April 8, 1948, 1.

18. Bartley, *The Tidelands Oil Controversy*.

19. E. I. Thompson, "Tidelands Controversy Fundamentals," *TR*, October 1952, 26–27; also see *TR*, March 1951, 15; July 1951, 10; and August 1952.

20. Clark, *The Oil Century*, 224; *Independent News*, May 24, 1948; *TR*, March 1951; July 1951; October 1952.

21. Clark, *The Oil Century*, 186n.; "Unitization Occupies Executive Committee Attention," *TR*, February 1949, 2; Weaver Moore, "S.B. 24 Is Not Voluntary Pooling and Is a Threat to Independents," *TR*, February 1949, 3. See also *TR*, January 1949, 4; and March 1949, 3.

22. David Donoghue, "TIPRO Protests Development on Spacing and Unitization," *TR*, November 1951, 8; David Donoghue, "Forced Pooling Parades under Conservation Label," *TR*, January 1952, 13; "Compulsory Unitization Refrain Has False 'Conservation' Theme," *TR*, March 1952, 13; Will Odom, "Independents Cannot Survive Under Compulsory Unitization," *TR*, August 1952, 10.

23. Moore, *West Texas after the Discovery of Oil*, 102–105.

24. William Murray interview, TIPRO Archives; Myres, *The Permian Basin*, 484–485, 503–506.

25. "Gas Monopoly Immobilizes Supply and Demand Forces," *TR*, May 1951, 18. TIPRO arranged for Mrs. Hill to testify before a Railroad Commission hearing (*TR*, March 1951, 18).

26. The challenge of how to deal with regulatory agencies such as the Federal Power Commission and how to approach the many factions in Congress was gradually perceived by TIPRO as two separate problems, both of them apparently contingent on short-term election results as well as long-term structural relationships within the oil industry. In the founding decade, it can be said that TIPRO's most active members believed they had two general types of grievances, those generated by the actions of major oil companies and those generated by state and federal governments. Attempts to deal with the second problem were often undercut by the continued existence of the first problem. From a historical standpoint, TIPRO faced an analytical task that became more complicated as new evidence about the task itself developed from day-to-day events in the first decade of the organization's existence. These events began to have a dramatic effect on TIPRO's stance in the 1950s—as becomes clear in Chapter 4.

27. Guy Warren, "The President Says," *TR*, December 1948, 1. See also *Independent News*, February 1948.

28. For a full review of TIPRO's successful achievement of the Standard Gas Measurement Act, see *TR*, July 1949, 1–4.

29. *TR*, March 1951; April–May 1951; and June 1952.

30. Myres, *The Permian Basin*, 1–6, 31–34, 277–278.

31. The trials of producers in the Spraberry Trend is the subject of an informed analysis in Olien and Olien, *Wildcatters*, 99–109, and, with as much emphasis on Railroad Commission hearings as on production problems, in Myres, *The Permian Basin*, 272–278. Over 800 wells, some 18 percent of all wells drilled in Texas in 1951, sought Spraberry production (Myres, *The Permian Basin*, 36). For a discussion of the sundry geographical hazards facing West Texas independents, especially prior to the development of the Canyon Reef, see Olien and Olien, *Wildcatters*, 27.

There were, indeed, many hazards. Much of the crude found in the region was both sour (laced with sulfur) and heavy (low gravity), conditions that caused pipeline and storage tank corrosion and also yielded lower amounts of gasoline and other profitable light products. Thus, with the exception of Big Lake crude, prices in the Permian Basin were for years among the lowest in the nation. Because of the nature of the crude and the remoteness of the region, a number of independents in the Permian Basin were somewhat more dependent upon the majors than was routinely the case in other sectors of the state. Even in exploration, major companies were always significant players in the region.

4. The Warning Years

1. "Importers Promised in 1949 Not To Supplant Domestic Oil," *TR*, February 1953, 14.

2. *TR*, October 1952, 6–7. The article was excerpted from a formal address by Bryan Payne to the Independent Natural Gas Association of America on October 6, 1952.

3. Four months into the voluntary imports program, monthly production allowables in Texas had declined to a twelve-day pattern (*TR*, October 1957, 37). After the mandatory program was implemented, allowables declined to seven days.

4. For a representative sample of TIPRO responses over a five-year period, see "If 'Voluntary' Cut Has Failed, What Next to Curb Oil Imports," *TR*, February 1956, 32; "Foree Cites Economic Pinch, Raps Importers' Tax Boons" (keynote address to Eleventh Annual TIPRO Convention), *TR*, June 1957, 27–28; "Claims, Charges Fail To Mask Voluntary Program's Failure," *TR*, April 1958, 40–41; "TIPRO Blasts 'Success' Claims of Government's Voluntary Program," *TR*, June 1958, 33; "Mandatory Program's Defense Goal," *TR*, April 1959, 33–35; and "An Agonizing Reappraisal: The Mandatory Program after One Year," *TR*, April 1960, 24. See also note 14 below.

5. Frank Pitts interview, TIPRO Archives.

6. Billy Thompson, interview with author, July 1995. Over forty years earlier, Thompson's fellow oil editor, Jay Hall of the *Dallas Morning News*, had written: "The Texas Independent Producers and Royalty Owners Association leadership has sometimes been guilty of overstating its fears for the obvious purpose of winning its point or garnering public sympathy. Newspaper people . . . learn to suspect overstatement" (Jay Hall, "Newspapers Must Resist Overstatement," *TR*, May 1952, 15). It is appropriate in this connection to note the work of Harry Heinecke, who for many years was the oil editor of the *Fort Worth Star Telegram*. A knowledgeable observer of the petroleum industry, Heinecke gradually developed a deep admiration for TIPRO's advocacy of the cause of independents and began in the late-1950s to place his reports on the association's initiatives within a sophisticated analytical context that was distinctive among oil journalists (see note 30 below).

7. *TR*, December 1954, 16–17.

8. Thompson's style was visible in his regular column in the *TIPRO Reporter*, "From the Hub" (March 1951, 11; May 1951, 16; December 1952, 18; and December 1954, 27). The difference in the two schools of thought within TIPRO was strategic and turned on differing understandings of both the industry as a whole and the power of different industry segments in Washington. For example, Woodward said, "What we fail to understand is that when the battle is between independents and the few large importing companies, it is we who have the initiatives [and] have all the advantage by virtue of our numbers" (*TR*, February 1955, 20). For many TIPRO activists, this line of reasoning seemed not only unrealistic and even complacent as a forecast for the future, but it had been contradicted by political outcomes that had already been set in place during the first postwar decade. Moreover, a number of these events, dismaying as they were, had not occurred in faraway Washington but in the very backyard of Texas independents—namely, the legislature in Austin. See below in the text and in notes 27, 28, and 29 for the details of the gas gathering tax.

9. The internal debate within TIPRO concerning the style of advocacy best suited for independent producers had an interesting personal dimension. As interviews with surviving early activists attest, the most tenacious opponent of the Porter-Thompson-Woodward school was R. L. Foree. After Thompson retired because of ill health and was replaced by W. Earl Turner as the association's executive vice-president, Foree acquired, in Turner, a well-placed ally. As TIPRO insiders knew, the irony here was that Turner had originally been brought on staff by Jack Porter soon after TIPRO's founding in 1946. Indeed, Turner was related to Porter by marriage. In this case, policy differences overrode kinship ties.

A number of contemporaries of the founders endeavored to restrain the more prominent swashbucklers. For example, in a subsequent retrospective, Edward Kadane of Wichita Falls found a graceful way to explain why Porter was elected first president—not because he was outspoken but because he was less outspoken than the obvious alternative choice, Houston's Glenn McCarthy. "Some of us felt Glenn was a little too colorful during those days," said Kadane ("Remembering the Early Days," *TR*, Spring 1985, 18, 34–35).

10. R. L. Foree, testimony before the House Ways and Means Committee, January 28, 1955, reprinted in *TR*, February 1955, 21–22. This was an early signal by TIPRO. The course change by independents would become generally visible to everyone in the industry by 1957.

11. *TR*, February 1957, 31; *TR*, February 1959, 5.

12. "TIPRO Committee Seeks Reinforced Import Controls," *TR*, February 1960, 29–31. The final chapter of Clark, *The Oil Century*, 229–254, entitled "The Problem of Imports," adequately reflects the anxieties among independents in the 1950s, when Clark's study was published. A contrasting view is contained in "Voluntary Program's Success Told by Administrator Carson," *TR*, June 1958, 13. See also Robert J. Enright, "What 8 Days Will Mean to Texas," *Oil and Gas Journal*, March 31, 1958, 47–49. Five years earlier, importers had assured the House Ways and Means Committee that the import problem was temporary ("Administration Expresses 'Hope' for Voluntary Imports Solution," *TR*, June 1953, 7).

13. American Petroleum Institute / Independent Petroleum Association of America / Mid-Continent Oil and Gas Association, *Joint Association Survey of United States Oil and Gas Industry, Annual Report*, 1960 and 1968 (Washington, D.C., 1961, 1969). See also Independent Petroleum Association of America, *The Oil Producing Industry* (1960, 1968). Annual figures on crude prices from intervening years show remarkable uniformity: $2.89 in 1961; $2.90 in 1962; $2.89 in 1963; $2.88 in 1964; $2.86 in 1965; $2.88 in 1966; and $2.92 in 1967. In 1959, the year the mandatory program began, the price of crude was $2.90. The contrasting rise in exploration costs is detailed in Olien and Olien, *Wildcatters*, 96.

14. The headline "Imports and Gas to Dominate TIPRO Seventh Annual Meeting" (*TR*, February 1953, 7) turned out to be the continuing theme of the journal for the next two decades. Independents were haunted by three issues that dominated the association's activities: (1) the transparent inadequacies of the mandatory imports program, (2) the FPC's interpretation of the Phillips decision to place independent producers under utility-type regulation, and (3) the deeply disappointing elements in all subsequent gas decontrol legislation. It would be an exercise in pedantry to cite the relevant issues of the *TIPRO Reporter* that dealt with these matters other than to offer this summary generalization: the helplessness of independents, in the face of price and gathering discrimination by gas pipelines and in the face of excessive imports, dominated every issue of the journal throughout the decade, were discussed in a tone of increasing urgency, and were the source of a series of proposed remedies offered by independents, none of which prevailed at the level of national policy. See notes 15 through 36, below, all dealing with these areas of intraindustry tension.

15. "New Gas Legislation: Producer Bill or Monopoly Bill?" *TR*, April 1957, 24–25; "TIPRO Asks Changes in Harris-O'Hara Bills," *TR*, June 1957, 17. By 1957, TIPRO's skepticism was well honed. Earlier, when President Eisenhower had surprised friends and foes alike by vetoing the

Harris bill in February 1956 (because of a lobbying scandal associated with its passage), TIPRO took the "loss" in stride: "The gas bill was far from a good one for independents, anyway" (*TR*, February 1956, 16).

16. "Federal Control of Gas May Be Industry's Own 'Comedy of Errors,'" *TR*, June 1957, 10–12; "Industry Unity and the Independent: Memo To Those Who Would Avoid Intra-Industry Squabbles," *TR*, August 1957, 5, 42. While TIPRO's indignation at the trajectory both of the FPC and of gas legislation fairly bristled throughout the summer of 1957, the association's location of the underlying cause in the actions of major companies could be seen at the very beginning of the year: "The antidote is not, as so many industry spokesmen have contended, greater 'industry unity.' The picture of a united petroleum fraternity linked arm in arm, smiling an 'all's well' to the world, can only contribute to the concept of it as a leering, profiteering, smug giant, intent on gouging the consumer and dominating the political and economic life of the country" (*TR*, February 1957, 10).

17. *TR*, June 1957, 10–12.

18. "The Case against Ike: International Companies and Government Policies," *TR*, April 1957, 42–45; "Industry Unity and Gas" and "Industry Unity and the Independent," *TR*, June 1957, 5, 10, 42.

19. "Smaller Independents Avoid Burden of Expensive Financial Reporting," *TR*, December 1957, 28–29.

20. "Special 8-Page Report on U.S. Oil Import Policy and Monopoly" and "Market Demand Proration and Oil Imports Control," *TR*, February 1962, 13–20, 21. In the same issue, with its heavy focus on the failed mandatory imports program, TIPRO president James West identified the political opposition to independents as "consisting mainly in those whose interest is in maintaining the present ineffective program" (West, "At the Crossroads," *TR*, February 1962, 26.)

21. "Fair Play—A Vanishing Tradition," *TR*, Summer 1965, 20; "The Future and Allowables," *TR*, February 1962, 8, 32–34; "The Texas Allowable Day System," *TR*, October 1962, 20–22.

22. This is not to say that relationships between the IPAA and TIPRO were not sometimes strained, as Lester Clark, among others, has emphasized (Lester Clark interview, TIPRO Archives). See note 23 below.

23. The origin of Lester Clark's determination to create a broad coordinating committee of producer associations lay in his testimony in the spring of 1957 before the antitrust subcommittee of the Senate Judiciary Committee in Washington. Only TIPRO and regional Texas producer associations showed up in support (Lester Clark interview, TIPRO Archives; "Lester Clark Testifies: Associations Charge Importers with Monopoly Grip on Industry," *TR*, April 1957, 27). With TIPRO executive committee endorsement, Earl Turner actively supported Clark's initiative and accompanied him to the Wichita meeting that resulted in the creation of the Liaison Committee of Cooperating Oil and Gas Associations with Clark as its first chairman. In a retrospective on the twentieth anniversary of the Liaison Committee, the editors of the *TIPRO Reporter* recalled the late 1950s as "a time of bitterness among the associations" (*TR*, Fall 1978, 50).

24. "Foreign Trade Panel," *TR*, April 1958, 12; "World Trade Views Are Aired at Height of Imports Battle," *TR*, June 1958, 10–12. Also participating in this TIPRO convention—a harbinger of things to come with respect to the association's relationship to oil-producing nations—was Venezuela's petroleum attaché in Washington, Dr. Eduardo A. Acosta.

25. Julian Martin, interviews with author, May 1993 and July 1995.

26. Ibid., May 1993.

27. How independents learned what they were up against when confronting pipelines in a legislative battle is evident in the reports in the association's journal. They reflect a rising trajectory of dismay:

At the outset, in mid-1951: "A Major Victory: Gas Gatherers Will Share Tax Load with Producers" *TR*, July 1951, 4.

In late 1951 (after pipelines contested the tax in court): Alvis Vandygriff, "Tax on Gas Is Justified and Fair," *TR*, October–November 1951, 14–15.

In 1952 (after the levy was ruled an unconstitutional restraint of trade): "Court Decision on Gas Gathering Tax Intensifies Demands for Legislation," *TR*, August 1952, 21.

In 1953 (during a new attempt to pass a gathering tax): "Gas Gatherers Lose Round in Fight To Escape Taxes," *TR*, February 1953, 31.

In 1954 (after a revised gas gathering tax is again declared unconstitutional): "New Gas Production Tax," *TR*, April 1954, 32.

28. On the gas gathering tax, TIPRO president Bryan Payne sounded a renewed alert early in 1952 that pipeline companies were maneuvering to "knock it out in the courts and shift the additional burden to producers" (*TR*, January 1952, 6). Though Payne assured the membership that "we are on that job," the real fight had been waged earlier in the specific shaping of the legislative language of the 1951 bill. As events were to show, this battle (over language that could be amended to make any pipeline tax constitutionally vulnerable) had been won by the pipelines.

For the same reasons of constitutionality, the legislative struggle in the late 1950s on the severance beneficiary tax also took place over the specific language of the bill. Pipelines were alarmed for two reasons, one general and one specific to the 1959 bill. The general reason was the intention to avoid a tax of any kind on pipelines on the theory that the legislature, reluctant to further tax Texas producers, would focus all future attention exclusively on pipelines once a tax was constitutionally sanctioned. The second reason the pipeline lobbying effort was so intense in 1959 was that the legal concept behind the severance beneficiary levy (which taxed a "right" or legal "benefit" rather than a commodity in interstate commerce) appeared much more constitutionally protected than had been the Hazlewood bills of the early 1950s. As pipeline strategists saw the options, the task in 1959 was to amend the language of the severance beneficiary levy so that it could be attacked in court as a restraint on interstate commerce. They were successful in adding amendments that achieved this effect. Before and after this struggle in 1959, the only way the Texas Legislature could acquire tax revenues from the petroleum industry was through a levy on production.

29. Said Eckhardt: "Governor Daniel was helpful to me. Attorney General Carr was not" (Robert Eckhardt, interview with author, May 1995). Though Eckhardt, who was not in the legislature in 1951–1952, could not know the personal details that later proved relevant, Daniel, as Texas attorney general in the early 1950s, had represented the state against the pipelines in constitutional litigation over the gas gathering tax. Daniel's resentment of pipeline lobbying tactics in 1952, which fatally weakened the language of the Hazlewood bill, carried over to the 1959–1960 contest.

While both Daniel and Eckhardt understood the legal subtleties that defined the actual nature of the political struggle, the coverage in the state's newspapers did not, to say the least, reflect the same awareness. Outside the ranks of TIPRO and close associates of Daniel and Eckhardt, few Texans had any grasp of the embattled effort to induce gas pipelines to pay taxes remotely commensurate to the taxes paid by producers. TIPRO wryly quoted an unnamed press observer who quipped, "The oil lobby was equally opposed to all gas taxes. Only some were more equally opposed than others. But any bill which would tax gas pipelines was opposed most equally of all" (*TR*, "Producers, 'The Lobby,' and State Taxes," August 1959, 11).

The fact that many independent producers were at the time saddled with near-confiscatory prices in their contracts with pipeline purchasers merely underscored the general absence of equity that surrounded the production of natural gas in Texas. These relationships constituted the essential message of independent producers—one that for the next twenty years proved virtually impossible for them to convey persuasively to the rest of the society.

30. The role of TIPRO and Bentsen in the depletion struggle in the 1970s is detailed in Chapter 5. In 1959–1960, both Price Daniel and Robert Eckhardt labored to lift the "Texas

umbrella," Daniel in his role as chairman of the Interstate Oil Compact Commission and Eckhardt by devising a market-sharing formula for producing states. Both efforts were carefully tracked by the oil editor of the *Fort Worth Star Telegram*, Harry Heinecke. In this period—so soon after the formation of the Liaison Committee of Cooperating Oil and Gas Associations—links between producing states were still too fragile to moderate the existing power relationships within the industry. Thus, despite the efforts of Daniel and Eckhardt and the careful reporting of Heinecke, the "Texas umbrella" created by major companies remained intact. The huge shut-in capacity of Texas crude was the single most enduring component of domestic production through the 1960s.

31. "Vance Foster and the Decade Ahead: What Route Should Independents Take?" *TR*, February 1960, 7–10.

32. "The Gas Problem and TIPRO Actions," *TR*, February 1955, 40–41; "Railroad Commission Tackles Problem of Inequitable Natural Gas Proration," *TR*, August 1955, 23–24; "Ratable Take for Gas Will Bring Equity without Depriving Any Present Markets," *TR*, September–October 1956, 35–36; "Pipeline Scarcity: Unconnected Wells Brings RRC Study of Common Carriers," *TR*, February 1957, 14–15.

33. Malcolm Abel, quoted in *TR*, Fall 1964, 7–11, 37–38; *TR*, Winter 1964, 7–20.

34. "George Garver Repeats Familiar Pipe Line Reservations on Decontrol," *TR*, Fall 1964, 24–25.

35. "Percentage Allowables Aid Market-Sharing Climb," *TR*, February–March 1963, 29.

36. "Members Underscore Opposition to Compulsory Unitization Law," *TR*, May 1952, 10; "Independents and 'Unitization,'" *TR*, February 1961, 8–12; "Co-Chairmen J. Ed Kendall and Walter Koch," *TR*, August 1963, 7–11.

37. Julian Martin, interview with author, May 1993. For the Normanna and Port Acres cases, see *TR*, Winter 1964, 24, and *TR*, Spring 1965, 22–23. For the Crown case, see *TR*, October 1962, 23; Spring 1964, 23; and Fall 1964, 15.

38. "Mobil's Plan Sparks Debate," *TR*, Fall 1970, 18.

39. William Murray, "Tell It As It Is," *TR*, Summer 1970, 17. Murray added: "If I am right, then some very responsible industry and government sources must be wrong or badly out of date. If I am right, then much of the policy guidance coming out of Washington is wrong or badly out of date. If I am right, it is past time for new policy directives to be forthcoming from government and industry."

40. Julian Martin, interview with author, May 1993.

41. Ibid.

42. In constructing this analysis of the oil crises of the 1970s, I wish to acknowledge my central debt to Julian Martin of TIPRO. Prior to his lengthy interpretation of the Arab embargoes in a 1993 interview with the author, I, like many other observers outside the ranks of independents, saw the crises of 1973 and 1979 essentially in terms of Middle East tensions and Cold War politics, without reference to the underlying loss of domestic reserve production capacity anchored in Texas. The timing of these two events—verification of the end of Texas reserve capacity in 1972 and the Arab embargo of 1973—fully explains why the nation had long lines of motorists at gasoline pumps in 1973, but not in 1967, when Texas reserves bridged the gap. Martin characterized the 1956 Middle East war as a "political alert" for the West and the 1967 war as a "supply alert."

5. Transformation

1. Concern about the narrow range of perspectives among CEOs of major oil companies engaged in foreign operations was not restricted to specialists in petroleum journalism or to observers in other segments of the industry. In the Eisenhower administration, a senior oil strate-

gist in the U.S. Department of State, Richard Funkhouser, believed the problem to be serious enough to require special advice to other State Department employees as to how best to talk to major company executives: "It is of critical importance to the success of any approach that oil men be handled most carefully and diplomatically. Oil officials seem overly sensitive to any indication that the industry isn't perfect. Emotion, pride, loyalty, suspicion make it difficult to penetrate to reason" (Yergin, *The Prize*, 471).

2. James David Barber, *Presidential Character* (New York, 1972).

3. Tenure as TIPRO president: Jerry O'Brien, 1957–1958; John Hurd, 1960–1961; Malcolm Abel, 1964–1966; Chester Upham, 1978–1979; Frank Pitts, 1980–1981; Bruce Anderson, 1983–1984; Jim Russell, 1989–1991. For a listing of all TIPRO presidents, see the Appendix.

4. George Mitchell, "The Problem Is Right Now," *TR*, Spring 1973, 4–5. For TIPRO's reaction to Nixon's decision to abolish import fees, see "President's Energy Message: Lacking Courage of Convictions," *TR*, Spring 1973, 1, and, in the same issue, "President Opts Out on Energy Policy," 7.

5. Mitchell, "The Problem Is Right Now," *TR*, Spring 1973, 4–5.

6. Both TIPRO leaders and staff members learned a great deal in the 1950s about the general lack of knowledge among elected officials concerning distinctions between segments of the oil industry—staff members perhaps a bit more fully since they were exposed to politicians on a more frequent basis. Stories and even jokes about this state of affairs were common at TIPRO meetings, though dismay rather than humor was the underlying ingredient of most such conversations. While it would be excessive to suggest that TIPRO ever embarked on a concerted program to "educate everybody," spokesmen for independents increasingly gave themselves permission in the 1960s to take aside prominent conservative and liberal members of Congress and brief them in great detail on the operative dynamics of markets and prices as both bore on the relationship of consumer interests to producer interests. By the time of the Arab-Israeli War of 1973, this method of advocacy had become a settled tradition within TIPRO and provided the basis for the general political approach described in this chapter. See, for example, "Independents and the Industry," *TR*, Spring 1973, 22. For insight into how this approach had begun to create some common ground between producers and members of the Carter administration, see "Gorman Smith: Educate Your Enemies," *TR*, Summer 1975, 32.

7. "R. L. Foree Testifies," *TR*, Summer 1973, 38–39.

8. George Mitchell, "The Energy Situation," *TR*, Fall 1973, 3–4; "Majors Get Tax Break," *TR*, Winter 1973, 22.

9. "Congressman Charles Wilson: Percentage Depletion and Independents," *TR*, Summer 1975, 30–31.

10. W. Earl Turner, "How It Happened: Fighting to Save Depletion," *TR*, Spring 1975, 2.

11. "Congressman Charles Wilson: Percentage Depletion and Independents," *TR*, Summer 1975, 30–31.

12. Julian Martin, interview with author, May 1993.

13. Turner, "How It Happened," *TR*, Spring 1975, 1–3. The important role of Bentsen's aide, Gary Bushell, is evident in this retrospective. See also "Breakfast Seminar, Gorman Smith and Gary Bushell," *TR*, Summer 1975, 16.

14. Julian Martin, interview with author, May 1993. The benefits of the separate legal definition for independent producers, which became evident in the windfall profits bills of the 1980s, was also a factor in the 1978 natural gas legislation, as described later in this chapter.

15. Turner, "How It Happened," *TR*, Spring 1975, 2; in the same issue, see also George Mitchell, "Assessing the Situation," 8–9.

16. *Oil and Gas Journal*, March 17, 1975.

17. "The Wilson Amendment," *TR*, Spring 1975, 27.

18. Gary Bushell, telephone interview with author, August 1995.

19. The preoccupation of some Texas independents with oil exploration and others with gas exploration is an interesting side feature in the oral interviews that now comprise the TIPRO Archives. Some of these preferences (or prejudices, as the case may be) have such deep and abiding roots that they are still present in the 1990s. The author was personally involved in two separate interviews in which, in one, natural gas was seen as an "infestation" and, in the second, as "the fuel of the future." As TIPRO veterans themselves know, such wildly divergent approaches of independents are scarcely restricted to the finer points of exploration; rather, they range over the entire gamut of social and political issues that routinely confront producers and, indeed, occupy contemporary American society generally. Be that as it may, scholars and journalists still routinely attempt to generalize about what independent oilmen think based on investigations that are hasty and confined to a handful of sources who are then taken to represent independent producers as a group.

20. *Middle East Economic Survey*, December 28, 1973.

21. Frank Pitts interview, TIPRO Archives; see also *TR*, Spring 1977, 16; *TR*, Spring 1978, 6.

22. Frank Pitts interview; *TR*, Fall 1977, 34–36;

23. "Gas Monopoly Immobilizes Supply and Demand Forces," *TR*, April–May 1951, 18. Also see Chapter 3.

24. Frank Pitts interview.

25. "The Case for Realistic Interstate Gas Prices," *TR*, Winter 1977, 10–11.

26. Robert Wiebe, *The Search for Order, 1877–1920* (New York, 1967), provides an effective historical overview of how the entire subject of large-scale concentration in the U.S. economy inevitably immobilized public officials, who faced real problems as distinct from theoretical ones. On the famous progressive, Robert La Follette, for example, Wiebe writes: "La Follette could talk earnestly about a sweeping antimonopoly crusade yet premise his tax program on the growth of big business in Wisconsin." Wiebe adds: "In a way only a few [regulators] fathomed, their alterations strengthened a scheme they disliked by weaving its basic elements into an ever-tighter and more sophisticated national system. A public bureaucracy sheltered as it regulated" (297). The emphasis in Wiebe is on bureaucratic accommodation to outside political pressure rather than on the sources of this pressure in the quasi-monopolistic corporations that were being "regulated." Two other interesting—if inconclusive—attempts to make sense of the modern state are Theodore Lowi's *The End of Liberalism* (New York, 1979) and E. F. Schumacher's *Small Is Beautiful: Economics As If People Mattered* (New York, 1973). For LaFollette, see David Thelen, *Robert LaFollette and the Insurgent Spirit* (Boston, 1976).

The entire issue of economic centralization of the American economy is one that has historically confounded scholars as well as political observers. It may be said that the internal records of TIPRO constitute—in terms of detailed evidential concreteness—one of the most remarkable sources of historical evidence available anywhere in the nation as to the negative impact upon independent entrepreneurship of large-scale economic concentration in America. Among studies of the larger topic of antitrust, see Harry First, Eleanor M. Fox, and Robert Pitofsky, eds., *Revitalizing Antitrust in Its Second Century: Essays on Legal, Economic, and Political Policy* (New York, 1991); William F. Shugart, *Antitrust Policy and Interest Group Politics* (New York, 1990); and E. Thomas Sullivan, *Understanding Antitrust and Its Economic Implications* (New York, 1988). The classic work is Hans Birger Thorelli, *The Federal Anti-Trust Policy: Organization of an American Tradition* (New York, 1955).

27. Julian Martin, interviews with author, May 1993, June 1995, and August 1995. The twelve issues of the *TIPRO Reporter* published from the beginning of 1977 through 1979 provide an intimate (if necessarily complex) commentary on the politics of regulating decontrol. If this TIPRO commentary can be faulted as transparently partisan, it also has a countervailing utility as an exercise in informed skepticism.

28. "exTIPROaneous," *TR*, Spring 1978, 5.

29. Bill Dutcher, "Independent Producer Exemption Has Best Chance To Survive," *TR*, Fall 1977, 17.

30. Chester Upham, "On Being Independent," *TR*, Fall 1978, 4–5; Turner, "exTIPROaneous," *TR*, Fall 1978, 49.

31. "Lynn Coleman Defends Corrected Version of Proposed Natural Gas Act of 1978," *TR*, Fall 1978, 8–9, 38, 41, 43.

32. Foree, quoted in *TR*, Fall 1978, 9; Frank Pitts interview, TIPRO Archives. In 1989, Pitts commented, "I think deregulation of new gas only, allowing the price to go up in the interim, is one of the finest things that could have happened to the producing segment of the industry and the consumers of this country" (*TR*, Spring–Summer 1989, 26).

33. Close observers of the 1971–1973 struggle over unitization within TIPRO agree it was the opposition of "the old hands" which doomed compulsory unitization in Texas. Foree did not, in fact, back off very far from his historic opposition, saying in 1973 that "forced unitization is forced monopoly" (*TR*, Spring 1973, 29). For contemporary accounts of prospects and results, see Jim Drummond in *Oil Daily*, September 1, 1971; and "Unitization Bill Dominates Meetings," *TR*, Spring 1971, 8. The results of the internal poll of TIPRO members on unitization were published in "TIPRO Effort Directed at Ensuring Safeguards," *TR*, Spring 1973, 10-11. In the same 1973 issue of the *TIPRO Reporter*, George Mitchell, TIPRO president at the time, referred to the internal struggle as "blazing hot" and conceded that "some bitterness ensued." For his part, Jim Russell, an outspoken proponent of statutory unitization, said "I still have scars on my back from that fight" (Russell interview, TIPRO Archives). See "Statutory Unitization, YES" (Russell) and "NO" (Robert Payne), *TR*, Winter 1970, 2–5. It should be added that another reason the last great effort to achieve unitization in the 1970s failed had to do with the fact that the East Texas field was continuing to produce dramatically but was also beginning to water out on the west side. Thus, certain producers in the field were looking for unit agreements before they were watered out. But most were not. Perhaps the larger historical point is that the long-term internal cohesion of TIPRO as a voice of independent producers was not decisively affected by these irreducible internal divisions.

34. Private interview with author, May 1993.

6. An Expanding Realm of Surprises

1. Oilwell completions in 1981 totaled 13,878, a 42.5 percent rise over the previous year (*TR*, Spring 1982, 12–15). See also "Abandoned Texas Oil Fields: Outstanding Prospects for Redevelopment," *TR*, Winter 1980–1981, 15–16, 76–77. Private interview with author, May 1993.

2. *TR*, Fall 1979, 42; *TR*, Winter 1979, 51; and *TR*, Fall 1979, 38–39.

3. Untaxed imports were, of course, centrally germane to any discussion of national petroleum tax policy—in the early 1980s as in the three previous decades. As in the earlier period, TIPRO's effort in Washington in the 1980s was inherently an uphill struggle against the most powerful lobbying consortiums in national politics. See "Tax Battle Rages in Washington," *TIPRO Target*, August 1982, 1; Francis R. Durand and Ernst & Whinney, "The Future Tax Bite on Oil and Gas Producers and Royalty Owners," *TR*, Winter 1982, 19, 62–74; "Issues and Questions," *TR*, Fall 1982, 11. For earlier assessments, see *TR*, Spring 1980, 9–13, 29; and *TR*, Fall 1980, 18–21, 42. The *TIPRO Target* was a newsletter, initially published on a regular basis between the quarterly issues of the *TIPRO Reporter*. After the mid-1980s, an expanded *Target* became the principal forum for producer views after publication of the *TIPRO Reporter* was cut back as an economy measure. The publication is hereafter cited as *Target*.

4. This process, acted out on three separate occasions in the Texas legislature in the 1950s, is detailed in Chapter 4 and in notes 27, 28, and 29 of that chapter. TIPRO's perspective in the 1980s is visible in a lengthy analysis, "Interstate Natural Gas Pipelines and Antitrust Immunity," *TR*, Spring 1982, 24–33.

5. TIPRO's historic opposition to unreformed import practices, dating from the 1950s, is tracked in some detail in Chapter 4. On repeal of the windfall profits tax, see "Repeal of Windfall Profits Tax Eases Administrative Burden," *Target*, September 1988, 3.

6. Greg A. Winczewski, "World Oil Prices and Macroeconomic Activity in the OECD," Table 8.3 ("World Oil Prices and the Balance of Trade in the United States, Japan, and West Germany, 1972–1989"), 104, in Siamack Shojai and Bernard S. Katz, eds., *The Oil Market in the 1980s* (New York, 1992). In 1973, the United States had a narrow—but favorable—international trade balance. The deficit was $8.9 billion in 1975, $31.1 billion in 1977, $112 billion in 1984, and $160 billion in 1987. From the beginning, TIPRO's proposals on oil imports had often been advanced in the context of world trade. See, for example, "World Trade Views Are Aired at Height of Imports Battle," *TR*, June 1958, 10–12.

7. An account of petroleum tax policies in the early days of the Reagan administration is available in Kent Hance, "The Bed Was Already on Fire When I Crawled into It," *TR*, July 1982, 24. Much of this ground has been previously touched upon in the context of the divergent exploratory and developmental practices of independents and major companies and also with respect to foreign tax credits (see Chapters 4 and 5). The strains of the new international trade balances are treated in Edward R. Fried and Charles L. Schultze, eds., *Higher Oil Prices and the World Economy: The Adjustment Problem* (Washington, 1975). In 1981, some 9,000 independent producers and royalty owners mobilized by TIPRO came to Austin by the busload to participate in a public hearing of the U.S. Senate Finance Committee, chaired by Senator Bentsen, which detailed the differences between independents and major companies as these distinctions bore on tax policy. For a later TIPRO effort in behalf of "the principle of equalization of federal tax burdens between domestic crude and imported oil," see Marvin Zeid, *Target*, January 1983, 2. Zeid was chairman of TIPRO's task force on oil import fees. For a similar argument in the 1950s, see *TR*, April 1957, 40–41.

8. Julian Martin, interview with author, May 1993.

9. For an extended discussion by TIPRO members of big oil's tax avoidance, see *TR*, Summer 1983, 36–37. For the contours of TIPRO proposals on import fees in 1986, see "A Way to Stop the Bleeding," *Target*, February 1986, 1. A report on the Zeid-Strake debate is contained in "The Great Oil Import Fee Debate: Marvin Zeid vs. George Strake," *Target*, May 1987, 8.

One of the most straightforward recent complaints about the antidemocratic impact of excessive lobbying on the American political process was offered by the *Wall Street Journal*, August 17, 1995. The scholarly literature on the subject, and the effect of this antidemocratic trend on the economy itself, is quite large, and much of it predates the controversies of the Reagan-Bush years. The assumptions underlying much of this scholarship, particularly that portion that attempts to explain the post-1974 economy in terms of conventional economic theory, has come under sustained assault; see Lester C. Thurow, *Dangerous Currents: The State of Economics* (New York, 1983). For some of the specific ramifications affecting independent producers, see Robert L. Lesher (president of U.S. Chamber of Commerce), "Oil Import Fees Are Bad," *TR*, Summer 1983, 52, 64; and Bill O'Fallon (independent producer), "Oil Import Fees Are Good," *TR*, Summer 1983, 53, 65–69. For a summary account, see George Mitchell, "Why the United States Needs an Oil Imports Fee," *TR*, Summer 1986, 16.

10. Special marketing left producers virtually devoid of options. See "Issues and Questions," *TR*, Spring 1984, 7, for a cogent summary.

11. "Change in Gas Rules Approaches," *Target*, November 1986, 1; "Task Force Recommends

Statewide Gas Proration," *Target*, December 1986, 1. The seven-hour Railroad Commission hearing on the issue is summarized in "Proration System Reviewed," *Target*, February 1987, 3. For an intimate account of how special marketing affected independents, see Neal Anderson's extended comments in Chapter 7. For a relevant summary report from the Natural Gas Task Force to a two-day summer meeting chaired by TIPRO president John Watson in 1987, see *Target*, September 1987, 1. For a time, producers also explored possibilities of gas co-ops: Bill Henderson, "Natural Gas Co-ops: Concept Evolving in U.S.," *TR*, Fall 1985, 57–58.

12. Shojai and Katz, eds., *The Oil Market in the 1980s*. The essay in this collection by Margaret A. Walls and Andrew S. Jones, "The U.S. Oil Industry Response," 115–130, is especially germane to this study: "On April 1, 1986, the price of oil fell to under $10 for the first time in nearly a decade" (115). Nominal crude oil prices peaked in 1981, exploratory drilling reached an all-time high in the same year, and then fell by more than 30 percent by 1985, continuing downward thereafter.

13. Walls and Jones, "The U.S. Oil Industry Response," in *The Oil Market in the 1980s*, ed. Shojai and Katz, 120. During the decade of the 1980s, the IPAA estimated the decline of independents nationwide at one-third, from 15,000 to 10,000.

14. Bill Rutter interview, TIPRO Archives. In 1981, the International Energy Workshop predicted real oil prices in 1990 would be $60 per barrel (Dominick Salvatore, "Petroleum Prices and Economic Performance in the G-7 Countries," in *The Oil Market in the 1980s*, ed. Shojai and Katz, 99).

15. Wall and Jones had this assessment: "Even more than the industry as a whole, independents have been hit hard" ("The U.S. Oil Industry Response," in *The Oil Market in the 1980s*, ed. Shojai and Katz, 116).

16. "Army Engineers Embrace TIPRO Suggestions," *Target*, November 1982, 3; "Dillard Gives Water Story to Environmentalists," *Target*, December 1982, 2; "Environmental Improvement for Giddings," *Target*, November 1982, 5.

17. "Right To Know Update," *Target*, August 1988, 3, 5–6. It was in the 1980s that independents first began to acquire more than a vague and generalized knowledge of the legal implications of environmental initiatives. See the analysis by TIPRO's legal counsel, A. Scott Anderson ("Implied Covenants and the Law of Surface Damages in Texas," *TR*, Fall 1981, 72–75), which emphasized that judicial understanding of what constitutes a "reasonable" duty or obligation of a mineral leaseholder changes over time and that the rights of both landowners and the general public also evolve. Similarly, producers were presented with an analysis of OSHA legislation and practices: Philip W. Blake, "TIPRO Legal Notes: Rights and Responsibilities of the Oil and Gas Producer," *TR*, Winter 1981, 24–30; and Allen Cluck, "Wetlands Production: A Balancing of Concerns," *TR*, Fall 1983, 13–15. For early TIPRO recognition of environmentalism, see *TR*, Spring 1973, 12.

18. "Russell Establishes New Environmental Committee," *Target*, September 1989, 1–3; "Environmental Committee Sets Priorities," *Target*, November 1989, 3.

19. "TIPRO Assumes Active Role in Migratory Bird Issue," *Target*, November 1989, 1. Independents were introduced by Dr. Carl Oppenheimer, University of Texas microbiologist, to "biomediation" techniques of contaminated pit control, a process that "could take hours or weeks, depending on the thickness of oil in the pit." TIPRO began to work with the state land office and outside specialists on developing biomediation remedies.

20. "Railroad Commission Addresses Statutory Changes," *Target*, January 1992, 4; "Statewide Rule 14 Governing Well Plugging Proposed," *Target*, December 1992, 6.

21. "Railroad Commission Establishes Pollution Prevention Program," *Target*, March 1994, 4. An earlier TIPRO-sponsored oil pollution prevention seminar in Dallas in 1993 focused on three important oil-spill contingency plans: Spill Prevention Control and Countermeasure (SPCC);

Oil Pollution Act Facility Response Plans; and Texas Oil Spill Prevention and Response Act Certification Requirements.

22. *Target*, March 1992, 7; December 1992, 5; and August 1995.

23. Amy Carman, TIPRO staff, interview with author, August 1995. On coastal management, see John Watson interview, TIPRO Archives; *Target*, August 1993; "Coastal Coordination Council Addresses Several Producer Concerns—More Progress Still Needed," *Target*, September 1993, 1, 6; see also *Target*, March 1994, 3, and May 1994, 6. Houston's Scott L. Anderson encouraged the EPA to "incorporate exemptions in the proposed Risk Management Program requirements to ensure that small, remote exploration and production facilities are not unduly subjected to economically burdensome requirements, specifically on facilities handling crude oil, natural gas or hydrocarbon condensate that have no human exposure within a designated radius of exposure" (*Target*, February 1994, 6).

24. As one measure of the diverse currents in TIPRO on the environment, in the mid-1980s George Mitchell pioneered relations between TIPRO and the Sierra Club to work on certain natural gas features of the Clean Air Act that would simultaneously help the environment and producers. Mitchell told Houston independents, "That makes a hell of a good coalition between us and the Sierra Club" (*TR*, Winter 1985–1986, 20).

25. *Target*, December 1985, 5; and June 1988, 1.

26. William L. Fisher, "Can the U.S. Oil and Gas Resource Base Support Sustain Production?" *Science*, June 1987, 1631–1637; *Target*, April 1988, 2.

27. William L. Fisher, "Oil in Texas: Yesterday, Today, Tomorrow," *TR*, Spring 1981, 10–14.

28. "Schlumberger Has 50th Anniversary," *TR*, Fall 1977, 32. Relevant historical evidence concerning the evolution of petroleum technology is contained in Olien and Olien, *Wildcatters*, 15–16, 24, 75–77, 97–98.

29. As noted at the outset of this chapter, technical developments in seismic testing and in unconventional exploration techniques had gained producer interest in the 1970s (*TR*, Fall 1979, 38–39, 42). Gradually thereafter, technology appeared in TIPRO publications as an increasingly focused topic. For early examples, see "Enhanced Recovery," *Target*, November 1982, 5; "Enhanced Oil Recovery for Independents," *Target*, October 1983, 6; "Enhanced Oil Recovery," *Target*, Spring 1984, 23–25, 34.

30. "Russell Appoints New Applied Research and Technology Committee," *Target*, February 1990, 2; "Association Reps Attend DOE Conference on Enhanced Oil and Gas Recovery Research," *Target*, February 1990, 4; "Technology Summit Features Independent Producers Forum," *Target*, June 1990, 2. Prominent in the new committee headed by Fisher were former TIPRO presidents Frank Pitts and John Watson.

31. *Target*, October 1990, 6.

32. "Technology Transfer Survey Reveals Independents' Needs," *Target*, January 1991, 6; "Advanced Exploration-Recovery Program Underway," *Target*, July 1991, 1; "Improved Recovery Forums Bridge the Technology Gap for Producers," *Target*, December 1991, 1–2; "Free DOE Workshops for Independent Oil and Gas Producers," *Target*, October 1992, 6. See also *Target*, May 1992, 4; and August 1992, 1–3. The results of the questionnaires were aggregated and published as "Technology Transfer Needs and Requirements of Texas Independent Oil and Gas Producers."

33. "GRI/TIPRO Technology Transfer Agent Program Established," *Target*, May 1993, 4; *Target*, November 1993, 5.

34. Julian Martin, interview with author, September 1995.

35. Pat Gratton interview, TIPRO Archives. As an example of evolving informational patterns within the independent producing sector, "GRI/Technology Transfer Corner," a column in the July 1994 *Target*, carried information on "Application of Shale and Tight Sands Research to the

Barnett Shale." Survival of the independent producing sector—and the revenues it generated from new field production—was, of course, vital to the Texas state budget. In 1994 Governor Ann Richards announced a $300,000 state contract to be used by TIPRO and the Bureau of Economic Geology in conjunction with the TIPRO/GRI technology transfer agent program and the newly formed Petroleum Technology Transfer Council.

36. Russell Taylor, telephone interview with author, September 1995.

37. Ibid.

38. Frank Pitts interview, TIPRO Archives. See also "Coffman and Gratton Helping to Head Up Texas Technology Transfer Network," *Target*, February 1993, 3.

39. The interchanges between independents and specialists yielded evidence that producers were more receptive to completion technologies than to the more costly exploration technologies (see *Target*, March 1993, 3, and December 1993, 4). Accordingly, the third stage of the internal education program on technology, styled the Improved Recovery Information Service, was focused as a conduit for oil and gas research as distinct from being an operational repository for exploratory ventures. This represented—for the time being, at least—a retreat.

40. A. Scott Anderson, interview with author, May 1995; "What's New on the TIPRO BBS/Website?" *Target*, August 1995, 5; *Target*, February 1994, 5, and July 1994, 1–2.

41. A. Scott Anderson, memo to author, September 1995.

42. Tom Coffman, interview with author, August 1995.

7. The Way of Life

1. Scott L. Anderson interview. This and all subsequent interviews cited in this chapter, unless otherwise identified, are deposited in the TIPRO Archives at the Center for American History, University of Texas at Austin.

2. Pat Gratton interview.

3. R. L. Foree Jr. interview.

4. This conversation, among Neal, Scott, and Craig Anderson, was recorded in the office of the Anderson Oil Corporation in Houston in March 1992.

5. Jon Rex Jones interview.

6. Bruce Anderson interview.

7. Pat Gratton interview.

8. Jim Russell interview.

9. Graham's Bruce Street provides a personal story corroborating Jim Russell's account of the state of waterflooding in the early days. Street and his brother got into oil by drilling 500-foot wells in a field about twenty miles from his hometown: "Those little 500-foot wells were particularly adaptable to waterflooding. We didn't know much about that. We knew we could put water in the ground and we were supposed to have somewhat of a pattern. We did it and it worked. That's about all we knew." Bruce Street interview.

10. George Mitchell interview.

11. Jim Russell interview.

12. Neal Anderson interview.

13. Jim Russell interview.

14. Chester Upham interview.

15. Bruce Anderson interview.

16. Jacqueline Anderson interview. The early hardships were a stark contrast for Jacqueline Anderson. Immediately before meeting Bruce in Los Angeles, she had been well into a promising Hollywood career, having played leads in several western movies. Her journey from the silver screen to "solid, steady winds" and "ground blizzards" in Wyoming came with great speed.

17. Catherine Terrell Smith interview.

18. Irene Wischer, telephone interview with author. Irene Wischer put her stamp on the Pinto Well Servicing Company in one other way—she had all the rigs painted pink! She adds: "We had the hard hats of the men painted pink, too, but OSHA frowned on that as a safety violation; but when I'd come around a rig, the men often put on their pink hats."

19. Lester Clark interview.

20. R. L. Foree Jr. interview; Della Foree interview.

21. Pat Gratton interview.

22. George Mitchell interview.

23. Jerry O'Brien interview.

24. Neal Anderson interview.

25. The author had this conversation at the 1961 TIPRO convention in Midland.

26. Foree's role in national affairs is detailed in Chapter 4.

27. Frank Pitts interview.

28. John Hurd interview.

29. An example of John Hurd's subtle style is his self-effacing account of how he came to be a fencing champion—through his fascination with rowing: "The high school I went to was on the banks of the canal that connects Lake Washington to Puget Sound. That is where the University of Washington, well known for its oarsmanship, used to row." But Hurd's father did not think a college should be selected on the basis of its crew, so he opposed John's desire to go to Washington. The University of California? "'No, son, they've got a rowing team too. Think some more.'" They settled for Harvard because, said John, "he didn't stop to think that Harvard had one of the finest crews on the East Coast." Two weeks of freshman rowing, and Hurd developed boils on his posterior. "They gave me everything, including chamois pants, and it didn't do any good. The doctor says, 'Sorry, your skin is too tender; you're just not going to be able to row.' I'm six feet tall and weigh 135 pounds, so I go out for lightweight football. I move good, but my hands aren't big enough—I can't reach and grab the football with one hand and hold it. So the freshman coach says, 'You've got good moves and you're fast. Come out for boxing; I'm the freshman boxing coach.' I spar around and everything is fine, so he puts me in the ring with a guy. I wake up and he's knocked me out. The coach says, 'You can't box. You've got a glass jaw. But I know where you can go. Next door. The coach is a nice man. They'll put a mask on your face so they can't hit your jaw. They'll put a glove on your hand and it doesn't matter how big your sword is, you can hold it. You stand up so you won't get boils on your seat. I think you will be a logical fencer.' And I was. Won the intercollegiates my senior year, was captain, and then two years later went to the Olympics in Berlin—1936" (John Hurd interview). John Hurd graduated from Harvard Law in 1937, went to work for the land division of Standard of California, married a Texas girl, moved to Laredo, and went into the oil business.

30. Bill Rutter, telephone interview with author, August 1995.

31. Bruce Anderson interview.

32. Malcolm Abel interview.

33. Shelby Pitts interview.

34. Watson's appointment of D. F. McKeithan of Milwaukee highlights the fact that roughly 15 percent of TIPRO's members live outside of Texas. They joined TIPRO either because they owned production in the state or because they wanted to lend their personal support to TIPRO's aggressive advocacy of the independent industry. Many became active spokesmen in the Liaison Committee. In addition to McKeithan of Wisconsin, this group included Clint Engstrand of Kansas, Bob Prewitt of Colorado, and Ben Cubbage of Kentucky. (Julian Martin, telephone interview with author.)

35. John Watson interview.

36. Gene Wright interview. Like John Hurd recalling his fencing days (see note 29 above),

Gene Wright recounted his work as a young lieutenant specializing in sonar equipment at the navy's submarine base on Guam in the Pacific during the late stages of the World War II: "The admiral had gotten twenty sets of underwater mine detection gear for a special project to send subs into the Sea of Japan. Before the old admiral would send the subs out, he would watch them do their mine detection work. A sub named the *Bonefish* was the last of the first group we were installing this equipment in, and the admiral decided that I was to go along on the *Bonefish*'s mission to see how the stuff worked. I had all my gear on the *Bonefish* and the admiral was with us on the final sea trial. When we got back to the base, the admiral changed his mind about my assignment: 'I am not going to send you forward, because we have nine more boats to get ready and I need you here.' So I did not go. And the sub did not complete its mission. The *Bonefish* was the last U.S. submarine lost during World War II. I guess that is the only reason I am here today."

37. Information in this paragraph is derived from interviews with Lester Clark, Jim Russell, and Jon Rex Jones and—concerning Coffman's technology initiatives—John Hurd, Bruce Anderson, Chester Upham, Frank Pitts, and Pat Gratton.

38. Jon Rex Jones interview.

39. Ibid.

40. Bruce Anderson interview.

BIBLIOGRAPHY

The principal sources for this study of TIPRO were the association's publications, the *Independent News* (1947–1948), the *TIPRO Reporter* (1948–1996), and *TIPRO Target* (1980–1996); the internal records of TIPRO (1946–1995); and the oral interviews that, together with the internal records, are now a part of the TIPRO Archives at the Center for American History at the University of Texas at Austin. These documents, periodicals, and transcripts constitute the evidential centerpiece of the TIPRO History Project, undertaken by TIPRO in cooperation with the Center for American History and its director, Dr. Don Carleton. The bulk of the interviews were conducted between 1992 and 1994 by Dr. Barbara Griffith, director of the Oral History Program at the Center for American History.

Interviews

Abel, Malcolm, Midland.
Abraham, Malouf, Canadian.
Anderson Family, Houston (Bruce, Jacqueline, Craig, Neal, and Scott).
Beecherl, Lewis H., Dallas.
Brown, Claude, McCamey.
Carl, William E., Corpus Christi.
Clark, Lester, Breckenridge.
Darbyshire, Bernard, London.
Egan, Jim, Austin.
Finley, Robert J., Austin.
Foree, Della, Dallas.
Foree, R. L., Jr., Dallas.
Frizzell, Allan D., Abilene.
Gratton, Patrick J., Dallas.
Holmes, Estelle Yates, San Antonio.
Howell, T. D. "Rusty," Marshall.
Hurd, John G., San Antonio.

Jones, Jon Rex, Albany.
Marr, Morton H., Dallas.
Mitchell, George, Houston.
Murray, William, Austin.
O'Brien, Jerry, San Antonio.
Pitcock, Roy and Lewis, Graham.
Pitts, Frank, Dallas.
Pitts, Shelby, Dallas.
Rosenthal, Betty and Stanley, Bay City.
Russell, Jim, Abilene.
Rutter, William, Midland.
Smith, Catherine Terrell, Fort Worth.
Street, Bruce, Graham.
Upham, Chester, Mineral Wells.
Walker, Jim, Amarillo.
Watson, John, Houston.
Wright, Gene, Tyler.

Secondary Sources

Adelman, M. A. *The World Petroleum Market.* Baltimore, 1972.

American Bar Association. *Legal History of Conservation of Oil and Gas: A Symposium.* Chicago, 1939.

Anderson, Irving H. *Aramco, the United States, and Saudi-Arabia: A Study of the Dynamics of Foreign Oil Policy.* Princeton, 1981.

Bartley, Ernest R. *The Tidelands Oil Controversy: A Legal and Historical Analysis.* Austin, 1955.

Blair, John. *The Control of Oil.* New York, 1976.

Boatwright, Mody C. *Folklore of the Oil Industry.* Dallas, 1963.

Boatwright, Mody C., and William A. Owens. *Tales from the Derrick Floor.* New York, 1970.

Burrows, James C., and Thomas A. Domencich. *An Analysis of the United States Oil Import Quota.* Lexington, Mass., 1970.

Breeding, Clark W., and A. Gordon Burton. *Taxation of Oil and Gas Income.* Englewood Cliffs, N.J., 1954.

Clark, J. Stanley. *The Oil Century.* Norman, Okla., 1958.

Commoner, Barry. *Science and Survival.* New York, 1966.

Conrod, Robert L. "State Regulation of the Oil and Gas Industry." Master's thesis, University of Texas, 1931.

Engler, Robert. *The Politics of Oil.* New York, 1961.

First, Harry, Eleanor M. Fox, and Robert Pitofsky, eds. *Revitalizing Antitrust in Its Second Century: Essays on Legal, Economic, and Political Policy.* New York, 1991.

Fried, Edward R., and Charles L. Schultze, eds. *Higher Oil Prices and the World Economy: The Adjustment Problem.* Washington, D.C., 1975.

Haigh, Berte R. *Land, Oil, and Education.* El Paso, 1986.

Hardwicke, Robert E. *Antitrust Laws et al. v. Unit Operations of Oil and Gas Pools.* New York, 1948.

Harvard Business History Review. *Oil's First Century: Papers Given at the Centennial Seminar on the History of the Petroleum Industry, Harvard Business School, November 13–14, 1959.* Boston, 1960.

Herald, Frank A., ed. *Occurrence of Oil and Gas in West Texas.* Austin, 1957.

Hines, LeRoy H. *Unitization of Federal Lands.* Denver, 1953.

Hoffman, Leo J. *Voluntary Pooling and Unitization: Oil and Gas.* Dallas, 1954.

Ickes, Harold. *Fightin' Oil.* New York, 1943.

James, Marquis. *The Texaco Story.* New York, 1953.

Karlsson, Svante. *Oil and the World Order.* Gothenburg, 1983.

Kemnitzer, William J. *Rebirth of Monopoly.* New York, 1938.

Klebanoff, Shoshana. *Middle East Oil and U.S. Foreign Policy: With Special Reference to the U.S. Energy Crisis.* New York, 1977.

Knowles, Ruth Sheldon. *The Greatest Gamblers.* 1958. Reprint, Norman, 1978.

Larson, Henrietta M., and Kenneth W. Porter. *History of the Humble Oil and Refining Company.* New York, 1959.

Lowi, Theodore. *The End of Liberalism.* New York, 1979.

MacAvoy, Paul W. *Price Formation in Natural Gas Fields: A Study of Competition, Monopsony and Regulation.* Yale, 1962.

McDaniel, Ruel. *Some Ran Hot.* Dallas, 1939.

McLean, John G., and Robert W. Haigh. *The Growth of Integrated Oil Companies.* Boston, 1954.

Miller, Aaron David. *Search for Security: Saudi Arabian Oil and American Foreign Policy, 1939–1949.* Chapel Hill, N.C., 1980.

Moore, Richard R. *West Texas after the Discovery of Oil.* Austin, 1971.

Murphy, Blakley M., ed. *Conservation of Oil and Gas: A Legal History.* Chicago, 1949.

Myres, Raymond. *The Law of Pooling and Unitization—Voluntary, Compulsory.* New York, 1957.

Myres, Samuel D. *The Permian Basin: Era of Advancement.* El Paso, 1977.

Nash, Gerald D. *United States Oil Policy, 1890–1964.* Pittsburgh, 1968.

O'Connor, Richard. *The Oil Barons.* Boston, 1971.

Odell, Peter R. *Oil and World Power.* New York, 1974.

Olien, Roger M., and Diana Davids Olien. *Wildcatters: Texas Independent Oilmen.* Austin, 1984.

Painter, David. *Oil and the American Century: The Political Economy of U.S. Foreign Oil Policy, 1941–1954.* Baltimore, 1986.

Presley, James. *A Saga of Wealth: The Rise of the Texas Oilmen.* New York, 1978.

Pope, Clarence C. *An Oil Scout in the Permian Basin, 1924–1960.* El Paso, 1972.

Prindle, David. *Petroleum Politics and the Texas Railroad Commission.* Austin, 1981.

Raskin, Marcus G. *The Politics of National Security.* New Brunswick, 1979.

Rifai, Taki. *The Pricing of Crude Oil.* New York, 1975.

Rostow, Eugene V. *A National Policy for the Oil Industry.* New Haven, 1948.

Rundell, Walter, Jr. *Early Texas Oil.* College Station, 1977.

Schumacher, E. F. *Small Is Beautiful: Economics As If People Mattered*. New York, 1973.

Schurmann, Franz. *The Logic of World Power*. New York, 1974.

Schwettman, Martin W. *Santa Rita: The University of Texas Oil Discovery*. Austin, 1943.

Sherrill, Robert. *The Oil Follies of 1970–1980*. Garden City, N.Y., 1983.

Shojai, Siamack, and Bernard S. Katz, eds. *The Oil Market in the 1980s*. New York, 1992.

Shugart, William F. *Antitrust Policy and Interest Group Politics*. New York, 1990.

Stocking, George Ward, and Myron W. Watkins. *Monopoly and Free Enterprise*. New York, 1951.

Stoff, Michael B. *Oil, War, American Security: The Search for a National Policy on Foreign Oil*. New Haven, 1980.

Sullivan, E. Thomas. *Understanding Antitrust and Its Economic Implications*. New York, 1988.

Tait, Samuel W., Jr. *The Wildcatters*. Princeton, 1946.

Tanzer, Michael. *The Political Economy of International Oil and the Underdeveloped Countries*. London, 1969.

Thelen, David. *Robert LaFollette and the Insurgent Spirit*. Boston, 1976.

Thorelli, Hans Birger. *The Federal Anti-Trust Policy: Organization of an American Tradition*. New York, 1955.

Tinkle, Lon. *Mr. De: A Biography of Everette Lee DeGolyer*. Boston, 1970.

Thurow, Lester. *Dangerous Currents: The State of Economics*. New York, 1983.

Trevey, Marilyn D. "The Social and Economic Impact of the Spindletop Oil Boom on Beaumont in 1901." Master's thesis, Lamar University, 1974.

U.S. Senate Select Committee on Small Business. *The International Petroleum Cartel. Staff Report of the Federal Trade Commission*. 82d Cong., 2d sess., 1952.

Wiebe, Robert H. *The Search for Order, 1877–1920*. New York, 1967.

Yergin, Daniel. *The Prize: The Epic Quest for Oil, Money, and Power*. New York, 1991.

Other Sources

The annual *Joint Association Survey of the U.S. Oil and Gas Producing Industry*, published by the American Petroleum Institute, Independent Petroleum Association of America, and Mid-Continent Oil and Gas Association, proved useful to this study, as did the IPAA publication *The Oil Producing Industry*. Also consulted were the *Oil and Gas Journal* and *World Oil*.

INDEX

SPRING BRANCH MEMORIAL LIBRARY
930 CORBINDALE ROAD
HOUSTON, TEXAS 77024